THIS IS POP

The life and times of a failed rock star

THIS IS POP

The life and times of a failed rock star

By Ed Jones

CANONGATE

First published in 1999 by Canongate Books Ltd, 14 High Street, Edinburgh EH1 1TE

10 9 8 7 6 5 4 3 2 1

British Library Cataloguing-in-Publication Data
A catalogue record for this book is available
on request from the British Library.

ISBN 0 86241 880 1

Cover design by Brian Cannon and Microdot.

Typeset by Palimpsest Book Production Limited,
Polmont, Stirlingshire

Printed and bound by WSOY, Finland

Endless gratitude etc . . .

Geoff Meall, Richard Thomas, Damian Liptrot, Simon Collett,
Sean Staunton, Peter Grant, Guy Keegan, Alan McGee, Brian Cannon, Spencer Leigh,
Chris Spriggs, Vera Dyer, Carys Williams and everyone at Canongate. Oh, Alison, of course,
I almost forgot.

For Elliot
Je vois mon destin dans tes yeux . . .

CONTENTS

FOREWORD

This is pop?

It's difficult to deal with not achieving your dreams. Everybody has them. I know how hard the music industry is, to get third on the bill at the Moonlight Club in Hampstead when you're a twenty-one year old kid. It amounts to zilch inches in the *NME*, yet after trying for two years you think you've climbed Everest.

When you want something so much and you fail, it hurts.

I changed course and started to put my friends' records out. I realised I was kidding myself on. I was never going to be a pop star. Success can be as damaging as failure but you have to be close to success. I know this as fact. The Tansads never got the chance.

This is the story of the people who don't get on *Top of the Pops*. This is the story of the vast majority. This is what it's really like to be in a British indie band.

Not everybody can be a pop star. Not everybody can be famous. Not everybody can be rich. Not everybody can fuck beautiful women.

This is what it would have been like if Oasis, Paul Weller, Primal Scream, Pulp, Blur, The Verve and Ocean Colour Scene, amongst others, hadn't made it.

This is the tale most people don't write.

With every big-selling album you should get a free copy of this book. This is the underbelly of success. This is how not to be famous.

This is not pop.

This is The Tansads.

Alan McGee
Creation Records, 1999

PROLOGUE

'Is that Kate Moss?'

'Where?'

'There, right in front, look. With the combat trousers.'

'Naah. Too short.'

'It is. Look, she's turning round.'

'Oh Christ, so it is.'

On Sunday May 24th 1998, for one glorious evening only, there was simply *nowhere* else to be, regardless of who you were, but standing on a golf course in the grounds of a former stately home overlooking the Lancashire town of Wigan. That's right, W.I.G.A.N. It was suddenly hip to come from the home of *Uncle Joe's Mintballs*.

If Manchester had been the new Liverpool, Wigan – astounding as it sounds – became the new Manchester, flat caps, whippets 'n' all. So forget about meat and potato pie butties or ten pints at the Bee's Knees followed by a punch-up on King Street West, because tonight, Matthew, Wigan is going to be the most glamorous rock-'n'-roll centre in Britain, if not the world.

Stars in your eyes, indeed!

'COOOOOME OOOOOON! Eight fuckin' years and here we are!' The band kick into 'This is Music' and the crowd erupts and like, say, the Stones at Hyde Park, the Stone Roses at Spike Island or Oasis at Maine Road, **The Verve** at Haigh Hall became one of those era-defining gigs. By 'eck.

We only lasted four songs, however. I turned to Guy Keegan (aged 32, married, father of three, occupation: car salesman; former drummer with Wigan band The Railway Children; three LPs released; highest singles chart position reached; 24; claim to fame: were once supported by a band called Blur. And the Happy Mondays) and before I, Ed Jones, (aged 34, married, father of one; occupation: journalist; former bassist with Wigan band The Tansads; three LPs released; highest singles chart position reached; 101; claim to fame: were once supported by a band called The Verve. And Kula Shaker. And Cast. And Dodgy) could speak, he nodded.

We had managed to procure freebie tickets and, when we collected them, a very nice girl with a very un-Wigan accent strapped purple bands to our wrists. This, we figured, could only mean one thing: backstage privileges. No time for questions and, as the gates opened, our little purple passes led us into the secret garden.

THE VERVE – 'Bittersweet Symphony', the breakthrough release, was actually their 9th single, but the first for almost two years, during which time the band had to all intents and purposes split after tales of big-daddy rows between singer Richard Ashcroft and guitarist Nick McCabe. The success of the single didn't reap any financial rewards, however, as the track's signature string section hook is sampled from an orchestral version of the Rolling Stones, 'The Last Time'. This led to former Stones manager, and owner of their back catalogue, Allen Klein to insist not only on keeping all the royalties but also on Messrs Jagger & Richards having a writing credit. Handy for negotiating with the marketing department at Vauxhall.

We fast discovered, alas, that we were only third-class first-class passengers. A further VIP area within the VIP area was accessible only with black and white bands and the hallowed inner sanctum beyond the further VIP area within the VIP area was out of bounds unless one was strapped with red. Still, we contented ourselves with sitting on the benches and watching Kate Moss walk in and out. The beer wasn't free but at least we didn't have to mix with the hoi polloi and queue for up to an hour to be served. We sipped our lager.

'It's not that I think they're crap, Guy.'

'No.'

'Far from it. I wish I did, it would simplify matters.' I paused. 'Do you know what I'm jealous of?'

'The money?'

'No.'

'The fame?'

'No. The Power. The Power to make all these people come here, to have burger bars and Amnesty International tents and car park attendants. And the Power to do what the hell you want with your life.'

And I remembered a quote from Richard Ashcroft which I read in *Q* magazine prior to the Haigh Hall gig: 'Can you imagine if we'd carried on releasing records and it'd never happened, what would we have done? Just disappeared and gone and lived in a fucking igloo? Because when you believe in something so strongly, for it not to happen would've been scary.'

They *had* made it, however. Thirty-three thousand souls, including every music journalist of note in the land, supermodels, pop stars (we only saw Tim Booth from **James** but I heard *everybody* was there), two giant video screens, and a BBC crew filming for a network transmission later that night, testified to that. What about the others, though? The ones that don't make it. What about Guy? What about ME?

That's what this book is about. No stars and no pat Hollywood endings. This is reality. THIS IS POP.

JAMES – It took James nearly eight years to score their first top forty hit, 'How Was It For You?' Their biggest success came in March '91 when 'Sit Down' reached number two. Incidentally, I was one of approximately 12 other people to see James headline Preston Paradise Club in 1985.

DISC ONE

March 1964 – July 1988

THE BEGINNING OF THE END

Being in a band is a bit weird really, isn't it? Actually *doing* it, I mean.

There's certainly nothing unusual about wanting to become a pop star. All boys have some kind of fantasy, and, together with being a footballer, it's one of the most common. Nowadays, opportunities abound to combine both worlds, be it Hoddle and Waddle duetting on *Top of the Pops*, Spice Boy Beckham with his Posh girlfriend, or Robbie Fowler celebrating a goal by mimicking the snorting of a line of coke. It's only rock-'n'-roll. And I like it.

But at a young age, when dreams cloud the head, you never stop to equate the glamour of fame with the necessary skill and, more importantly, the application. In other words, what falls between wishing it and being it.

Take Richard Ashcroft. One day he was a skinny college kid in Wigan, the next he was a skinny pop star from Wigan. For most, though, the idle notions of pop stardom are soon shelved somewhere between puberty and adulthood, when a combination of sceptical careers officers, peer ridicule and parental pressure destroys self-confidence and the Sensible Job Syndrome subsequently kicks in. The dream then fades with the puppy fat and the arrival of your first pay cheque, your first kiss (and more!) and your first legal pint. I could have been a contender. Yeah, right.

That's what happens in most cases. There are those, however, who are just too stupid to know any better and whose absurd level of self-confidence (or delusion, as it inevitably turns out) knows no bounds. That's me. Ed Jones. A mild-mannered, well-educated, white, middle-class boy with no great artistic genes. (The most rock-'n'-roll thing I can glean about my heritage is that Mum and Dad met at **100 Oxford Street**, later to become legendary birthplace of punk; the decadent youth of their day was (a presumably thin) George Melly rather than Sid Vicious.)

I believe January 16th 1978 was the day that triggered everything. My father died from cancer at the age of 47, five months to the day after Elvis Presley passed away. All shook up. It was a few months before that that Dad told me. We stayed at the Richmond Gate Hotel, situated opposite the grand entrance to Richmond Park. Dad and I shared a room and during *Match of the Day* (Man City versus Nottingham Forest), he suddenly turned all serious on me.

'Old chap, turn the TV off for a minute. I've got something to tell you.'

I thought that, when my parents came to see my sister Lucy and me at

100 OXFORD STREET – The legendary basement club in the west end of London where The Sex Pistols took up a residency of sorts in 1976, soon developing a reputation for violence, drug use, drunkenness and general foul-mouthed debauchery. And that was just on stage. The band effectively split shortly after the release of their legendary debut album *Never Mind the Bollocks, Here's The Sex Pistols*, when singer Johnny Rotten bowed out onstage in San Francisco with the immortal phrase "Ever feel you've been cheated".

our boarding school in Surrey, it was something to do with the unhappiness of our two months thus far. Frensham Heights was a horrible place. I was stuck in unfamiliar surroundings away from everything and everybody I loved, I was bullied, and I knew something was terribly wrong at home. The gravity of Dad's tone made me realise that it was nothing to do with the bullying. From this moment on, life would never be the same again.

'You know I had the operation last winter. Well . . .'

How much courage must it take to tell your 13-year-old son you only have months to live? Heartbreak Hotel. I saw him only once more, when Lucy and I returned home for Christmas that year. He was making plans for a family holiday to the US the following summer; Mum knew the reality.

Had Dad not died when he did, though, I know I would never have had the same level of personal drive that would see me lunge into everything like the proverbial headless chicken. It provided me with a hunger and stubbornness that I would never again be denied anything and it also created a desire for revenge, against whom I haven't still quite worked out yet.

There lies an uneasy contradiction in the loss, however. His death was good for me. Can I say that? The pain taught me lessons about myself I may never otherwise have learned. I can trace every ambition that has ever breathed its life through my veins back to the darkness it generated. How I pity those kids who grow up in a stable, loving, financially comfortable two parent family. They're doomed, aren't they? No chip on the shoulder and nothing to scream at or tear down. I was one of the lucky ones, granted a bona-fide trauma at the most impressionable of ages. I recommend it to all budding artists.

When the reality stopped, the myth took off. My image of my father will remain. The rose-tinted specs are welded to my face and there is nothing I can do about it. I am forced to look at him through the eyes of a 13-year-old, one of the most crucial parts of my personality frozen inside the body of a child. And that's what still hurts. Even after twenty years. Especially after twenty years. The longer it goes on the worse it gets. In the immediate aftermath of his death, I filled the void by creating a fantasy world. I transported myself to a place where nobody could touch me and where I looked for answers but never really found them. It was simply a place where I was alone with him. It was my secret hideaway. I dreamed about him all the time, wrote about him, willed myself to have visions of him. And I forgot the first anniversary of his death. My mother sent me a single red rose and a card that read simply 'In Loving Memory'. No signature. I was genuinely perplexed. Why would anybody send me a flower? And what did 'In Loving Memory' mean? He was still alive. Always on my mind.

It soon became clear to me that my destiny lay in following Dad to King's College, Cambridge. Ever since he had taken me there a couple of years before he died, the place had developed a mystical aura in my mind. I convinced myself the longer I could retrace his footsteps, the longer he would remain alive inside me.

I chose to do a course in Russian and French; he had read German and Russian. I studied ferociously, and impressed sufficiently at school to be put forward as an Oxbridge candidate. Bingo. Soon afterwards, King's called me for interview. This was a piece of cake. I travelled up on the train, and I could feel Dad was with me. I signed myself in at the gatehouse, and emerged into the magnificent main quadrangle, a huge lump in my throat.

'Why have you chosen King's, Edmund?'

Naturally, I lied.

I talked about a deep-seated desire to learn Russian and my passion for modern French literature. I remember the view out of the window, overlooking the rolling lawns to the river, in the shadow of the beautiful Tudor chapel. Everything felt perfect. I even fell head over heels in love with one of my fellow candidates, Anita from Shepton Mallet. We spent most of the day together, talking and walking around the college and sitting in the sun just soaking in the atmosphere. I even missed my train back so I could stay with her an extra couple of hours.

Meeting Anita felt like a sign. Everything I wanted was here. It was a moment of utter clarity and, when I got back to school, my faith was vindicated almost at once. King's invited me to take the entrance examination that autumn. Another hurdle gone. I spent the entire summer reading. And I kept in touch with Anita as promised. Reading her letters made me feel as though I had known her forever. She even invited me up to her birthday party one weekend, which was great. Back at school, I buckled down once more. Finally, the big day arrived. The exam was held at school and I was ushered into a room. The paper sat waiting for me on the solitary desk.

'You have three hours. Good luck.'

The sun was shining. I stared out of the window for a moment. Then I launched myself at the work, looking for the question on *L'Etranger*. I was particularly strong on existentialism, all that Albert Camus stuff about inner freedom. I could rattle it off in my sleep. I can't remember what else was on there but I felt it went well. The result would be posted to me in the Christmas holidays. For days, I rushed downstairs first thing in the morning to scan the mail. Each time there was nothing. I became twitchy until the next morning. At last, there was the envelope addressed to me with a Cambridge postmark. I stared at it for ages. I knew my life could hinge on this one moment. I wanted this so badly. I opened it.

Sorry, son.

Up until that point, failure had never once been part of my vocabulary. Now it was. Failing the exam was a blow, but failing where Dad had succeeded was absolutely devastating. I'd not just let myself down; I'd let him down. Mum tried consolation in reminding me that Dad had never really enjoyed the Cambridge experience. Rather, he felt he wasn't cut out for a life of academia and had been forced into it by his parents. The last thing he would have wanted was for me to go through the same torment. That just made things worse, however. He had got in *without even trying*. And of course, Anita wrote to say she had been offered a place. In the letter, she also referred to her boyfriend.

It took a long time to pick myself up. The lure of academic work certainly lessened, though I passed my A levels and secured a place at Lancaster University to study Theatre Studies and French (I never did want to learn Russian, let's face it). Although I was still excited at the new life ahead, nothing quite filled me with the conviction and belief that I had felt that glorious day in Cambridge and on my subsequent crusade towards and through the entrance exam. A little faith in myself had been chipped away and, at the same time, I felt Dad's influence diminishing slightly. I didn't think about him quite as much any more and I didn't base everything I did on trying to match myself up to him. Maybe, at last, as I turned 18 and officially became an adult, I had begun to behave like one a bit.

Then I discovered music.

BAD MOON RISING

MARCH 1964 – A band by the name of The Beatles sat at number one on both sides of the Atlantic with something called 'Can't Buy Me Love'.

March 1964 was a great month for rock-'n'-roll. I was born. Alas not in bohemian Paris, swinging London or even Liverpool, but in Geneva, Switzerland, a country where the national sport is time-keeping. My father's linguistic ability had earned him a job as a translator for the International

Labour Organisation, and my sister Lucy and I were thus brought up in the city of conferences.

This is the only unusual aspect of my early childhood, give or take the fact I learned French before English, spoke a different language at home than with my friends, and my grandparents lived 500 miles away. It also provided me with my earliest pop-star link: Lucy was in the same class as Petula 'Downtown' Clark's daughters and I once attended a birthday party at their heavily swimming-pooled house on the shores of Lake Geneva. Maybe if I had been able to drive a Rolls Royce, it would have ended up in the pool *à la* Keith Moon. I certainly thought about shoving a trolley full of cream cakes to its watery demise. Does that count?

By the time I was 15, however, I was beginning to assemble a rock CV that read like a half-Moon.

Substance abuse

Aged four. Infants' school. The leafy playground. The snack break.

'NO, EDMUND, NO!'

The teacher snatched the biscuit from my hand. My crime? Heinous. Separating the bourbon cream, scraping the chocolate off with my teeth, before scoffing the remnants in a decadent feast of dry biscuit.

'You can't eat it like that! Where would we be if everyone did that?'

Where indeed?

Animal abuse

Aged seven. Unpacked boxes from a recent move. The basement. Dad and I.

'Daddy, daddy, look, there is!'

After hearing him complain that there was not enough room to swing a cat in the room, I scampered off, scooped up our unsuspecting kitten Hector and soon returned to disprove his theory.

It was not to be the last time that playing around with pussy was to get me into trouble.

Hotel abuse

Aged nine. Okay, so it wasn't a Holiday Inn or a Marriott. But it could have been. I had been sent to my room by the Man (well, Dad) and told not to re-emerge until my twenty-first birthday or something, and all because of something I can't exactly recall now. It couldn't have been anything that bad, I'm certain. Anyway, brimming with genuine injustice,

I decided to voice my protest by emptying the contents of my room into the garden.

Kids didn't have tellies in those days, but if I had . . .

Supermodel abuse

Aged fifteen. Frensham Heights. Along with two friends, I was able to bribe a sixth former to obtain a bottle of vodka for us, which was duly knocked back with suicidal breakneck speed together with copious quantities of Lilt (I still can't touch either to this day, incidentally). Naturally, I was violently ill the next morning, shivering and sweating. Nobody had warned me about hangovers. I was still conscious enough, however, to get up and leave my bed. Mistake.

One of my classmates (I use the term loosely) was called Emma Woollard, an object of such rarefied beauty and perfection that I had never been able to speak to her in two years. She went on to be a model, fittingly. My whole being craved for her day and night (mostly nights, ahem). Imagine the abject horror, then, when she made a beeline for me: fantasy in a 100 mph head-on collision with reality, a cocktail more lethal than vodka and Lilt.

'Ed, I need to ask you a question.'

That voice, those eyes, her face.

'Oh, hi, Emma, I, uh—'

My head, my sweaty brow, my breath. Ugh.

'How are you feeling?'

Oh, my Lord, I'm going to faint.

'Oh, oh, a bit rough, actually. I got a little drunk last night.'

'Did you have a nice time?'

I blushed.

'Well, I can't remember that much about it. I—'

'Oh really?'

Ah, that'll be the sarcasm.

'Well, uh—'

'So you don't remember talking to me, then?'

Oh God.

'Talking? Uh, no. I mean, yes, yes, of course.'

'You *do*?'

Oh Christ, I didn't ask her out did I? Did we kiss?

'Well, you know. Bits.'

'Do you like me, Ed?'
'Like? Yes, of course, I like you, I think you're the most beaut—'
'Why did you piss on my feet, then?'

So, before that first string on the guitar was ever plucked, the signs were there. Not only did I share a birthday with Eric Clapton, 60s wild-man guitar-hero-turned-Grammy-dripping-member-of-the-Establishment, my behaviour had me marked as a natural.

Rock-'n'-roll!

THIS IS THE VOICE OF THE MYSTERONS

Fender Musicman, black, £90.00. The ad, pinned on a notice board near my room on the campus of Lancaster University, reached out and spoke to me.

'Come to me, come to me,' it whispered and I came the instant I laid eyes on the beast. It was love at first sight. I had to have it. That classic Fender shape, that light maple neck and that black body with its scratch plate and control knobs, together with the genuine Fender logo stamped on the head. No cheap imitations for the Jones boy. It was mine. All I had to do now was learn how to play.

Easy. I immediately purchased a big blue volume entitled *The Guitar Handbook*, which taught me every single chord ever invented, when and where to use them, and a lot more besides. For instance, did you know that Gibson's original 1952 Les Paul only had two high-impedance single-coil pick-ups? Or that the ground-breaking humbucker didn't supersede them until 1957, although that name – get this – only came into common parlance three years later, the new system at first being referred to simply as PAF, Patent Applied For.

I still don't know what a humbucker is. Nor can I play a G flat seventh augmented ninth with an E root note. But the book still helped me to progress in my own way, though I was not patient enough to mimic my record collection, hence the inability to this day to trot out 'Stairway to Heaven'.

Until now, music had always been a spectator sport for me. I cheered on passionately from the terraces for the likes of The Jam, Elvis Costello and Echo and the Bunnymen. I failed, however, to make much of a connection between listening to other people's songs and playing them, let alone writing my own. That was soon to change and, although it may sound terminally naff, it was Morrissey that completed the transformation. Just as I was discovering the joys of rock-'n'-roll, the cardigan-wearing, flower-in-the-back-pocket Mozzer gave a voice to bedroom philosophers everywhere and from the closet we emerged. Suddenly it was the height of fashion to use pop music as a vehicle for more than inane songs about cars and girls. You could sing about shyness and death and still be famous and sexy. And Johnny Marr was a guitar genius to boot.

THE SMITHS – In his time Morrissey has variously been accused of being a Myra Hindley sympathiser ('Suffer Little Children'), a militant animal rights campaigner ('Meat is Murder'), an anti-royalist ('The Queen is Dead), a racist ('Bengali in Platforms'), a fascist ('National Front Disco') and a plain, old-fashioned wanker. His pro-miserablist and openly celibate stance made him the first real 'bedsit' non-pop star, and who can forget the sight of Morrissey sashaying and shimmying across the Top of the Pops stage complete with hearing aid and gladioli sprouting from his back pocket. I still love you, Moz.

The **Smiths**' historic first major UK tour stopped off at Lancaster University Great Hall, only 200 yards from my room. I stood in the audience utterly transfixed, the sheer excitement and volume sweeping me away in its tide of euphoria. Marr also had a black Fender. That night opened my eyes and I discovered the reason I was put on this earth. Planet Pop.

Being quite an instinctive and impulsive person (I'm told it's an Aries thing) my reaction was that I had to quit college immediately and simply play music. Immerse myself totally, man. That's what I wanted but retaining a modicum of common sense, I decided instead to spend a few months improving on the guitar first. It would come, however, and midway through my second year, I could bear it no more. If only to keep Mum quiet, I arranged to take a year off university rather than quit completely, even if at this stage I had absolutely no intention of returning.

So while my flatmates Jon and Rog headed off to France for their teaching year, I stayed on in the flat for a sabbatical of my own, courtesy of Her Majesty's Government's generous dole money. It was idyllic. The digs were part of Wyreside Hall, a converted old monastery, overlooking the River Wyre. If ever an artist had wanted a muse-inducing lair, this was it. Ahh . . .

I had worked through previous holidays to buy a bass, two amps and a drum machine and, having just turned twenty-one, I was now entitled to the £1,500 my grandfather had left Lucy and me each in his will. I thought it only right to spend the loot on music, my vehicle to keep the Jones genius alive. So I bought a 1960s Hofner semi-acoustic (the Fender was sacrificed in the name of progress), a four-track porta-studio and a VW Beetle to carry me around. I was on my way. Movin' on up.

I would lock myself away for hours, sometimes days on end, writing and recording. Some of the early results were admittedly horrendous, but I wasn't to be deterred. It doesn't happen overnight, I told myself, it never does. What I was finding, however, was the whole new dimension that songs allowed in expressing my feelings about Dad. At first, I tried to write love songs, but it was just awful slush. I hadn't the wit to articulate my longings and, let's face it, I had a pretty shallow well of experience to draw upon. Songs about Dad were different, though. There was a genuine intensity and the beginnings of a renewed belief that I was now doing something I cared about.

The year soon flew by and I decided to swallow my pride and finish the degree. It meant, though, that I could use the university facilities. Let's be honest. A couple of abortive musical dalliances with fellow students eventually led to the creation of The Mysterons (as in Captain Scarlet) with some other Wyreside flatmates.

My first proper band. Aged twenty-one.

The original singer was Niall Ashdowne, who has since, it pleases me hugely to say, become quite a big noise on the alternative comedy circuit in London (by the way tosser, I've still got that horrible pink and green sweater you left behind). We hate it when our friends become successful.

He made way for Dave Cattermole, a Buddy Holly fan. I was happy to wear my bass hat as nobody else owned one and completing the line-up was Pete Ryan, one of that rare breed, a tasteful rock guitarist. We had no drummer, so had to make do with good old metronomic Dr Rhythm. The best song was one of Dave's called 'Shane', inspired by the Alan Ladd western. He had written the words and basic tune, but I recorded a version adding a killer riff and a couple of distorted guitars. Yes. It was the first song I had been involved in that really rocked.

Our first gig was a showcase of the Lancaster Musicians Collective (we had only joined for the rehearsal space), upstairs at a pub called The Priory, by the bus station. The historic date: May 16th 1986. We played three or four tracks and went down well. Fuelled by the response, I got The Mysterons three more gigs around various Lancaster pubs.

Amazing fact No.1. The shows were full: of friends, friends of friends and their friends.

Amazing fact No 2. They cheered.

'Dr Freedom' & 'Mr Rock 'n' Roll' in the university paper *Scan* were less generous. We were, and I quote, '**The Sisters of Mercy** on a health-food kick, typifying the pain in the arse mediocrity of the slightly left of centre (but only slightly) devil-may-care hell-raising modern student. These good blokes are pretty crap. They would be well advised to stop this silly nonsense and get on with their degrees.'

THE SISTERS OF MERCY – I can safely say that Leeds' finest are the best band I ever saw. Or rather, didn't see. The Sisters' live experience (original version) featured so much dry ice that I only ever caught a glimpse of Andrew Eldritch's hat, the tip of Gary Marx's guitar and Wayne Hussey's leg (not sure if it was his right or left). In terms of power, noise and sheer excitement, however, nothing in the intervening fifteen years has come remotely close.

Hmm, what did they know?

It certainly didn't put off the bulky shape of Andy Tennant; definitely mutton dressed as lamb.

'I'll manage you,' said Andy.

'Okay,' agreed the greenhorns.

Andy was a serious scholar of hedonism. In theory, he was at university to study; in practice, he partied. He was loud, lazy, unreliable, and unashamedly fun to be with. Because he would usually spend all his money on beer, he could never afford the petrol home to Peterborough, and would therefore drain the brake fluid on his ultra-hip black Hillman Minx, get as far as the M6 and then rely on the fourth emergency service to tow him home.

'It's worth the subs if you do it a few times,' he explained.

Perfect manager material.

I don't know if he ever made it through his time at Lancaster and beyond because one of the last things I heard about him was that he was rushed into hospital with a malignant ulcer. After months of a lifestyle that involved two day long benders without food, then eating several loaves of toasted bread at once, his long suffering body finally slung the proverbial pencil on the table and said, 'Enough is enough.'

Not before, however, its jovial owner had attempted to derail our fledgling musical careers with his peculiar brand of management.

The first of the two gigs Andy booked was at a Morecambe nightclub called Porky's. The sign outside read: 'Porky's, because you're a fat pig'. Gulp. Luckily, the residents of Redneck City decided not to frequent their local that night, a couple of barflies notwithstanding. We lasted four songs before the landlord pulled the plug at the beginning of the fifth.

The other gig, meanwhile, never even happened. We refused after he'd booked us to play at a country and western night at another choice Morecambe watering hole. The landlord was assured we were pure checked-shirt-and-chewed-tobacco material. I mean, what else would a band called Rawhide be like?

Andy Tennant became the first victim of Jones' ruthless axe.

Over that summer, a new demo was prepared and I packaged it off ready to send to record companies. I studied the sleeves of my favourite records, got names and addresses of companies, and stuffed copious Jiffy bags into the postbox. A month later and I was able to begin my rejection letter collection. At least I had seen EMI headed notepaper, though.

During the final year at university, study did begin to take on much greater significance. At least for the others. I was quite happy to squander more time in the name of music. We had the addition of two new members – Graeme on guitar and drummer Sean – and one final gig, which I billed 'An Historic Farewell'. Yes, I *was* a drama student.

And that was the end, my friends, the beautiful end to The Mysterons. While Pete was serious about a career in engineering and had a determination to ride the train all the way through to Jobsville, Dave and I – degree certificates in hand – embarked on a spiritual and literal journey of our own. We couldn't just leave music behind, we told each other, it meant too much. There was a bond between us and we owed it to ourselves to carry on. And we also owed it to the Public. I mean, where would we be if all the great artists – Vincent van Gogh, James Joyce, George Best, and Cilla Black, to pick but four – had given up?

A desert with no cultural pool to sup from, that's where. We were going to provide that oasis. We were on a mission and this time it was personal. With equipment and dreams we relocated, lock, stock, and two smoking barrels, to Manchester-ra-ra-ra.

Hallelujah!

DON'T LEAVE ME THIS WAY

In the summer of 1987, Manchester was the musical capital of the world. It gave good sound. The Smiths and New Order were happening and there were dozens of other indie hopefuls: The Railway Children, James, The Fall, The Stone Roses, The Happy Mondays, The Charlatans and Inspiral Carpets (roadie, as we know, Mr Noel Gallagher) were amongst the boys who done good (I loved a band called **The Chameleons** that nobody else ever seems to have heard of – for me still the greatest). London never entered our consciousness. Manchester was the epicentre of (our) music in the late 80s. No question.

And, boy, did we get off to a good start. Things moved quickly. As expected.

From the ashes of The Mysterons, Those Famous Red Shirts rose majestically and soon our first demo, featuring Dave's voice and me on everything else, was being reviewed in a magazine called *Underground* by none other than John Peel.

THE CHAMELEONS – There were warning signs within the career of my favourite band ever – the record company politics, the financial ruin and their final dissolution into acrimony. Even with major US label muscle (Geffen) behind them, they still couldn't break the Top 40, coming closest with their third and final album *Strange Times*, which reached number 44 in 1986. They have never been matched.

'Their appeal is in the application, which shows some imagination and no little songwriting talent.' Dave's voice was described as 'a trifle maudlin but attractive nevertheless'. An instant catch phrase.

Then, out of the blue (or red, depending on your Manchester team), another stroke of good fortune. The girlfriend of Pete Brookes, one of our lecturers at Lancaster, was the viola player for the chart-topping Communards, and they needed a second support act for their upcoming Manchester Apollo show. Well, (i) we knew it wouldn't be an accurate reflection of our current material; (ii) it wasn't exactly our target audience; and (iii) we didn't have a band. But how could we refuse?

Pete and Graeme (bless 'em) drove up for a single rehearsal, and off we went. The Apollo was overwhelming. With no soundcheck, we played a 20-minute set of which the only recollection I have is Dave introducing 'Shane' by saying it would be our single. If we had one, that is. I don't even remember if we got paid.

A couple of days later, I got a letter from Paul MacDonald, then A&R scout from London Records (later to go on and work for The Verve's record company Hut, ironically), following up John Peel's review in *Underground*. He wanted a tape, and were we playing any shows?

Kiss my face.

Dave and I settled into a flat over a butcher's shop in Sedgeley Park. The smell of rotting flesh in the morning was less than refreshing, especially when accompanied by the additional sight of the old man chopping up the carcasses, fag in mouth. But there weren't any neighbours and we could rehearse without fear of offending.

I found work at the Securicor parcels office in Manchester. It was only part-time, but this allowed me more hours for music. Perfect. Like Dave's temporary admin job, it was dull and poorly paid, but at least we had managed to get a foothold in the big city, and were surviving, just, our enthusiasm batteries still full to the brim.

Our search for new members didn't take long. One of Dave's workmates, John Eastwood, knew a bass player, Barrie Stanhope. He was a bit older than us, married, with a young boy. He was from a different galaxy, into jazz and knew nothing of the current scene, but it made for an interesting hybrid; sort of Jaco Pastorius meets Buddy Holly in an echo chamber. Nice.

The recruitment was nearing completion when our advert for a drummer was answered. In strolled Mad Bob, the shortest biker I had ever met. The nickname came from these huge, bulging demonic eyes but he assured us he was good, loved the material and was really, really keen. Better still, as he worked for a TV production firm in Salford, he had access to the best rehearsal room I had ever seen. A brilliant studio that was spacious, dry, clean and FREE. One problem, however, as within a microsecond of our first session with him, we discovered he was hopeless, with time-keeping to match Lord Lucan. Worse still, he was utterly convinced of his brilliance.

Problem.

'It's the others, Bob,' I lied. 'They were looking for somebody, you know, a bit different. They don't think you'd fit in, you know, socially, nothing to do with the music. That was great.'

There's nothing like rejection to cut down even the greatest of deluded egos. Poor Bob was virtually in tears. Jones-the-Axe had struck for the second time, and we learned never to be seduced by a sexy rehearsal room again.

Next came Chris, whom Barrie had been in bands with in the past. Chris was excellent, no doubt about that. He was not into **Van Halen** (unusual), a little unsure of himself (bizarre), open to criticism (unheard of), contributed to arrangements (incredible), and didn't practise his Cozy Powell drum solo whilst the rest of you attempted to communicate (totally mind-blowing). More than this, he was a great laugh. Things are never that straightforward, though. We soon found out he was an alcoholic and a junkie, and was suffering the emotional trauma of trying to come off both while being dragged through a nasty divorce.

VAN HALEN – With his not inconsiderable wit, charisma, sly humour and effortless cool, there was a time when original vocalist 'Diamond' Dave Lee Roth made heavy metal desirable. It never lasted, however, and rather than remember any of their songs, I like to recall Van Halen as the band whose rider included a bowl of M & Ms with all the brown ones picked out and disposed of.

Drummers. Everything they say is true.

Dave and I, though, decided to take things at face value. Chris said he was off the smack and the booze and, despite never quite believing him, in the short time we were together, his problems never reared their ugly head. Chris was determined to use music as a path to rehabilitation and his arrival and enthusiasm duly propelled us forward. After the rigidity of the drum machine, suddenly there were dynamics to the songs. The honeymoon period was so successful in fact, that the three of us decided to move into a flat together, in Whalley Range, halfway between our work in the city centre, and the textile company in Stockport at which Chris was a quality controller.

It was early summer 1988. We had been in Manchester almost a year. Chris and Barrie were not football fans so we (reluctantly) changed the name to The Playthings. Our debut occurred on July 31st in the surroundings of a Dorset country garden in front of 20 people. Ostensibly, it was a birthday party for Dave's brother, but he never turned up. The local police did, however, and they pulled the plug after barely half a dozen songs.

Dave Simpson in the *Melody Maker* wrote: 'The Playthings attracted my attention by mixing their highly promising tales of lust, sex and terror with emotive, effects-laden pop hailstorms. Tonight they confirm their potential.' He referred to the guitarist as 'a genius in the mould of Dave Fielding' (from The Chameleons, one of my all-time heroes), then concluded, 'I'll be back, if only for their god-like guitarist.'

Unfortunately, this The Playthings gig took place at the White Horse in Hampstead, West London, in February 1991 and did not feature any of the four chancers from that glorious English summer of '88.

Barrie was the first to announce his departure.

'The music does nothing for me any more,' he said.

'You cannot be serious,' I said.

He was.

At first I hedged my bets, telling the band that we would look for a replacement bassist, while in the meantime, on the quiet, still doing separate stuff (musical term) with Barrie. Then, in a life of bad decisions, I made the worst and decided to split the band. Artistic Differences.

Throughout the year in Manchester, Dave had occasionally threatened to pack it all in and go home to Oxford. I would call his bluff. I cancelled the few gigs we had booked, as well as a session at Out of the Blue studio. The monster had killed its creator. The saddest thing is that we never got to commit any of the material to immortality. On a whim and in a huff, I threw away everything Dave and I had worked for. I can't explain it. Maybe Dave can.

'You are the lowest form of back-stabbing scum it has ever been my misfortune to mistakenly call my friend,' the letter started. 'It is only that I find your belief in your own musical superiority so laughable which prevents me from really hating you with real fire. The meanest of your insults came when you said that if I stayed around you would probably choose to work with me. Clearly this patronizing lie was meant as a charitable gesture as you were sure I would move south. How worried you must have been as I dashed around looking for a new bassist. How you must have fretted about the potentially awkward situation. Well things have fallen nicely into place for you now, haven't they? Yes, indeed, the relief on your face when I announced I would, after all, be moving away was <u>disgusting</u>. Jesus, Barrie must have been flattering you like hell lately. The fact is that whatever recognition your work has received to date has been in large part down to my writing, performing and playing flair.' Absolutely correct, of course. 'You are an above-average, workmanlike guitarist, and you'll need to find a collaborator of at least my standard to give you a hope. Dear old Barrie just doesn't measure up now, does he?'

Of course, this was the truth. But I couldn't let his letter go unanswered. I wrote back.

'Barrie's decision to quit came as as much of a surprise and bitter disappointment to me as it did to you. For a time, I believed genuinely (but a bit naively) that I could be in two bands at once, hence my initial enthusiasm for a replacement bassist. However, I then found myself in a position of having to make a choice. Never was this a slight on you, nor me claiming superiority, but I feel closer to Barrie musically since circumstances have forced the issue to a crunch.'

Dave finished our final communication in style.

'All the times in the past week when you said I'm not sure. You knew all along, you bastard. Bullshit, Ed, fucking patronizing BULLSHIT. To use a well-worn phrase, if I never see you again, it will be too soon.'

I attempted the final word with some kind of counter-attack, but it was a little half-hearted. Dave didn't just hold the moral high ground, he'd moved in, and built a shopping centre on it.

'You have always said you would stay in the band as long as it was good for you. Why should I not adopt the same policy, your policy? Take it or leave it, that's the truth. I'm sorry it has to end this way.'

What a fucking, stupid, short-sighted, arrogant, foolish PRICK. My musical ego had been well and truly seduced. Barrie always praised my guitar playing and, his technical knowledge being greater than mine, he was always looking to stretch me, experimenting with new feels and timings. I thought it would be more challenging, and I had enough confidence in my own songwriting to believe it was the right thing to do.

How wrong can one person be?

Barrie was a good player, but he was no songwriter, no poet like Dave and, much more importantly, no friend like Dave. The magic of the band was in the songwriting partnership. We had brought out the best in each other. It was obvious. How did I not see that?

We were not the finished article by any stretch of the imagination and, listening back, there is an embarrassing amateurishness to the demos. But there was also an emotional rawness to some of the songs, giving them a real edge. The despair and melancholy in Dave's lyrics was potentially the stuff of greatness. We had managed to achieve substance without being pompous or resorting to rock clichés. Had I had the wisdom to see it, maybe I wouldn't be writing this. Perhaps, though, retrospect and unfulfilled potential are blurring reality.

Immature ego is the most common cause of death for young bands. Fact.

I set myself up in a studio flat in Salford but very soon discovered the mistake I'd made. Barrie and I got on well, but we never really fused musically. We enlisted Dave's old workmate John Eastwood as the singer, and rechristened ourselves The Rain (a drab name for a drab band, and nothing to do with Liam Gallagher's first outfit, alas). It never felt quite right. The enthusiasm was gone. John had a very theatrical voice and though he wrote well, his tones grated on me. The music was far too indulgent, a mish-mash of ideas with no coherent direction. Dave was no Caruso, but I missed him and his a-trifle-maudlin-but-attractive-nevertheless tones.

Reverting back to the old name, I began writing on my own again and demoed on a four-track as That Famous Red Shirt; ironic, but symptomatic of my self-induced musical solitude. I packaged the cassettes with a colour picture of Roy of The Rovers and, Jiffy bags at the ready, the demo did the rounds of the record companies again, something for which I didn't feel – hopeless task as it was – The Rain material was even near being worthy. I didn't get anywhere, of course, but there was one favourable review by Mick Middles in the *Manchester Evening News*. The music lacked some dynamism, he said (bastard) but the lyrics were very promising.

The Mancunian experiment having clearly failed, I applied for a job as trainee journalist at the *Wigan Reporter*. On the strength of my interest in football, I got an interview and, amazingly, was offered the job. The money was crap, but I needed a change. I phoned Barrie and John to tell them the news. Geography was a great excuse but I'm sure they still felt the swoosh of Jones' axe down the line.

The future beckoned and it came in the guise of Alison Gladwin.

LOVE BUG

My ideal girl always had to have three essential prerequisites: black hair in a bob and a Northern accent. On that score, Alison didn't let me down. Picture the scene: Lancaster student disco, circa 1985. If you were cred, you were into The Sisters of Mercy, otherwise, you didn't show your face on the dance floor (unless for The Smiths). Anyway, on comes that anthem of gothdom 'Temple of Love', and there she was, black velvet dress, bangles, pointy little boots, not only dancing but also singing the words.

She liked The Sisters because Scott, the guy she had always fancied (who already had a girlfriend) was a fan. If it wasn't bad enough that I wasn't number one on her hit parade, it became clear that she also had her eye on two of my friends, Jon and Roger, both of whom were spoken for.

Fourth choice, then.

Still, I was clearly ahead of number five in the pecking order, Richard, then boyfriend, who was unceremoniously dumped when I started expressing an interest. Actually, there's a funny little (this being the operative word) tale to be told at this juncture.

Richard and I shared some other common ground, a stunningly beautiful drama student by the name of Cath Tozer. Anyway, yet another ex-girlfriend, Tricia McGrath (yes, yes, university is one three-year-long orgy), shared a house with Cath, and I was told later that Cath reckoned Richard and I had boasted (if that's the right word) the two smallest, ahem, gentlemen, she had ever seen. Maybe that's why I bought the VW Beetle.

Alison didn't seem to mind, although she might just have been too polite to say, and we were eventually married on June 10th 1989, the day after Dad would have been sixty.

DISC TWO

December 1988 – March 1992

BASS – HOW LOW CAN YOU GO?

The Tansads must rank alongside Bogshed as one of the worst band names of all time. I had nothing to do with choosing it, though, let me make that plain from the outset. Its origins came from Tansad Limited, a Birmingham-based firm who manufactured small, open prams known everywhere as buggies. That is, however, everywhere except in certain murky backwaters of Wigan, where the locals refer to them as tansads.

To call ourselves such a thing, then, was stupid on two counts. Not only is it highly naff to call yourself after a pram, but the word in itself is so utterly unmemorable. It soon became more misspelled than Sheik Spear (Tramsheds, Tanzards, Tin Czars, Transard, Tanzed) and nobody outside Worsley Mesnes or Pemberton a) knew what the fuck it meant or b) could pronounce it properly (literally, Tan-sads).

I can't remember precisely when I joined The Tansads. My new life in Wigan had begun on December 12th 1988, at 9:15am, when I strode into the offices of the *Wigan Reporter* on Library Street, round the corner from the Ritz Cinema where Buddy Holly had played his first ever north-west show in 1958. My first decision was to start a music column, which I called (ahem) 'Finger On The Pulse'. I had seen fly-posters all over the town advertising gigs at a venue called The Den and featuring bands with such names as Thorns from the Flesh of Troy and Doctor and the Crippens. It was proof of a thriving musical underworld and one that I couldn't wait to infiltrate and influence.

The first substantial interview was with underground shakers The Volunteers, who had just released the wonderfully titled *Bladder of Life* LP. They blew me away when I went to hear them rehearse. Driven by two in-yer-face electric guitars, they had anger, songs, and commitment. Their open-top double decker bus of a sound was never going to be giving guided tours round Pop City, but their appeal lay in a sort of punk anti-appeal.

ALISON says, *'I hadn't spoken to John since school, so when Ed met him it was strange. It ended up that my husband spent more time with my ex-boyfriend than with me. When I was with John, everything I ever wanted was in Wigan. But I went to university and discovered a big wide world and fell in love with a posh Southern boy who could have taken me anywhere. Unfortunately, he just followed me back to Wigan.'*

The rhythm guitarist was John Kettle, **Alison**'s old boyfriend from school. She dumped him while they were still at school and hadn't seen him since. They met again for the first time when Alison and I went to a Railway Children gig at Wigan's only sizeable venue, The Mill At The Pier, the day after I started at the paper. We were standing near the back when a stranger with a moustache came up to her and gave her a hug. Very alarming. The moustache, I mean.

Some weeks later, John appeared at the office with a cassette, recorded independently from The Volunteers with his current girlfriend Janet singing. He didn't want a review, he said, but was after a guitarist for the new band. He knew I played, asked if I would listen to the songs and, if I liked them, was I interested?

Well, the tape was genuinely impressive, far more accessible than The Volunteers. Janet sounded like Sandy Denny, the music was guitar-driven and a bit Smithsy but rockier. I was interested. I reviewed the tape in the column, and it was by far the best demo I had so far received. I suppose it must qualify as The Tansads' first genuine press, although I wasn't a member at the time it was printed, April 25th 1989:

'Finely crafted guitar pop, destined surely to adorn many a tasteful record collection. The songs are intelligent, melodic, and wonderfully understated, the end result is truly magnificent.'

And I meant it.

Soon after, I drove up to John's house for a practice. He was a far better player than I was. When he asked me to strum in 2/4 or 3/4 I struggled. Absolute basics of course, but I had always been prone to attempting to run before I could even walk. We persisted, however, and he gave me some tunes over which to write some lyrics. Of these, the only one to catch his eye was 'Father's Day', a slightly sentimental but totally sincere poem I'd written about Dad. Over his subtle ballad, the words fitted perfectly.

I miss you more with every day
But time won't take the pain away
The shops are full of greeting cards
That say it's Father's Day

The song apart, though, things did not go well, and I soon came badly unstuck at my first practice with the rest of the band. It was held at Wayward, a converted garage turned eight-track studio belonging to John's friend Steve Edwards. The Volunteers drummer Bug was helping out, and studio engineer Dave Fillingham filled in on bass. That left John, Janet, the oddly named Shrub on keyboards, John's brother Robert on harmonica and acoustic guitar, and me on second electric guitar.

Tragic.

'You're out of tune,' barked John.

'But the tuner says—'

'Switch that thing off. Can't you even tune your guitar?'

We struggled through the tracks on the demo, which I'd spent hours learning.

'You're overplaying, there's too much delay, turn yourself down.'

John blamed me for the disjointedness of the overall sound. He was a transformed being; the patience and encouragement previously displayed had given way to arrogance and a supreme aura of confidence. I was devastated, the tears were choking inside me; humiliated not only because of what had been said, but because I had believed there was an equality in our musical relationship.

He said he'd call.

My ego was well and truly shattered. I had assembled a hotchpotch technique, learning advanced jazz chords without understanding the rudiments of scales, and how each chord related to others. Not only that, the majority of my lyrics had been overlooked as well, but I decided to greet the news of my sacking with dignity. I would admire John's determination. He knew what he wanted, and he wasn't scared of telling people. It just was not meant to be. I would wish him every success and promise not to let the past hinder coverage in the paper. Bastard.

When he called me at the office later that week, I closed my eyes, and took a deep breath, anticipating a taste of the medicine I had dished out to others in the past. I remember even feeling slightly sorry for him because I knew how difficult it was to make those calls.

'I'm sorry about the other day,' John started. 'I think I went a bit over the top. I thought you were the big music-journalist ego-man and I was a bit hard. I didn't realize I was hurting you so much.'

His tone took me by surprise. I stammered something out.

'Oh, oh, don't worry about it,' I think I said.

'The thing is,' he went on, 'there's no easy way to say this really.'

Oh-oh, here we go . . .

'I took it out on you but really I was frustrated because I thought our styles would be more suited. The fact is, what you were playing just didn't work, and that guitar sounded crap.'

OK, he's getting somewhere now. Come on, let's have it straight.

'I don't want you as a guitarist any more.'

Surprise surprise.

'But the thing is, the way you reacted to my criticism made me respect you a lot more.'

Don't damn me with faint praise, Buster, just pull that trigger.

'Do you want to play bass for us?'

I didn't know what to say. Having expected the sack, it felt like a death-row pardon. There was an awkward silence.

'I don't think the songwriting partnership thing is going to work, but if you write stuff which is right, there's no reason why the band can't play it.'

Sounds good.

'I understand if you say no, though. I don't know if I could handle that sort of abuse from somebody. But I like you, and I think you're right for this band.'

I said I'd think about it. It was a lot to take in. I was under no illusions that what he liked most about me was clearly not musical ability. He knew I had some experience of bands and that my position at the paper would help for publicity, also indicating, perhaps, a flair for organisation and administration, things that all bands need but which most are hopelessly ill equipped to deal with. John was shrewd enough to know he needed the right kind of band members who would pull their weight, and take some of the burden of responsibility off his shoulders.

It was big decision time once again.

On the one hand, this was not the band for me, clearly. I wasn't on my preferred instrument, I wasn't in a position of control and the music, though I quite liked it, wasn't completely me. Forget what I said earlier.

On the other hand, what could I lose? My recent efforts to get a band started had proved most strenuous (why was everybody obsessed with playing Queen covers?) and I was convinced that – despite the abysmal name – The Tansads had a great chance. Besides, all was not lost, as some of my songs might be played. Ultimately, I felt I had more to lose if I didn't jump on to their train. It may not have been going to the exact destination I had in mind, but it was definitely moving in the right direction. I would ride along for a time, I told myself, then hop off when I was ready to do my own thing. With the memory of Dave and my previous decision-making blunders still looming large, and bearing in mind my less than bulging self-confidence after the practice, I chose to eat humble pie and accept. I even convinced myself it would be good not to be weighed down with the creative load for once.

Yeah, right.

Given that I had always been a driving force creatively in other bands, that I was primarily a guitarist and heavily into the indie scene, to become a non-songwriting bassist in a group who would one day grace the cover of *Folk Roots* magazine may seem a little odd. And indeed it is, with the wisdom of hindsight. But there was no way I was going to become a Pete Best and soon I was drawn into a completely new musical vortex.

For folk's sake, Jonesey.

THE MAGNIFICENT SEVEN

'Comin' outta Wig'n town, these arrr Tha' Teaanzaaaads . . .'

By the time a Canadian DJ on our local Rock FM cheese-station by the name of Adam Kelly inexplicably played two tracks, 'Diamonds in The Rain' and 'Pendle Hill', we had become the magnificent seven, due to the recent addition of John's eighteen-year-old brother Andrew. Kek, as he was also known, was by far the youngest in the group and was appropriately shy in the beginning. It often seemed that he was only in the band under duress, John having press-ganged him into The Tansads after overhearing Andrew singing one day. Certainly, the pop-star bug never really bit Kek and throughout his time in the group, he was something of an anomaly: unmotivated by success but happy to develop into the closest thing we ever got to a classic rock-'n'-roll icon. He was also in possession of the thickest, most impenetrable (if he was in the mood) Wigan accent you could wish to hear.

I'm jumping forward a bit, but the only time The Tansads got a mention on Radio 1 in the latter half of the 1990s came when Stuart Maconie (a Wiganer as well) was standing in for Mark Radcliffe late one evening. Maconie played a track from Hull band Kingmaker, before recalling a story drummer John Andrew once told him.

'They were recording their album at the same time as Wigan band The Tansads,' says Stuart, 'and one day John was in the kitchen making a cup of tea when singer Andrew Kettle walked in.

'Whur's kuklurah?' growled Andrew.

'Sorry?' John said.

'Kuklurah?

'Eh?'

'Kuklurah, whur's kuklurah?'

'Dunno. Cornwall?'

At first Andrew and I were a bit wary of each other (fear of the unknown probably), but over time we got pretty close, and he's one of the few members of the band I genuinely miss these days.

As for the others, we were a most disparate bunch. Music often has a way of making people stick together and, while not going as far as making opposites attract, it certainly makes them hang around long enough to take a closer look.

In the clean living corner were John, Janet, Shrub, and me: low alcohol intake, short hair, clean clothes, and early to bed types.

John's world-view was probably closest to mine, though our apprenticeships had differed wildly. College dropout and eight years on the dole, he was totally single-minded about music. While I was messing around studying, playing football, and fiddling with echo pedals, John was busking in Nice and sleeping on the beach. He was a brilliant guitarist, a prolific songwriter, and the creative driving force of The Tansads.

But he had a moustache. As Scottish broadcaster, writer, and ex-*Tube* presenter Muriel Gray once said, anybody who dons a moustache may as well have the words 'I'm a dickhead' tattooed on their forehead.

'He had one at school,' remembers **Alison**.

ALISON says, *'John told Ed I was the reason he started writing songs and why he wanted to be in bands. I'm sure that's why Janet never liked me, because the songs were about me and not her. Could she have been jealous of that? Silly…'*

I was incredulous.

'In those days,' she continued, 'he was a lot thinner, and he always wore a black suit. I didn't particularly fancy him actually, but everybody else did so when he asked me out, I was hardly going to refuse. He was a catch.'

With a tash?

As far as I was concerned, rock-'n'-roll lead guitarists DO NOT have moustaches. I impressed this point on him repeatedly, but the upper lip slug was not to be budged.

'Besides,' he said, 'Janet likes it.'

Janet was The Tansads' pillar of society, the clearest evidence being her job at the dole office; ironic in that most of the band signed on. She was totally supportive of John and, although a fiercely headstrong person herself, she always took her lead from him when it came to music. Had he suddenly chosen to be a landscape gardener, for example, and forget all things musical, she would have followed him quicker than you could say Alan Titchmarsh. Her dependence on him musically was reciprocated by the fact that she organised his life for him, including, it seemed, facial hair. She could sing a bit, though.

On keyboards, we had Shrub – David Atherton's nickname coming from a former hairstyle that resembled one. He was definitely no mean-living dude. Rather, Shrub was a gentle and sensitive soul, too polite and reserved by half to be a rock-'n'-roller. Considerably older than the rest of us, he'd been in and around the music scene for decades and, like me, his ultimate ambition was to branch out on his own. The musician was the man: tasteful and understated. I liked him, but it was soon to become obvious that Shrub was a passenger on the Tansads train.

All drummers drink. It's industry standard. Some more than others, granted, but few as much as Bug – Christopher Atherton. With his long flowing locks and an ever-expanding belly, Bug was a ferocious drummer. His character matched his style of play: loud, energetic, extroverted, highly entertaining, but wayward and unpredictable. At this stage, he was still 'just filling in', which roughly translated meant he was waiting to see if we became a viable proposition before switching his allegiances from The Volunteers. A classic amateur bands ploy.

As for Robert, the middle brother in the Kettle line, his poison was more of the herbal variety than liquid, the procurement and consumption of said stimulant playing the dominant role in his existence. A childhood tendency towards epilepsy had apparently changed him from insular youth into universal being. It left him with a slight speech impediment and a brain the size of Jupiter. He could be most beguiling, engaging anybody in conversation, but there were drawbacks, not least in the field of personal hygiene. Toothpaste and shampoo did not feature highly on his list of favourite playthings, he never wore underpants, and his Mum had to rip his jeans off him every few weeks and hurl them screaming and shouting into a reluctant washing machine. Like all big-time potheads, his mind would drift above day-to-day drudgery, but had the ability to be uncannily focused as soon as arrangements were being made for the next score. As a result, I was always a little suspicious of his ethereal genius. Music gave him a convenient hook on which to hang his lifestyle but, for all his philosophising, he couldn't change a plug, let alone a string on a guitar, and would never have got anywhere without his brother's patronage. That said, and despite playing guitar and mandolin like a penguin wearing mittens, there's no denying his presence became an integral aspect of the band.

There were also a few significant others in and around The Tansads.

Every band has its Terry. He was with us all the way through, jack-of-all-roadies who developed into an excellent lighting engineer. Half Pakistani, half broad 'Wiggin', in a former life he had been a wild man, an Asian Nazi sympathiser (the tattooed Swastika on his forehead had to be surgically removed) who had spent his early days fighting, drinking, fighting, crashing stolen bulldozers, fighting, then drinking again. Following a spell in Strangeways (debt evasion, I think), he discovered ganja and Pink Floyd, and transformed himself into a human being, albeit one of the scruffier variety.

As long as you didn't get on the wrong side of Terry, he was great. But his infrared bullshit detector soon let you know when you strayed from the righteous course. Thing is, nobody spewed out more crap than Terry after a few spliffs, and he could be one hell of an argumentative bastard too, especially if he drank, which, thankfully, was rarely. But he was definitely on our side, a trusted and valued companion.

Stuart Felstead was John's friend, and he knew about guitars. I had never come across the concept of a guitar technician before, but it's a pretty good invention. While you're on stage taking the glory, employing (I use the term loosely) somebody to tune the spares, change strings, and generally make sure everything's running smoothly. Stuart harboured desires of playing in the band, but, as he was the worst bass player I had ever heard, with as much rhythmical sense as a baby learning to walk, there was little chance of that. I think John offered him the job to cushion the blow of rejection and he became the first in a long line of guitar roadies, both peripheral and crucial at the same time.

For the first few shows, we used a combination of Dave Fillingham from Steve Edwards' studio and Steve himself as sound engineer. Fillingham was a shifty character who eventually let us down badly, but Steve was one of the foundations on which the band was able to survive and grow. Ostensibly, he had given us hours of free time for him and Dave to 'learn' the studio, but even after the guinea-pig arrangement had run its course, he carried on with his support, and gave us thousands of pounds of time for virtually nothing. Again, a long line of engineers followed suit.

Only one more, honest, and that's Simon 'Fat Man' Collett. He looked like a pair of Morrissey specs on stilts (hence the 'hilarious' nickname) and had lived in the first flat I had moved into in Wigan. We instantly bonded. He was a brilliant graphic designer, and was health-threateningly generous with both his time and his money, funding and designing posters and demo covers. The Fat Man soon sculpted the image of the band, and his financial contribution would be critical in the months and years to come.

In all cases, apart from Fillingham, and all sound engineers as they were paid, the currency was goodwill. Why were they so devoted? Music has this debilitating effect on the senses and there was a chance we would make it.

Did we abuse their loyalty? Probably, but there was no alternative to getting heavily into debt; financially and especially morally. It was all in the name of progress.

Let's folk-'n'-roll!!

PERAMBULATORS ARE GO!

Monday March 26th 1990. Upstairs at a pub in Widnes called Players, and The Tansads make their first public appearance. Promoter Tony Dagnall paid us £75 – I think – which was really pretty good for a debut gig in a town where the only previous claim to rock-'n'-roll fame (Sporty Spice hadn't been invented yet) was its station platform, upon which Paul Simon penned 'Homeward Bound'. But while he couldn't wait to get out of the place, we couldn't wait to get in.

As the gig approached, rehearsals became more intense and we'd be spending double sessions on Sunday afternoons and twice during the week playing at the aptly named Dead Fly studios in St Helens. Included in the price were two flights of dimly lit stairs, a continuous and nauseous stench of adhesive from the factory below, soundproofing akin to damp cardboard, and a drinks machine that didn't work. All the greats start somewhere, I kept telling myself, and while those days were hard, eight hours at work, straight over to The Fly, back home in the early hours of the morning, up at seven and off to work again, the excitement and tension was building as we moved ever closer to that elusive first gig.

ALISON says, *'What was I supposed to think? We had just got married, just bought our first house, it was the start of an adventure. But he just didn't take it seriously, didn't take me seriously. All that was in his mind was the band.'*

The band was shaping up well, and developing a real edge. John's songs reflected his heroes: Paul Weller and 70s Mancunian folk-rock legend Roy Harper. Underneath all this was Bug's highly physical presence. He was into Funkadelic and The Red Hot Chili Peppers, who were just breaking at the time. As for me, I didn't have much chance to influence the sound, although I was discovering the concept of 'the groove'. While the others sat around, Bug, John, and I would develop an idea and I always did think that this stripped-down part of the group was best, a classic rock sound with no folky tangents to water things down.

John's head, however, was in a different place altogether. His arse. He wanted The Tansads to embrace as many genres as possible, and said a great band should be able to play any style, any time, anywhere. Maybe, but whereas The Beatles' various incarnations took place over nearly a decade, he wanted us to do it in forty-five minutes. The ability to do this with admittedly varying degrees of success was our greatest strength. It would, however, soon become our greatest weakness.

The PA stacks (translation: speakers) John hired for Widnes cost more than our fee and wouldn't fit up the stairwell of the pub. 'Welcome Spinal Tap' read the sign above the door as we attempted The Guinness Book of Records entry for the most ever musicians to stand on a staircase holding a speaker. We eventually bullied the brutes into submission but the incident was a significant omen – attempting to fit the square peg of ambition into the round hole of reality. A futile exercise we spent virtually the whole life of the band trying to achieve.

It also illustrated the differing 'management' styles John and I would develop. He was the impulsive one, intransigent, never letting finance or practicalities get in the way of a good idea. I was the boring one, the worrier, who poured cold water over his enthusiasm. John had decided that we would bring our own rig, because, he said, he didn't want the band's confidence to be wrecked by the shoddy PA the promoter was bound to provide (PAs are always the first place promoters save money).

'OK,' I said, 'but does it have to be so big?'

'You look after the publicity and book the gigs, and I'll handle the music' was the put-down.

I can't remember anything about the soundcheck that day but I know we were all very nervous. Not surprising, really, as after all the preparation this was the moment of truth.

Hello, Widnes!

There were thirty people there, some of whom we knew, and most of whom were sitting on chairs and on the floor. The applause was polite, apart from Andrew's mad mate Frank who completely freaked out at the end. Unbelievably we got an encore, more because we wanted to play another rather than being invited to by the audience. **Tony Connolly** also became our first proper fan (i.e. one we hadn't known previously) by asking us to sign our demo. Where are you now, Tony?

TONY CONNOLLY – Tony's favourite Tansads' song was 'Father's Day' (good man), which he heard for the first time at this gig, it's only ever live rendition. As a special favour to Tony and his girlfriend Lorraine, who along with various members of their families soon became regular attendees at gigs (Tony even guesting on the spoons very occasionally), John agreed to play it once more at their wedding the following year – yes The 'Sads did a wedding. But never a barmitzvah.

Fortunately, we were spared a repeat performance with the speakers on the way out. A disco was going on downstairs so the emergency exit stairs that had been conveniently been locked on our arrival were now opened. We were delighted the impending corridor burden had been lifted, but the relief was short-lived when we encountered the landlord's ferocious dog chained up on the terrace. The brute was none too happy about a convoy of heavy-duty musical equipment being trawled past his kennel at such an undogly hour, and he related his chagrin most eloquently. Thankfully, the chain was stronger than his straining muscles – just – and I was glad to be wearing my brown trousers that evening. I mean, have you ever tried tiptoeing down a stairwell with a missing stair and around a salivating Doberman at one in the morning and in the pouring rain whilst carrying a 16-ton weight?

Quite.

The Widnes date was to have been part of two warm-up gigs before our hometown debut five days later. Unfortunately the date at a St Helens nightclub called Crystals was cancelled at the last minute due to a double booking with a stripper, and The Den, Wigan was to be the next performance.

Playing at home is always more daunting. Although there are friendly faces present, there is a sizeable contingent of those who come with the express intention of seeing you fall flat on your face. The Den – The Wigan Greater Manchester Buses depot social club, no less – was the town's only regular venue and, as there was no promoter involved, I booked the room. Again John hired the PA. Again it was too big and again very costly. We had made a considerable loss in Widnes ("Well, that was a useful lesson for the future anyway," said John) and tonight threatened to be similar. We had to pull 130 people to break even. Gulp. Even The Volunteers gigs pulled less than 100 at The Den, and they were an established name. Incredibly, however, by the time support act Peter James Mercer had finished his set, the room was full like I'd never seen it before.

Hello, Wigan!

Opener 'Shandyland' was cheered. Thank God for that. In the end, we got two encores – audience-induced – and exactly 130 people paid to see us.

Wigan is small, its band scene even smaller and, like any town, there is an overwhelming sense of apathy towards anything new and untested.

Make no mistake, this was a major, major, result.

PULL UP TO THE BUMPER, BABY

There was an inevitable anticlimax after our thousand-megaton blast onto the rock-'n'-roll stage. Two other Tony Dagnall gigs apart, back at Players and at a pub called The Royal in Runcorn (the box office had been jammed for weeks, allegedly), there was nothing.

The ultimate irony in a land which has produced – and celebrated – so many great bands is that the system is arranged to positively discourage originality in new music. Or perhaps that's the point: only the hardiest creative genius survives the freezing winter of universal lack of interest. Probably not.

The lucky ones get noticed straight away and avoid the pathetic scramble even to get on the first rung of the ladder. The majority, however, fall by the wayside before they even learn what A&R stands for (thankfully in many cases). Artists and Repertoire, by the way, in case you were wondering.

Getting gigs at this level is a question of blag, hence the need for a pushy manager (or a pushy mate posing as one). I have about as much aptitude for salesmanship as for handcuffed caber-tossing, but in a moment of weakness and admittedly, pique, I volunteered myself as chief gig-prospector and was determined to succeed. The first step was to create the impression we were bigger than were. Publicity. Solution – black-and-white photo shoot in the local park. Cliché – by the bundle, mate.

Simon used the picture along with a more dramatic shot Alison had taken from The Den (with crowd – i.e. following – visible) to design (and fund) a glossy handout. The band's image was all over the place – bank clerks meet vagrants at a cider festival – but the illusion clearly worked. Suddenly, things started moving and ten gigs were arranged between August and the end of the year at pubs and clubs across the North-west.

Hardly an arena globetrot, but it was a start.

The first show, on August 15th, was in Wigan, supporting *NME*-touted Swervedriver at a horrible, vacuous rock club called Maximes. Despite their huge desirability, support gigs with established groups are the ritual humiliation all bands must suffer sooner or later. The worse the venue, the worse the nightmare. This place was shit.

Maximes has a disproportionately tiny stage, like a sumo wrestler with a tennis ball for a head, and when there's already another band's gear on it and they refuse to move even a drumstick, things can get tricky. Especially when there are seven in the band. We subsequently spent our entire allocated soundcheck time (a good ten minutes) arguing with their tour manager and the promoter, until a compromise was reached: they moved one of the amps a couple of inches backwards or something. Thanks, boys.

Fraught from this particular battle, we squeezed onto the stage like a truckload of startled sheep and attempted to perform. With enthusiasm. The PA subsequently broke down when Terry turned the lights on. Twice. Any illusions of glamour had long since vanished as we stumbled through the rest of the set in semi-darkness, willing the end.

Then, in the final twist of the knife, just when you think it's safe to hide your face and vanish, we had to get back onstage to clear up before the main band came on, thus killing off completely any notion of the performer-as-star.

At least, in this instance, people had come to see us, and we were relatively well received. When you get a hostile crowd or are simply just ignored after all the traumas of setting up, your head-butted ego ends up with less self-esteem than a beggar on Wall Street.

And remember, these are the good gigs.

A fortnight after our career-enhancing Swervedriver extravaganza, we fell for the local-bands-night trick. Doh. The management of the Boardwalk club in Manchester assured us that if we brought a Wigan Showcase to the Mancunian mother ship, we would undoubtedly be offered support gigs in the future. And A&R scouts always come to local bands nights, we were told.

We believed them. We organized a night. Inevitably, we made a loss. The convoy that came trundling down the M61 consisted of The Tansads, Peter James Mercer, and the excellently titled Those Naughty Corinthians (whose party piece was to perform a ten-song set in 15 minutes) along with 80 lost and lonely souls who paid loads for a gig they could quite easily have seen for a quarter of the price in Wigan.

There was no publicity, therefore nobody else turned up, and the nearest **A&R** man was playing with his mirror and razor blades in the toilets of a club in Camden. Finally, we rowed with the promoter over ticket money, and he promptly refused to put us on again, thus conveniently unarranging the arrangement about further gigs.

There's no business like show business, there's no business I know.

It was clearly time for a boost, which duly arrived in the form of our second Wigan Den show, on September 14th. The room was full to bursting with over 200 fans, and another 40-odd were turned away. That's right, turned away. Unbelievable.

The cassettes we sold at shows were hardly a money-spinner, but they served to spread the word. Now the people knew the songs. Now the people cheered at the beginning of songs as they recognised the introduction. Now the people danced. And now the people sang. The atmosphere was transformed. Our self-belief was magically restored. John and Bug both finished

A&R – These people are employed to liaise between the artist and the record company. They get a lot of bad press, but to be fair, they do have the unenviable task of keeping both sides happy. Not easy given that the record company is interested solely in the bottom line and musicians are invariably prima donnas. Then there are the long hours scouting the nation (well, Greater London), listening to dreadful bands and the pressure of knowing that if the next 'big one' isn't discovered quickly, then plenty of eager beavers are just waiting to step into their shoes. That said, most of them are still wankers...

completely with The Volunteers, and we had a new member in Dominic Lowe, accordion, occasional trumpet and 'I'll help out on guitar if I have to.'

Aah, the Dom phenomenon.

He had just returned from Cornwall, and talked about nothing else but wanting to go back. His girlfriend at the time was Janet's best mate. Dom appeared at rehearsal one day, and the next thing I knew, he was in the band. From day one, he showed about as much enthusiasm as a child did on the way to the dentist.

'John's a twat,' he said to me after rehearsal one night.

'So why did you join the band?'

'Dunno.'

We shall be meeting Mr Lowe properly a little later.

The successes we had in Wigan made it a lot easier to take the knocks that came thick and fast in the shape of the truly awful gigs further afield. It had taken me six months to get a show at Storeys, a nightclub in Widnes; a gig there was a considerable notch on the bedpost.

When we arrived, we found a sparsely attended student disco, upstairs in the over-mirrored function room of a fun-pub.

The show must go on.

We were told to be there for 7.00 p.m. An hour later, the promoter turned up. We struggled with the gear up the narrow, painfully steep emergency stairs and soundchecked at 9.00 p.m., just as the doors were opening. We then had to wait until midnight to play.

The dance floor, though previously full, emptied in one unanimous movement when we turned our amps on, only to return as soon as the last note was played. It was as though we hadn't even existed. I can't remember anybody responding, not a jeer or a catcall. We then had to hang around like bored gatecrashers until the club closed at 2.00 a.m. Around 4.30, my head hit the pillow.

I soon developed an irrational fear of alarm clocks.

Similar strength-and-morale sappings occurred at various other North-west dives but we were once again invigorated by our third and final Den show on October 19th. God bless Wigan. Even more people were turned away this time and our support act was Monkeyland, a local four-piece I had been praising in the paper (we insisted on treating them well). The gig was mayhem and, in complete contrast to elsewhere, the shows in Wigan had become something of a celebration. One thing had become abundantly clear, however, and it was time to look for a new venue. The only suitable place was the Council-owned, 500-capacity Mill at the Pier. It cost £300 to hire. We would need a much larger PA and more lights, of course, but it was a risk we had no choice but to take. I booked January 4th, the first available Saturday.

There was one other bit of good news to come.

The IDEA project was a worthy Arts Council-funded promotion for unsigned local bands (those were the days). It was a chance for wannabes to be committed to immortality via vinyl. The track we submitted was 'Right On', a low-key, groove-based song with a catchy singalong chorus. Compared to all the ramshackle rants and grunts on the record, it stood out like blood on snow. The thinking behind IDEA was not only to promote the North-west to London, but also to give bands the chance to get an audience in different towns. The Volunteers had a following in St Helens, so we were given a support slot at a local venue, The Citadel, on December 22nd. Because of John and Bug's former affiliations it was definitely a friendly support, i.e. no arguments over drum kits or guitar stands, and colliding egos were placed on hold (for an evening at least).

Then we got the news.

Dave Elyatt, an A&R scout from Red Dot, a subsidiary of Chrysalis, had heard the album and liked our track. Dave Evans, the promoter of the Citadel gig, told us on the day of the show that Elyatt would be making the trip. Especially to see us.

Well, that was it then, wasn't it? Driver, put that stretch limo on ice, The Tansads are coming.

ALISON says, *'Other people's girlfriends may have watched them rehearse, but I didn't. I don't mind hearing a song once but I don't care to listen to it fifteen times over in a row. Besides, I hardly needed to. They still used the house for so-called quiet practices, and I could hear it all perfectly well through the walls, thank you very much. Some of them never even said hello to me. How was I supposed to react? I would be sitting in the next room with the cats, or ironing his shirts for work, and I couldn't even hear the television. Oh yes, those were happy days alright.'*

PIER PRESSURE

Dave Elyatt told me he enjoyed the Citadel gig. Honestly. He asked for more material, and three days before the Mill gig, our biggest show to date by a mile, he phoned to say he wanted to come up and see us again.

Woooooooooah!

To come once was amazing, to come back for more was the strongest possible statement of intent and of interest. I punched the table in delight after putting the phone down and soon set about publicising the gig. We couldn't have done any more. Posters were plastered all over town, hundreds of flyers were handed out and I plugged the show to death in the paper:

'After the chaos of the last Tansads gig at the Den, when people were turned away and those that did get in were crammed in more tightly than the Tokyo subway, the band felt it was wise to move to a bigger venue. Let's hope there's room for everybody this time round.'

When we arrived at the Mill at the Pier, the room seemed even larger than I remembered; anything less than 250 people and it would look painfully empty, 350 people was our break-even.

Sphincter muscles, stand by.

In total contrast to the rickety old Den, the stage was immense, there was room to swing a full cattery, never mind a solitary kitten. John hired a massive PA, which meant fat speaker stacks on either side of the stage, a mixing desk with more knobs than a foxhunting convention, a monitor speaker *each* on stage, a separate engineer for the on-stage mix, and the drums and keyboards placed on separate risers.

ROCK-AND-ROLL-ER!

Without a crowd to soak the noise up during the soundcheck, the drums were immense, the guitar bounced off the walls like rubber balls, the voices, incredibly, were audible and my bass thundered down below, ripping up through the ribcage. We sounded amazing.

How could Elyatt fail to be impressed?

When the support band, More Perfect Watchers, had finished their soundcheck at around 7.00 p.m., everything was in place. The tension was unbearable. You could have taken a knife to it and cut a large slice out. I was due to meet Elyatt at 9.00 p.m., but I couldn't stand just waiting around, counting the trickle of people coming in, and subsequently fretting over numbers. I decided to go home. It was no better there. I tried eating something but felt sick. I had a shower, agonised over what to wear, and decided that the combination of my Wigan Athletic football top and ripped old 501s was bound to bring me luck. I drove back to the venue.

The tension had been charged to an incredible excitement. I was a young child awaiting the arrival of Santa on Christmas Eve.

9.00 p.m. Still an hour to go before we were on. As I entered, I asked if Elyatt had turned up yet. No. Plenty of time, don't panic. I walked sheepishly into the auditorium, my hand over my eyes, too scared to look. How many punters are in? I then poked my nose round the corner . . . people! The room is full. Not completely. But there's a crowd. A lot of them sit on the floor, watching the support. I can't estimate exactly, but we're over the embarrassment threshold.

Thank God for that.

9.15 p.m. Still no Elyatt. Shit, he is going to come, isn't he? Were the directions right? 9.20 p.m. Still no sign. Come on. I'm hovering between the door and the hall, as twitchy as an entrapped wasp in a glass jar. The rest of the band arrives. Nobody else seems bothered about Elyatt, their minds set on the show. I talk to Simon. T-shirts have already been sold. I go back to the door. Nothing. Where is he? More people come in. 9.30 p.m. Still no sign. I've just thought of something. Is it naff to wait for A&R men? I suppose it is. Damn. But I said I'd meet him and it'll look bad if I'm not there. Won't it? 9.35 p.m. Come on, come on. 9.40 p.m. This is now beginning to look bad. 9.45 p.m. Fuck, we're due on in quarter of an hour. Come oooooon. 9.50 p.m. I'm going to have to—

'Guest list. Dave Elyatt.'

I look round. The howls of delight are all internal. Thankfully.

'Sorry I'm late.'

'No worries.' LIAR!

'I got a bit lost.'

'I'm going round to the back, do you want to come round and say hello?'

'No, it's all right, I'll catch up with you afterwards.'

At least he intends to stay until the end. I get back to the dressing room too late to prepare properly. My mind's in a spin, the knot in my stomach would make a boy scout blush.

10.00 p.m. Time. The lights go off. Simple murmurs. Where are the cheers of anticipation? We come on stage and there are a few claps and whistles. Everybody is still sitting towards the back. In front of the stage is an uninhabited pool of darkness.

It looks so crap.

The band kicks off. Lights dazzle me. The sound is huge. We're giving it loads. Nobody stands up. For fuck's sake, don't you know our future's at stake here? This is a rock-'n'-roll concert, not a madrigal recital. STAND UP, YOU CUNTS, impress the man! Two songs. Three songs. The reception is warm, but still they sit. Twats. Selfish twats. Four songs. Then it happens. *Right on*. The groove is so simple, so spacious, so infectious. A couple rise.

Thank Goodness!

Two more follow, then an irreversible tide sweeps everybody to their feet and, all of a sudden, we have a gig on our hands. The band responds. I relax and start to enjoy it. We get an encore and finish with the anthemic 'Shandyland'. We depart the stage to rapturous applause.

The dressing room is immediately awash with liggers, which pisses me off no end. I want to bask quietly in the euphoria of it all. No chance. Anyway, I have to go and find Elyatt.

He was waiting in the fast emptying hall. With the house lights on and a thousand plastic glasses all over the floor, the gig's spell had been broken.

'It was great, really,' he said and I noticed that he wore the obligatory A&R baseball jacket, despite the sauna-like conditions. John came and joined us.

'I'm still a bit worried about the size of the band, though,' Elyatt continued. 'It's a hell of a commitment. But I think you've got something, definitely.'

'You got the cassette, then, Dave?' I asked

'Yes, thanks. I liked the material, but I still don't know what we would choose as a single. We need a single, something to pin the whole campaign on.'

How could he be so matter of fact after such an emotional rollercoaster?

'Listen, I better get off. It was good, really good. I've seen the band in a different light tonight, I think we could well be onto something. But I've got to convince other people in the office, y'know. I'll be in touch. Maybe come and see you again. Make sure you keep me bang up to date with what's happening, OK?'

We nodded and then he was gone

It was brilliant that he had come, but seeds of doubt had been sown. I didn't know the logistics of bands getting signed but you heard tales of jabbering A&R scouts begging bands to agree to deals there and then. That was the legend. The reality is always duller. For The Tansads anyway. I reasoned Elyatt was going for the more measured approach. After all, a lot of money was potentially at stake.

JANUARY 16TH, 1991 – Another January 16th. I've just finished the best song I've ever written, 'Sometimes I Wish'. It's about Dad. John says he likes it, but doesn't think it would work in the band. Why do I fucking bother? *'January 16th 1978/the unthinkable pain one day would create…'*

Nevertheless, something didn't feel quite right. Elyatt talked in negatives, not positives. I didn't transmit these feelings to John. I didn't have to. We certainly didn't let the uncertainty darken our mood, however. The gig had been another overwhelming success. We had pulled just over 350, far in excess of our Den trawls.

We had conquered the North Face of Wigan Pier.

ARE YOU BEING VERVED?

It was just a demo. Badly presented, poorly recorded and with no information attached aside from track titles. It was no different from those I received by the bucket load at the *Wigan Reporter*. I wasn't to know that this band would evolve into a giant, that their albums would shift more in a morning than The Tansads would sell in a lifetime, or that they would achieve all my ambitions and more, while I watched, riddled with envy, from afar.

It was my policy not to slag off demos when reviewing them for the column. I knew what was involved in the making of them and the dreams each contained. I became a diplomat of language. When Verve's arrived, I remember thinking that it was nothing special. Reprinted for the first time since that fateful week, here is the historic text in full, the band's first ever press, in the *Wigan Reporter*, delivered free to 80,000 homes (and a few dustbins) in Wigan, Lancashire, England, stardate January 31st 1991:

'Verve are a 4-piece from Wigan and judging from the fact I've never heard of them before, this is presumably their first offering. The music is downbeat **Velvet Underground** kind of stuff, not completely lacking in lighter moments however, and not unpleasant at all.'

Classically patronizing.

'Overall I liked it, the band have a definite sound and there is soul and self-belief in what they do, musicianship and arrangements are not that important if the songs are OK, which I think these are. Given time and a little commitment, they could progress to better things, I'm sure.'

It was only an honest opinion. Hindsight has a cruel fondness for making you look like a complete prick. I used to fervently believe that Verve, or The Verve as they became, would come and go before The Tansads (or Tansads, as we became) had even reached their peak.

Difficult though it may be, having just read the above milestone (millstone) in rock journalism, you must believe that I was never comfortable sitting upon the falsely elevated stool of the music critic. After all, who the hell was I to judge other people's work? Just a guy in a band (I suppose that at least gave me some authority) who had the opportunity to get his views in print.

There is no greater arrogance than that of the critic, because the power they wield is so often abused. I never did that, I hope, but, however hard I try to squirm away, bad reviews always come back to haunt you. My only regret is that I don't have the consolation prize – the original Verve demo to flog to collectors. Much to my financial chagrin, it went the way of most of the dozens of others I received every month, heartlessly converted into a (nearly new) blank cassette.

I've still got Monkeyland, though, that any good?

VELVET UNDERGROUND – Nico (born Christa Paffgen, 16 October '38) was invited to join the band by manager Andy Warhol and featured prominently on the debut album *The Velvet Underground and Nico*, released October '67 on the MGM-Verve label. She died on the 18th July '88 after suffering a brain haemorrhage due to a fall from her bike while on holiday in Ibiza. Incidentally, it was after threatened litigation by the Verve label that Verve the band were eventually forced to add the 'The' to their name. We never got any such credibility-enhancing threats from Tansad Limited, alas.

Anyway, John and I agreed that Verve would be the perfect support fodder for our next Mill at the Pier show, which I booked for March 23rd. This time the audience target was 500. They appeared to have a bit of a following, and were good without being brilliant. Or so we thought. This represented the perfect combination: the swelling of crowd numbers with no better way of making your own band look good than coming on after an inexperienced, stage-shy support act who are given half the power and half the lights.

That's the theory.

This marriage of convenience was soon on the rocks, however. A friend of Verve's, Nik Clark, started a music column in the *Wigan Reporter*'s sister paper the *Wigan Observer* – not a patch on mine, of course. Under the headline 'Band War Breaks Out', he printed a picture of Verve, and in true 'this town ain't big enough for the both of us' style, inserted a caption about how they were going to blow us off stage.

We should have risen above the jibes, as reaction was a sure sign of insecurity. Still, there's nothing more dangerous than a wounded ego, and John's had certainly just received a swift kick in the balls. He was outraged, and wanted them kicked off the gig.

Ever the diplomat, I attempted to calm the stormy waters. My first reaction had been one of surprise, because I knew drummer Pete Salisbury and it seemed totally out of character, as he had always been so quiet and humble. Pete was a bit of a local band tart. He had been around. Not only was he in a group called The Comedians I had recently interviewed but he was also a member of The Rayne Props, a review of whom had just gone to print. Elasticity of membership, especially when it comes to that rarer specimen, the drummer, is the preserve of small town amateur scenes, which we had seen with Bug.

RINGO STARR – born Richard Starkey. In 1975, Ringo had a number three hit in the US with the Elton John/Bernie Taupin penned 'Snookeroo'.

As a muso aside here, I should have known that Verve were going to be huge there and then, because Pete followed in a tradition (**Ringo Starr**, Rick Buckler) of famous crap drummers. To quote biz vernacular, there are two types of timekeepers: twatters and ticklers. Bug was definitely the former, he virtually jumped on the skins to make them go louder, launching his entire being into every beat. He was in a different universe musically from Salisbury, who stroked the drums like he was spreading cold butter on a particularly crumbly piece of toast. Still, which one gets to throw TV sets out of hotel windows today? Or indeed, which one's even still drumming?

I digress. Verve were managed at the time by a friend called Dave

Halliwell – responsible more than anybody for their initial success. He was one hell of a pushy bastard. Through his telephone call, they swiftly apologised for the fighting talk in the *Wigan Observer*.

'We didn't say any of that stuff to Nik, he took it upon himself to write it all, honestly. He was only having a laugh, I'm sorry it came out the way it did.'

Dave's tone was satisfyingly apologetic. I didn't believe him for a second, of course, but the furore had only served to hype the gig further, so, mercenaries to the last, and after much metaphorical finger-wagging in order that we felt big and strong again, the matter was dropped.

Things were further patched up when I went up to interview Verve at bassist **Simon Jones**' house for a preview in the column. They were all there, along with Halliwell, and were politeness and gratitude personified. My journalistic technique was pretty laid back and unstructured then and I stressed that, as a musician and one of them, it would feel more like a chat than a formal interview.

SIMON JONES – I once bought a second-hand upright freezer from a house three doors away from the bassist's mum. It cost a bargain £30. Sweet.

My device for breaking the ice was always to ask silly questions at first. The current theme in the column surrounded cheesy music, so it seemed appropriate to head in a dairy-products sort of direction.

'If Verve was a cheese, which one would it be be?'

Choice of cheese, I believed, like that of a daily newspaper, is clearly an accurate litmus of personality.

'Garlic Roulé,' said Richard.

'Edam,' said Simon.

'Mature cheddar melted on crumpet,' said Nick.

I don't remember what Pete said.

The conversation deteriorated into a sensible chat about music. Yawn. We talked about their heroes, and I got the usual 'we're not here just for laughs, we've got a sound all of our own' platitudes; and a list of influences: Sonic Youth for Nick; Richard and Simon said Tim Buckley, **Neil Young**, and Can. Pete didn't say anything.

NEIL YOUNG – Having moved to the Geffen label in the early '80s, Young's work consequently became directionless and confused, with ill-advised forays into rockabilly and MOR country. His time with the label came to an end when Geffen sued him for making records that didn't sound like Neil Young!

What struck me right away was their self-belief.

'We plan to be around for a long time,' Richard told me. 'Obviously, it would be great if we got signed straight away, but we are determined to make it anyway, even if it takes longer.'

I'd heard this a hundred times before, college kids outlining the familiar manifesto for world domination. I had been one myself, of course, though I never got the chance to spout my philosophies in print.

I don't wish to be presumptuous by comparing myself to superstars (would I?) but I instantly recognised in Richard the same absurd self-confidence I had at his age. Where mine had been all fluffy intellectual drivel floating somewhere in orbit, however, his was frighteningly focused already. It may have been just the drugs working, of course, but, when he stared through those big round eyes, you could see he meant it. Translated into band-talk, the fundamental difference between us now was that he knew Verve would be signed. I hoped The Tansads would.

It is terminally ironic, but they soon went on to ask me for advice about record companies. I mustn't let retrospect cloud the fact that at the time our status was far greater than theirs; we had a big following, and I suppose my position as local rock journo gave me a kind of aura.

How I now cringe.

I explained we had hardly got beyond the rejection letter/ 'sorry, he's in a meeting' stage until Dave Elyatt. Dave Halliwell reeled off the places he was trying, and the positive responses received: London Records, East West, Polydor, Rough Trade.

'Sounds to me like they're bullshitting, Dave,' warned wise old bird. 'They're wankers, all of them, they'll only let you down, keep you waiting, then look elsewhere.'

Spot on with the prognosis, Jonesey.

We parted on amicable terms. I even drove Nick and his girlfriend Monica home miles out of my way as a 'no hard feelings' parting shot. However, the episode over the Nik Clark article had still left a scar of animosity. Despite the superficial niceties, we still wanted to show the whippersnappers who was Daddy in Wigan.

33,000 **Haigh Hall** tickets sold out in two hours? I think we can safely say who eventually won that argument.

HAIGH HALL – The Tansads actually played here first, back in January 1992, in the main ballroom to a crowd of at least forty doctors and nurses from Wigan Infirmary.

I made no allusion to the troubles in my feature, which duly appeared in the column two days before the gig, March 21st, embarrassingly headlined 'We just lerve Verve', alongside the same picture that had appeared in the *Wigan Observer*.

On the Saturday there was a real edge. We were still nervous about filling the hall, but Verve was the overriding itch we had to scratch. It must have cut both ways. This was also a big night for them, their first public show on home soil, their biggest attendance by far, and they were being watched by Dave Gilmour (not the Pink Floyd guitarist, but a then scout for Island), and let us not forget, a certain journalistic prophecy needed to be fulfilled.

Their fans stormed to the front of the stage when they came on, giving them a fabulous reception. I had never seen that at a local gig before. The audience became instantly divided. The majority stood back, reticent, leaving a halo around Verve and their people. The band were brilliant, mesmeric even then, and frighteningly unselfconscious. Ashcroft always got the plaudits, but for me the star was McCabe; his guitar had real danger lurking within it, immense, but still understated. Sure enough, this was competition like we'd never had before.

The room was absolutely packed with over 500 people. Fretting about audience numbers had given way to armour-clad band egos at ten paces and Verve fans had certainly thrown down the gauntlet. I was standing near the stall, at the back of the room. Simon looked at me and I could see it in his eyes: they were going to blow us off that stage right enough. Our fans never rush to the front like that, *never* treat us with such adulation.

Humiliation, thy name is rock-'n'-roll.

To make matters worse, the lights tripped out on them, so for the last quarter of their set, all they had were a few house fluorescents. I'm sure they thought we'd done it on purpose. Once they finished, the hubbub of anticipation rose. We retreated to the dressing room. John gave the team talk. We huddled round. He was in defiant mood.

'We can't control the crowd, but it's up to us to create a response like that. We've got to play like we've never played before. For fuck's sake, they're just a bunch of kids. We're the fucking headliners here.'

We were silent as the minutes ticked ever closer to stage time. I couldn't bear the tension. It had started getting pretty noisy outside. I had to look. Peaking round the backstage curtain, I fully expected acres of gleaming parquet flooring in front of the stage. But instead, a sea of faces stared back at me, jostling for the best vantage-point, shouting, whistling, and chanting our name. By carrying out the simple act of going to the front of the stage before we came on, the audience had plainly demonstrated that we were a proper band, who played proper gigs, and had proper fans.

Yeeeeeeees!

There was no reticence from the crowd as they went ballistic from the first chord. We leapt about like salmon on trampolines, the tension fizzing away from our bodies like air from a pricked balloon. The crowd was alive, dancing and singing the words to the songs with a daunting passion and the excitement created in us an unprecedented intensity of performance. It was total commitment to the moment. Songs like 'Shandyland' and 'Cobbly Back

Yard' turned into anthems, the gig never waned, and we finished off with two encores and a stage invasion for the mad, incongruous 'Ska Track'.

Afterwards, we collapsed, mentally and physically shattered. What impact Verve had had in the end is hard to say. How much the crowd was provoked into reacting so positively, and how much would have happened anyway, I don't know. Whatever, we had definitely won the battle – the odds had been stacked pretty heavily in our favour, let's face it – but little did we know then just how spectacularly we would lose the war.

The signs were there that night actually, only we didn't spot them. The bastards broke their toilet seat, and didn't even report it. Now that was decadence we could only dream about emulating.

THE MORE YOU IGNORE ME, THE CLOSER I GET

The phone rang at the office. It was Dave Halliwell, anxious to maintain the momentum of Verve's growing profile after their Mill at the Pier support.

'Thanks for the coverage, Ed. We really enjoyed the gig.'

No mention of band wars or broken toilet seats.

'I was calling to let you know the latest news. We're getting loads of interest: A&M, London, Virgin, CBS, Island, East West. It's a question of weighing up what each one has to offer, then choosing.'

'Thanks for letting me know,' I replied. 'I'll put something in this week. And make sure you keep me informed of what's going on.'

Shit. In an ideal world, this shouldn't have caused me any problems. I didn't mind Verve doing well; in fact, I would be more than happy for them to be successful. That is, of course, if The Tansads were doing better. We weren't. I was caught, therefore, between the inter-band jealousy that forbade me from applauding them and the pride and enthusiasm I had to display when writing about them in 'Finger on the Pulse'. I tried my best. Honest.

Meanwhile, in the land of A&R, if it weren't for bad luck, The Tansads would have had no luck at all. The nadir was to be The Powerhaus, London on May 17th. Before then we had got ourselves a manager. Since the association with the IDEA project in St Helens, Dave Evans from the Citadel and The Volunteers manager Damian Liptrot (a psychology lecturer by day), also heavily involved with IDEA, had been working on our behalf. Damian made the mistake, in fact, of working too hard on our behalf. We asked him to become our manager and foolishly, he accepted.

Our search for management had by this time become quite urgent. We had toyed with the idea of asking a guy called Mike Dutton who owned the local music emporium Music 90. But the alarm bells rang two minutes into our meeting with him at the Pear Tree pub.

'What's your vision for the band then, Mike?'

'Well, I know a bloke who runs a club in Southport . . .'

Thanks.

We didn't sign a contract with Damian, naturally. Money was such a foreign concept to us at this stage that it never entered our thoughts. Damian's first task was to try and tame the great A&R beast. So far, only Dave Elyatt had expressed real interest in us but, as he was dithering somewhat, we had to spread our wings further. Damian contacted dozens of companies, despatched demos like there was no tomorrow, and made a hundred phone calls.

'Play in London and we'll come.'

The old ones are always the best. And we believed them.

The only way we could secure a decent venue such as The Powerhaus was to take no fee and guarantee a coachload of punters. Effectively it was **pay to play** and it was a gamble. No question. But Elyatt and Martin Toher at A&M said they would definitely be there and others expressed an interest. Verve's recent history proved that it took only one of the buggers to bite, and the rest would follow like lemmings.

PAY TO PLAY – The majority of local band venues now adopt this reprehensible policy, sometimes disguised as bands having to sell tickets in advance. If all musicians united and boycotted these venues, things would soon change. However, bands realise that if they don't play, somebody else will and an opportunity to impress will have been lost.

On the night, however, instead of a throbbing pub full of cockney punters and a pack of eager-beaver A&R scouts (they were probably all back in Wigan negotiating with Verve), we played to fifty heavily subsidised Wiganers and one bloke who paid on the door.

Shortly afterwards, the first rejection letter arrived. Then another. And another. Island, Chrysalis, Sony, A&M, East West, London, Polydor, RCA, Go Discs, MCA, Phonogram, IRS, One Little Indian, China, Cooking Vinyl.

Were there any other companies left?

Nothing, though, arrived from Dave Elyatt. Eventually, I plucked up the courage to call him.

'I was always keen,' he said, 'honestly. I love the band's sound, but nobody else was convinced in the office, and unfortunately the decision's not only up to me.'

In truth, we had known soon after the first Mill date. But until he actually said no, there was always that glimmer of hope. By the time we received a personal letter of rejection from Dave Gilmour, the Island scout who had been so keen on Verve, we all knew it was time for Plan B.

The contingency to record something ourselves had actually been in planning for some months, a case of anticipating the bad news rather than waiting for it. We had hoped it wouldn't be necessary, but the band could not afford to tread water, or, more importantly, be seen to be doing so.

The problem was money. There was none. The cost of manufacturing 2,000 records was around £2,500. As Janet and I were the only band members with a regular income, we gave all we could. John made a little bit doing removals and the others chipped in a few quid. Again, it was a case of relying on our benefactors: Simon, Damian, and Steve, the unwritten understanding being that the people who helped us now would stay with us forever and consequently reap the rewards.

That's what we all thought.

Recording the LP, which we finished on May 1st, brought home to me just how marginal my role in the band really was. The live set comprised John's songs, and the ones co-written with Robert's lyrics. John could have done my parts and nobody except me would have noticed the difference. I was part of the album, but the adrenaline didn't flow in my veins or pulse to the beat of its rhythms as it did for him. My only writing credit was for 'Cobbly Back Yard', one of the very rare numbers to come from the band messing about at rehearsal.

I had worked on becoming an integral part of the band's structure, of its internal machinations, but musically I was a stranger in a strange band. I had always known this, of course, but doing the album was an uncomfortable reminder. The fact that Robert had credits littered throughout annoyed me more than anything. John argued that artistic coherence was crucial and that my songs (and Shrub's for that matter) were at a tangent from the way the band was moving.

He was waving a flag of convenience, of course, because the whole ethos of the group had always been variety. The (hardly) hidden agenda was clear: it was his ball and he was keeping it. My role was to organise, while his was to write and arrange the songs.

I was beginning, not surprisingly, to feel used. Here I was busting a gut for the cause without reward, not to mention the money I was sinking in, while Robert, on the dole, and who spent most of his time in spaced-out oblivion, would be far better off financially if we ever broke big time. Of course, we were talking hypothetically (very hypothetically given recent progress on the A&R front), but the principles were important: no songwritng credit means no songwriting royalties.

You'll find out more looking at songwriting credits on the back of any CD than from a thousand biographies: tectonic plates of raw ego crushing each other into submission. The history of rock-'n'-roll is rife with financial rifts, it goes with the territory. The only truly righteous path for bands on the way up – the only way to guarantee unanimous commitment – is to share everything equally. Only an enlightened few tread such hallowed turf – The Beautiful South, **Manic Street Preachers** and Radiohead are three – because it goes against the grain of accepted practice. Yes, John wrote the basic songs, but those songs had a voice because other people sang and played them in a particular way. Without that they would still just be fantasies played out in John's mind and bedroom.

MANIC STREET PREACHERS – Not only have the Manics always split their royalties, they have also set up a trust fund for all monies due to guitarist and lyricist Richey Edwards, who disappeared from the Embassy Hotel on February 1st 1995 and has never been heard of since. After his car was found by the Severn Bridge two weeks later, it was thought he committed suicide.

HEAR MY SONG

Dave Elyatt had been scared off by numbers. So what did we do? Yes, another Tansad was born.

Cudo – known to the taxman as Paul McKeown – drifted into the band over a period of months. Despite a sanity-sapping obsession with Pink Floyd, he was a quite brilliant drum programmer with a unique ability to make a machine sound like the real thing. Quite why he had to join the band was something else entirely, and another of John's democratic decisions. Cudo's 'crucial' presence in the studio during the recording of the LP evolved into 'helping out' at bigger gigs (on percussion and backing vocals) but then grew into permanence.

Thirty-five and still living at home may have been something of a giveaway. Paul was a strange man. He could be the funniest, sharpest conversationalist on the planet – his impersonation of upper-crust Scottish golfers still has me in stitches just thinking about it – but such lighter moments were rare, and usually occurred when the rest of the world had long since entered the land of nod. Mostly, we were subjected to varying degrees of unsociability. On a good day, silence and general lack of interest were akin to approachability. On a bad day, sultry molten aggression suggested human contact was not advisable. And on a really bad day we would get The Face.

This frightening apparition came only when his spectacles were removed, and at such dangerously cross-eyed moments you knew you were in for trouble. Cudo would slide into an impenetrable abyss, the look in his eyes communicating quite plainly any attempts at conversation would result in your liver being instantly ripped out and eaten fried on toast.

His demeanour directly correlated to the marijuana level in his bloodstream, which in turn regulated his insomnia and the grumpometer. His intake made Robert Kettle seem like a middle-aged vicar who had inadvertently come across a pretty plant with pointy leaves as a young missionary in the West Indies and brought back a cutting for his back garden in Shropshire.

Not wanting him in the band was never anything personal, because The Face notwithstanding, and for all the idiosyncrasies, I liked Cudo and his apocalyptic sense of humour. He helped me a lot with my own material, and we always got on really well. It was just that, even given my misguided belief that it would all be fine when we eventually signed to EMI, I could see another member was like waving a piece of paper in the air and saying Hitler was actually a really decent chap. But such thoughts were sacrilege, and would have exposed me as the odd one out.

It was another Catch-22. John saw the musical benefits, the stage presence of so many people while I just saw the cost.

'The band only gets noticed because of the way it is,' he would say.

'But can we survive if we take on one more?' Dull Ed's reply.

Positive versus negative, interesting versus boring. It doesn't take a genius to work out which got the popular vote. I knew my staff rationalisation bill would never get parliamentary airtime. We didn't operate that sort of constitution. John wanted Cudo on board, so he came on board. If anyone apart from me had any objections, they were certainly never heard in public.

In retrospect, maybe this was the time to leave. But then one of my songs at long last made it into the set and I got all happy again.

'Gelignite' was a mad, silly thing I had recorded in Cudo's bedroom. The process of showing John material was always a tortuous one. After listening to the songs, the conversation that followed always involved a dissection and explanation as to why they weren't suitable for The Tansads. I had sometimes got round the problem by asking him to contribute to the song with a guitar break or something but even that usually didn't work.

Since 'Father's Day' had briefly made it into the set, my success on the songwriting front had been very poor. Just three tracks, 'Say It With Flowers' (Lyrics: Jones, Music: Kettle, J.), 'The Parachute Song' (mostly John's but a few of my words) and one totally of my own called 'Spike' (as in Milligan), enjoyed brief flirtations with the rehearsal room but, even there they were soon overlooked.

This time I employed a different tactic: Andrew heard the demo first. Cunning.

He enthused satisfactorily, then bullied big brother into trying it with the band. Cudo's production skills had made the track sound a thousand times more confident than previous efforts, and John was impressed enough to give it a whirl. It sounded great in the rehearsal room, maybe not lavished with quite the care and attention one of John's own songs would have been, but I didn't mind as long it was in there. And anyway, it suited the track to stay raw.

I get high using natural means,
A piece of toast and a can of beans
I get my kicks being with my lass
One in the teeth, and one up the . . .

My attitude was instantly transformed. It really did feel like I'd reached an oasis after crawling through a desert. The song was a way off being performed live, but the initial reaction from the band was really positive, essentially because it was fun to play, with lots of ups and downs, and a big shouty bit at the end:

If you want to see the light, chew a lump of gelignite,
If you want to see the light, change the bulb and say delight!

The song received its 'world premiere' on July 3rd, during a low-key acoustic soirée we put on in the Citadel foyer. John left it up to me if I wanted to do anything. I'd never actually sung in public before and I was pretty nervous. After all, there were 20 people watching.

I bit the bullet, stood up, belted out the song, and everybody clapped. Was it really that simple?

Had John been a politician, he would have noted that a song in the set means a happy and contented Ed Jones, with lots of endeavour and no hassle from the usually obstreperous so-and-so.

He wasn't.

THE BEAUTIFUL GAME

One of the problems for The Tansads was that we made no bones about our heritage. This was the Wigan of pre-Verve success days. At best, the town was considered a joke and any articles about Wigan bands had by law to include in the headline the word 'pier' (or 'peer', if the sub-editor was really clever). Mind you, with a pop-musical history consisting of little else than George Formby and Limahl from Kajagoogoo (a fresh-faced Chris Hamill was a paper boy round the corner from Kettle Towers), it's hardly surprising local luminaries had traditionally kept their heads down.

Our most successful other band at that stage was **The Railway Children,** signed to Factory Records in Manchester, based at The Boardwalk, and therefore conveniently tagged as Mancs by the press. And I bet you didn't know Roy Kinnear and Sir Ian McKellen are (were in RK's case, sadly) pie-eaters.

THE RAILWAY CHILDREN – Originally called Awareness Party, then Back Then Beyond – it was the early '80s – The Railies were signed to Factory in 1985 by Mike Pickering, the subsequent 'brains' behind the horrendous M People. Their one and only hit, 'Every Beat of the Heart', reached number 24 in 1991, while follow-up 'Music Stop' was demoted from the charts for alleged (strenuously denied) chart-rigging. They never made the charts again alas, and were dropped by new label Virgin in 1992, reportedly owing £750,000.

Time for a brief savoury-flavoured tangent. The term pie-eater does not in fact stem, as is usually assumed, from the natives' inability to eat anything unless it's covered in pastry; nor by extension, from our town's unnaturally high quota of bakeries per capita. It actually derives from the time of the General Strike when Wigan miners were the first to eat humble pie and go back to work.

No backbone, it's clearly in the blood.

Unlike everybody else then, we decided, foolishly perhaps, to actually celebrate our home for what it really is, a screwed up little hole like so many others in the North, scarred beyond repair by a dwindling mining industry, and full – in the main – of moaning buggers. As such, the place has enormous comedy value, not in the ho-ho-ho Wigan Pier sense, but the sort of dark, self-deprecating humour borne out of desperation. A wee example. Four or five years ago, a theme pub by the name of Czechs opened in the town centre. A friend of mine overheard two locals talking outside.

'What sort of a name is that, Kazechies?'

Of course, everything changed with The Verve.

'We're so proud of them,' said The Mayor, who was at Haigh Hall bopping away with the rest of them, while the *Wigan Evening Post* produced a thirty-two-page special edition for the big day. A thirty-two-page special, can you believe that? I used to battle for quarter of a page for my column.

Despite our concert with Verve in 1991 being a charity gig to send local terminally ill kids on holiday, the same council not only failed to waive the hire charge for the hall, but also threatened to fine us £200 for each of the dozens of posters we had put up around town advertising the event. They later refused point blank to provide a town-centre notice board for local bands, despite a 1,000 signature petition instigated through the column. That's the real Wigan.

As Morrissey once wonderfully put it: 'If Prince had come from Wigan, he would have been slaughtered by now.'

At times we may not have been as focused as we should have been lyrically, but an industry devoid of subtlety completely failed to get the message, and mistook us for silly professional Northerners:

> Oh I never miss, with a perfect Northern kiss,
> Down in Shandyland
> Chips and egg would make them high,
> But God has poked them in the eye,
> God loves Shandyland.

Despite all this baggage, however, and the fact that London and the industry were displaying a general lack of enthusiasm, the spirit within The Tansads was excellent. Especially mine since the birth of 'Gelignite'. Whatever format the album would eventually take, and however successful its release, it was at least a positive step in the right direction. It would lift us onto a new level.

We had to remain upbeat. After all, the history of rock-'n'-roll is littered with groups who took years to make it. **Space**, Pulp, and Chumbawamba are the most recent examples, and the list dates back all the way to the Beatles, who were rejected by Decca. I was confident that one day Dave Elyatt would see the folly of his rejection of us.

The unshakable truth was that our success in the field couldn't have been further removed from experiences in London. Wigan was in the bag, our first headline show at The Citadel in St Helens had been a massive success, and although we were still struggling to get on the national circuit, Damian's

SPACE – Songwriter, singer, bassist and former apprentice French polisher Tommy Scott spent many years 'paying his dues' around his native Liverpool before the haunting 'Female of the Species' broke into the Top Ten in 1996. Tommy eventually handed the bass duties to Yorkie – real name David Palmer – a local legend because the cellar of his mother Gladys' house in the Fairfield district was used as a rehearsal space by early incarnations of The Teardrop Explodes, The Mighty Wah and Echo and the Bunnymen. In his book *Head On*, Julian Cope says Pete Wylie thought of the name 'Yorkie' because, like the chocolate bar, David Palmer was 'good, rich and thick'.

arrival as our manager definitely pushed the gigging up a notch. This was exemplified by our greatest single slice of exposure, credibility and nepotism to date: a support to The Beautiful South at the St Helens Show on July 27th.

Wow.

Citadel promoter Dave Evans had known frontman Paul Heaton from the days of **The Housemartins**, and Heaton agreed partly as a personal favour. I suppose he would never have done so had we not built up our own following and he also (quite) liked the demo.

THE HOUSE-MARTINS – The fact that this quirky four-piece bizarrely spawned both comfy armchair brigade The Beautiful South and everyone's favourite DJ Fatboy Slim has been extensively documented. Less well known, is that former guitarist Stan Cullimore became a successful children's book author and that original drummer Hugh Whitaker was charged and sentenced to six years imprisonment in 1993 for wounding with intent and three arson attacks on a business acquaintance. Gangsta' Trippin'.

For Heaton, it was just another show, but, to us, it was like a non-league team playing a Premiership side. It was our cup final. The most we'd ever played in front of was 500. Once. The attendance for this was going to be over 2,000.

Gulp.

The first thing that struck us when we arrived for the soundcheck was just how big everything was under the giant empty rectangular marquee. I'd been to dozens of gigs in my time, but standing in the audience in the dark is a world away from strutting by day on a 10-foot high stage surrounded by towers of rigging and lighting. The mixing desk was so far away that you couldn't communicate with the engineer just by shouting at him.

And backstage was another world. Our dressing room/Portacabin was right next door to theirs. Starstruck? Not me. A few muffled 'aw'rights' when you walk past each other on the way to the toilets is just about acceptable, though still a little risqué. Far more correct is to adopt the I-can-be fucking-hard-as-well-you-know approach and actively ignore your illustrious neighbours. Unless, of course, they make the first move. That changes everything. Then you respond, but don't be over-bearing, mind. The key is never to expect the main band to converse with you, and as such, like well-behaved children in 50s British films, only speak when spoken to. Rock-'n'-roll etiquette: very complicated.

So it was right and proper therefore, that as Dave Evans, Simon and I were chatting outside our 'cab', Paul Heaton made the first move.

'Hi Dave, fellas, how's it going?'

Be nonchalant. Be cool. Don't let on that this is the biggest-ever gig you've played and you're actually really, really grateful and really, really shitting yourself. Simon adopted his usual stand-in-the-background-say-nothing-and-shake-a-leg routine.

'Great,' I said.

Heaton spoke again.

'There was one song of yours that I thought was really good. Laid back, empty, not the sort of thing you would expect. It was on that LP.'

'Oh, "Right On"? Just bass and drums at first?'

'Yeah, that's the one. That was excellent. I thought the band sounded great on stage before, by the way. I hope it goes well tonight, good luck with it.'

And off he went, coming across as far more nervy than me, I thought. Maybe not.

We spent most of the afternoon kicking our heels backstage, soaking in the atmosphere of the B.I.G. T.I.M.E., certain that it wouldn't be the last such occasion.

Proof positive that we were an odd band was that cricket was our only communal sport. The footie standards – Simon and Andrew excepted – fell short of even my still-reckons-he-could-have-been-a-pro efforts, and when confronted with a total lack of enthusiasm, I was restricted to the odd, usually solitary, kickabout. Imagine my horror then, while my back was turned, The Beautiful South nicked my football. I stood watching as they began using it for a full-scale game, with headers and everything! Heaton brought the ball back in person, rolling it towards me as I sat by the Portakabin with a casual 'Cheers, mate'. Giving us a support gig was one thing, it seemed, but letting us play football with them was obviously quite another.

The show went really well. We were greeted by hundreds of screaming girls at the front, intermingled with our own fans and went off to such rapturous applause that Dave Evans insisted we go back on, unheard of for a support band. Simon was inundated with inquiries on the stall, we got literally hundreds of names on the mailing list, sold dozens of T-shirts, and we received a huge injection of self-confidence, not to mention our fanbase virtually doubling overnight.

Just as well, given what was waiting round the corner.

DEVIL IN DISGUISE

It's all very well releasing your own record. That's the easy bit. The problem is getting rid of the blighter. The relevant industry term (RIT) is distribution. Even if you physically go round every shop in the land, retailers are still not interested in littering their racks with a record by unknowns. In our case, one or two local outlets took a few copies on a sale or return basis because they knew we had a following, but ultimately this would just be preaching to the converted. We wanted – and needed – to reach a new audience, away from the region.

Getting a distribution deal was worse than hunting for a record contract. Distribution companies work together with indie labels, we were told. Unless you've already got a record deal, then you don't get a distribution deal.

'But we have! Well, nearly,' we lied.

Our protestations fell upon deaf ears.

'Anyway, we've got a big following, everywhere we play we go down a storm, just look at those (record-buying) girls at the front of The Beautiful South audience. Give us a chance and we'll make it worth your while, you're supposed to be into music, can't you see something when it stares you in the face?'

Apparently not.

The Cartel, Revolver, Backs, Pinnacle, APT – all the indie distributors at the time – wouldn't touch us with a six-foot stylus. Bastards.

The same scenario occurs when you send a record away for review by the music press and/or radio stations. The sad truth is that the majority of self-financed LPs flounder on the rocks of market forces before they hit the open sea, and end up merely as 'posh demos'. And their use in that field is limited, because, if the A&R tigers didn't roar when the same material was on cassette, they're hardly likely to be seduced by a bit of black plastic or shiny CD just because it's got a glossy cover (RIT: tough shit, buddy).

Talk about back to square one. And you wonder why aspiring bands sell their souls to the devil given the most minuscule whiff of interest?

We certainly did. Except for us the devil didn't have horns, he wore pink dungarees. Geoff Davis opened Probe Records on Button Street, Liverpool, a stone's throw away from The Cavern, in the 70s. The shop became a symbol for the new Mersey Beat scene: The Teardrop Explodes, Echo and the Bunnymen, The Mighty Wah, et al. Davis then founded Probe Plus, the label, which shot to fame (at least within indie circles) when John Peel championed the maverick Half Man Half Biscuit, who were completely crap in a completely crap sort of a way (though that was kind of the point, I think) but were nevertheless responsible for some of the greatest song titles of all time: 'The Len Ganley Stance', 'All I Want For Christmas is a Dukla Prague Away Kit', 'Outbreak of Vitas Gerulaitis', and dozens more.

Their claim to fame was turning down an appearance on Channel 4's seminal *The Tube* in the early 80s because it clashed with a Tranmere Rovers home match; they even refused after the show offered to fly them back for the second half by helicopter.

On with the story.

When we met him, Davis no longer owned the shop but was still very much in charge of the label, based upstairs. To us, Probe was a big name. Obviously not our first choice of label (if we'd had a choice, which we didn't) but we had knocked on their door several months previously and been turned away in no uncertain terms.

There were two bands called The Levellers at the time, both were roughly equal in status and, naturally, some confusion-stroke-conflict arose between them. So the Blackburn-based Levellers added the number 5 to their name and disappeared into oblivion, while the Brighton-based soap dodgers kept same said monicker *au naturel* and enjoyed (still enjoy, at the time of writing) a glittering showbiz career as Kings of Crust.

Damian went ahead and booked us to support the Probe-signed Levellers 5 at Bolton Crown and Cushion. We were suitably delighted with such a prestigious support slot. Impressing the label was never uppermost in our collective mind, even though Damian approached Davis with a view to distributing the album, and this probably showed in our performance. We knew it hadn't gone that well. There wasn't so much a stage as a cramped, oddly shaped 'raised bit' in one corner surrounded by wooden banisters, ensuring that half the crowd couldn't even see. In the audience of 18-to-20-something students was a balding 50-year old wearing pale pink dungarees: Geoff Davis. He was hard to miss.

On the strength of the performance, which obviously can't have been that bad, we struck, if not quite gold exactly, then at least something that could, with the lights dimmed (very) low, just about bear a passing resemblance. **Fools gold**. Never mind distribution, Davis wanted 'Shandyland' as a fully blown Probe release.

OK, so Probe was a small company run by an enthusiast and there were no oak-panelled offices, no expense accounts, no advances and the bastard didn't even offer to buy us a drink but, however crap Geoff Davis' offer was, we knew – and he might well have suspected – we simply didn't have any other options. As far as he was concerned, he loved the music (so he said

FOOLS GOLD – A seminal guitar-funk workout that exploded into the Top Ten in November 1989, this single marked the creative highpoint in the career of The Stone Roses. After a few one-off shows and a solitary single, 'One Love', the band went to ground, not appearing again until November 1994. The intervening years were rife with controversy and speculation, from the protracted court battle with label Silvertone to their eventual signing with Geffen for a reported four million pounds. Unfortunately, the release of their second album *Second Coming* in late '94 only served to highlight the internal cracks – firstly with departure of drummer Reni in April '95 and the subsequent and fatal exit of guitarist and songwriter John Squire the following year. The Stone Roses were officially no more in November 1996. It was a sorry, messy end for a band that had it all and it remains a bitter irony that their duller, Manchester progeny, Oasis, have inherited the success that tragically eluded The Roses.

anyway – I learned quickly not to believe a syllable uttered from his mouth), the LP was already recorded, and therefore we were a low-risk investment that might bring him in a few bob into the bargain.

For us, on the other hand, Probe would open the magic door of distribution (the company had a deal with APT), enable us to release 'Shandyland' on CD, and, most importantly, make the band be seen to have a deal.

Everyone's a winner, baby.

The shambolic way the label was run, and its precarious financial position were of no consequence when it came to the great biz credometer, because Probe oozed the stuff like oil from a clapped-out old Morris Minor. Public perception, especially locally where I had filled the column with stories of A&R interest from the majors, was that we had turned down a big deal in favour of Probe, to stay true to our indie roots.

What a joke!

Time for another (eventually relevant) tangent. If you ever want evidence that the music biz resides inside its own rectum, then look no further than the myth of the indie. Let me pick up the Verve story. Dave Halliwell rang me up at work towards the end of May to tell me that although they had received A&R interest from an incredible 20 companies and agencies in one form or another, the only one to come up with a concrete deal was Norwich-based label/distributor Backs Music, who were offering a one single arrangement.

Dave explained that there was interest pending from indie label Hut, but that they had decided to go ahead with the Backs offer in the meantime, in order to get an EP out quickly (the whole Backs episode seems to have eluded Verve's biographers). I duly announced the news (May 30th) under the headline 'Verve are Backs'. Ahem.

Putting my jealousy to one side, I also invited them up to the office for a chat and a photo; their success was a major story for the column. The interview and picture, headlined 'Verve Are Poised For The Big Time', was duly printed on June 20th, and was a substantial review of an extraordinary first six months.

'We know it will happen some time,' Richard told me. 'It has to. In a way we're better off waiting for a bit, building up more of a solid base that way.'

Bollocks!

We were hardly in the same boat, but ultimately, it was identical to the Probe situation: desperate wannabes snatching the hand of the first person to offer anything definite.

Even though the tab Hut ran for Verve at the (now infamous) Adelphi Hotel in Liverpool was (according to Dave) greater than the money Backs offered for recording the single, and even though Dave told me drooling A&R tongues said they were the 'greatest unsigned band in Britain', methinks no 17-year-olds on the planet – however self-confident – would have the guile to risk everything playing multinational corporations off each other. I may be wrong and hats off if I am, but somehow I doubt it.

Verve were just covering their (no pun intended) backs but, as it turned out, they needn't have bothered. The biographers correctly note that following their London debut at the Fulham King's Head on July 3rd, Dave Boyd from Hut came up with the readies – a somewhat more productive evening than our maiden voyage to the capital had been – and two months later they signed. True to his word, Dave rang to tell me, and under the headline 'In The Hut for Verve', I ran the story on September 12th.

The point is this.

Hut is not an independent label, it's a subsidiary of Virgin, which is in turn is a subsidiary of EMI, which (probably) has its fingers in a thousand unmentionably atrocious corporate financial pies and has as much in common with independence as the Young Conservatives. However, at the time, their produce was distributed by an independent company, thus qualifying it for the indie charts and maintaining its credibility. But that's akin to saying a tin of Tesco Yummy Poppet cat food is not in fact a can of Tesco Yummy Poppet cat food because it was delivered to the supermarket by a bloke in a flat cap riding a rusty bike, not in the big articulated 32-ton truck with Tesco painted on the side in huge 10 foot letters.

These days it's an accepted marketing tool for a major label to up a band's cred by putting the album out on a so-called indie label. Back in the murky early 90s, however, contempt hadn't yet bred familiarity, and it seemed a far shadier practice, simply because it was highly uncool to be signed to a major. The Railway Children were a case in point. Their first LP (released on Factory) hit the top of the indie charts, but their credibility and coverage in the *NME* and *Melody Maker* plummeted when they signed to Virgin.

How times have changed, but I've digressed from the digression.

Every cloud has a silver lining, though, I think, and the flip side of the indie coin was that, using a neat bit of reverse logic, The Tansads could keep their heads held high. Verve secured a five-figure, four-album deal with Hut/Virgin, okay, and we got a no-figure, one (already recorded at our expense) album agreement with Probe. But technically, we both secured hip indie deals. I was thus proudly (and just about legitimately) able to announce the news in my August 8th column, under a big close-up of Janet and the suitably ambiguous headline 'Sads sign up'.

We officially released the LP on our own label Wayward, in association with Probe, and retained full artistic control, merchandising, and publicity rights, but that was just a ploy to make ourselves feel better.

I made a valiant attempt at blowing the trumpet of independence in the column, attributing the following quote to our manager Damian:

'We want success on our own terms, and, with the backing of Probe, we can make a name for ourselves at the same time as keeping a degree of control over our destiny. This is the best way to achieve our aim.'

The theory was that we went halves on the manufacture, printing, and distribution of a thousand CDs and a thousand vinyl. It would cost only £2,300 each as we were told – hush, hush – that Davis kept the costs down by having the albums manufactured through the back door, the mate of a mate's uncle used to know a bloke who went out with a girl who was two-timing a security guard at a pressing plant and still had a key. Or something.

In practice however, it didn't quite happen like that. We paid for an initial run of 500 cassettes, while Simon provided camera-ready artwork, designed and printed an insert for the vinyl, designed and printed a 'Shandyland' poster, and produced the cassette sleeve, all at his own expense. As far as Geoff was concerned, if we wanted to provide artwork, manufacture T-shirts, and hire a publicist, it would all be less money for him to spend.

The Probe deal still felt like a victory.

After 18 months (the length of Buddy Holly's career) of trying, we had at last managed to climb onto the first rung on the ladder of pop stardom: we were officially a signed band. Damian, John and I travelled to Liverpool on the afternoon of Tuesday August 6th to 'seal the deal'.

Probe HQ was a complete tip. There were records stacked up to the roof, boxes of CDs everywhere, tattered posters on the wall, paper strewn all over desks. Geoff glanced briefly over a basic letter of agreement drafted by Damian the night before, and signed it straight away, no questions asked.

It was all so simple, so matter-of-fact.

We celebrated selling our souls to the devil on the way home with a cup of tea at the Little Chef on the East Lancs Road.

MESSAGE IN A BOTTLE

When I was 21, I set myself the target of being on vinyl by the age of 25. It seemed a generous, easy-to-achieve ambition.

I wish.

If you count the IDEA album in November 1990, I clocked in over a year and a half behind schedule, aged 26 and eight months. However, that wasn't a proper release. The implication of my original time scale was that I would be in an established group releasing records. *Shandyland* came out on **October 14th**, so using the revised criteria, I passed the ticker tape two and a half years late, hardly the first flush of youth in pop-age terms, but at least I still looked twenty-one.

OCTOBER 14TH – The week that was. As *Shandyland* was being released, the NME raved about a new band from Aberdeen, Seattle – Nirvana. Chapterhouse, however, graced the cover of the paper. Shane McGowan left The Pogues and later that week on the 19th, a roadie for the Inspiral Carpets called Noel played his first gig at The Boardwalk in Manchester with a band that had his younger brother Liam on vocals.

A veteran and an embryo simultaneously.

The LP 'sold out' straight away in all the local shops, because trustworthy retailers had only bought five copies each. Eventually they got the message, and had to quickly re-order, and for a glorious week or two, The Tansads were rubbing shoulders – in Wigan anyway – with the biggest names of pop. I sauntered around town with my mate Paul from the office. As we wandered into Our Price records, he turned to me.

'How the hell can you be walking round this shop without a massive hard-on?'

'I'm not.'

Having sold (we were told) 850 copies in the first week, the album should have made the indie charts. But Probe failed to register the release so the sales weren't recognised.

Thanks, Geoff.

We weren't too downhearted, however, as the important thing was to have the record out and onto the streets. And then the reviews came in.

Fellow *Wigan Reporter* journo Steve Brady didn't let me down:

'As catchy as Kylie, and sticks to your brain like a slug on steroids. After a few listens, you become quite intoxicated.'

Nepotism-Factor: fair to middling.

Better was to come. Damian was an old friend of Stuart Maconie (a then staff-writer on the *NME*), who had seen and liked us with The Beautiful South. The contact was instrumental not so much in having the album reviewed – Probe's mysterious cred would probably have done the trick on its own – but in giving the album a fair crack of the whip.

Just a few isolated ticks on the nepotism Geiger counter.

Stuart gave it seven out of ten, which was good if not brilliant, but I found myself agreeing with all his reservations; they were were my own fears in print. Paraphrasing slightly: 'On paper – big band line-up, accordions and the like, folky roots – they're decidedly dicey. On record, they're much more attractive, but it's on stage that they truly make sense. A ragamuffin, ingenious lucky bag of pop, rock and folk, it's at its most charming when nearest to pop, and least appealing when the finger-in-the-earisms are most evident. Their regionalism is part of their pull, even if this can lead them into sounding disturbingly like the Houghton Weavers. But a not inconsiderable – as John Major would say – cult is developing around this, the best group ever named after a pram, and you may love them. Go and find out.'

Reviews followed afoot from a hundred different sources, from the ultra-hip *Select* ('a wealth of musical invention to bite into, four out of five') and *Folk Roots* ('If only they were all this refreshing, bliss') to local papers and fanzines. There were criticisms, but generally, the response was massively positive and uplifting. A second run of a thousand CDs was ordered within a month, and that quickly sold out too.

Closer to Double Decker than Double Platinum, but there you go.

Damian was able to book a number of new venues on the combined strength of the album release and The Beautiful South show, but our one remaining shortfall was the inability to infiltrate the proper UK indie live circuit. As a result, our schedule had a definitely lopsided look ranging from the sublime to the ridiculous.

ALISON says, *'I would go to bed dreading the noise of that horrible van drawing up outside, waking me and the whole street. Goodness only knows what time it was. I just lay there upstairs cringing as they tried pathetically to be quiet while loading everything into the front room. My front room. But I heard every bump, felt every chip and every scrape. Why did it all have to be in our house, other people's filthy, smelly, ugly amps and guitar boxes? I nearly killed him the day I found those huge oil stains on the carpet.'*

The Mill at the Pier *Shandyland* Launch Concert, as we pompously called it, was another monster 500 sell-out, and was soon followed by brilliant responses at The Citadel and Bolton Crown and Cushion. The rest was all a bit hit and miss. Liverpool Institute (ignored by 500); a pissed student extravaganza at the vacuous Morecambe Empire (ignored by 1,000, twice); Ashton-Under-Lyne Witchwood ("You'll never play The Witchwood again,' said promoter Darren Poyser after we cancelled another show of his at the glitzy Bolton Oscars nightclub); and our worst-ever-attended show, at Legends, the social club of Preston North End FC (or Knob End, as we Wigan fans quip), where we were watched by three people, two of whom were Shrub's relatives, and the other a wino in for the cheap ale.

And then there were the downright bizarre gigs. We were supported by *pétomane* Mr Methane at Cambridge Junction (who was paid twice as much as us – kids, don't let anybody tell you farting's not good for you).

Morecambe Crazy Horse was a mock Wild West bar full of swinging saloon doors and Stetsons hanging from walls. We also played support to an indie bingo at the Preston Caribbean Club. This was deeply surreal. In one room, the old West Indian guys chapped their dominoes on tables, while in the other, after we had played in front of a garish painted backdrop featuring a Bermudan beach scene, a rather fey student stood up and called numbers in a particularly camp voice: 'eleven, community burglar' is the one that sticks in my mind. I think I won a packet of condoms and a Chinese cookery pocket book.

Then, at a café in **Bury** called the Metropolitan (for which we got a listing in the *NME*, no less) we were supported by a poet called Hovis Presley who came up with the timeless: 'If you want to buy my book, it's available at all good Asda carrier bags at the back of the room.'

BURY – Within a fifty-mile radius on this very night, Primal Scream were at Liverpool University, OMD sold out Preston Guildhall and The Den in Wigan had thrash band The Sons of Ishmael playing.

And then there was Widnes Studio.

We already knew first hand that Widnes was a crap place to play, and on the face of it The Studio would be no different, tucked away in a nondescript side street in a town that made Wigan look like a vibrant metropolis. The PA was non-existent, the dressing room was the toilet but when we shuffled out on stage however, we were greeted not only by a packed house, but a cacophony of screaming girls in their Tansads T-shirts, who knew the words and soon went about creating a mosh-pit.

What? A proper gig? In Widnes? Impossible.

But there it was, in front of our disbelieving eyes. What was even more amazing was that the girlies were stood in front of *me*, shouting out *my* name.

Nice.

After the show, there was a clamour round the dressing room door. When they refused to go home (it must have been about 11.30pm by now, way past bedtime), Janet, who had been fending them off, came to find me.

'You're going to have to talk to them,' she smirked. 'It's you they're after.'

Sniggers in the dressing room. That's jealousy for you.

'There he is! Ed, Ed, Can you sign *Shandyland* for me?!'

'Can you sign my poster?'

'She fancies you, you know!'

'No, I don't.'

'Yes you do, liar, and so does Joanne!'

'And why don't you fancy me, then?'

'I like Dom. I spoke to Dom, and he signed my album.'
'Have you got a girlfriend?'
'I'm married, I'm afraid.'
'Married? He's married!'
'Where's your wife?'
'Is she here, then?'
'No she's at home.'
'Is she pretty?'
'I bet she's gorgeous, being married to you.'

By this time, the rest of the band were creased up, watching the gaggle of hormone-happy lovelies poached from The Beautiful South audience giggling hysterically and poking my jeans and my T-shirt. The most ardent was called Joanne Hill (she breathlessly informed me several times), who must have been around 15 or 16.

'Wait till I tell my Mum I've spoken to you. She won't believe me. Can I have something of yours to keep?'

'What do you want? I've not really got anything on me.'

'Empty your pockets, then.' Phwoar, eh?

'You can have my plectrum, or a penny. Here.'

She eagerly snatched them from me. I stretched over to the stage and for a laugh picked up the empty lemonade bottle I had drunk during the show.

'Here, you can have this if you want!'

Not only did she take it, but it was the start of her Ed's Lemonade Bottle Collection. At all subsequent gigs she attended, she made it her purpose in life to pester Damian until said empty plastic container was retrieved. I dread to think what she did with them, or indeed what happened to them. Joanne, if you're reading this, write to the publishers and tell them what you did with all my lemonade bottles. Please.

HALF A PERSON

October 15th 1991. With the help of a calculator, taking into account leap years, I worked out that today I have lived exactly half my life without Dad. I was 13 years and 283 days old when he died. I am now 27 years and 200 days old.

I miss him so much I feel sick.

TAKING THE BISCUITS

Aside from the general upping of our profile, there were two direct consequences arising from *Shandyland*'s success. One great, the other disastrous. And it wasn't long before they were on an agonising collision course. So Tansad.

First the good. The brother of producer Phil Tennant spotted the *NME* review, passed it onto his sibling, who then faxed us requesting a copy of the album with a view to working together in the future. In his fax, he referred to a selection of previous and/or current clients: The Cure, The Waterboys, The Levellers, and **The Saw Doctors**. The album was despatched within the hour.

THE SAW DOCTORS – The band from Tuam, near Galway are unique within the UK music industry in that they manage to regularly fill the biggest venues in Britain without anyone really knowing anything about them. They have never received any support from the British media, nor did they get much help from their former record company Warners. Thus, they bought themselves out of their contract, and made – and make – far more money releasing their records themselves.

Now the bad. Geoff Davis wanted to record and release a single.

'If they were your songs you'd be interested too.'

John's tone was aggressive. If only I was in that situation, I mused.

'Yes, but we can do better,' I said. 'I know we can, and I know you know we can.'

The meeting in Simon's flat was getting strained. I had made the *faux pas* of suggesting that Geoff Davis had (in a strictly artistic sense, of course) seduced John.

'As far as I know, I may never get another song released. This is the first person that's taken me seriously as a songwriter. I've got to look at it.'

'But it goes against everything you, everything we stand for!'

I was getting frustrated and nobody was backing me up.

'What happened to production values, what happened to taking care of what we release? It's absolute madness.'

It was no good, John had decided to take up Geoff's offer of recording six tracks in two days at The Pink Museum, a 24-track studio in Liverpool, and there was nothing I could do about it. Not only that, John had agreed to Geoff's suggestion for a fiddle player to session on 'Up The Revolution', the song he wanted as a single. This was a total anathema to me because a) I can't stand fiddles and b) more importantly, thrashy guitars and a violin would have us pigeonholed as Levellers clones faster than you could say dog on a string. An industry devoid of imagination eventually did this anyway.

Thus began one of the most ludicrous chapters in our history; John Kettle the perfectionist, versus Geoff 'lo-fi'Davis. No contracts, just the sort of verbal understanding that had us believing the recordings were primarily demos, with 'Up The Revolution' being done with more care because that would be a single, and Geoff believing (as we later discovered) that he was getting an album.

Geoff was simply not used to working with musicians. Technical proficiency, timing, instruments in tune and multiple vocal takes were never things that had troubled Half Man Half Biscuit. The Davis motto was simple: if you want the real thing, just set up, smack it on tape, and release it; better feel, and cheaper into the bargain.

It was a marriage made in hell.

What really pissed me off was that I was being painted as the villain, both by John who wanted his songs recorded, and by Geoff, who thought I was poisoning John's mind with doubt.

Sometimes, you just can't win.

Geoff's 'production' technique was simple: smoke inordinate amounts of Black, let the band come up with the ideas, employ engineer Colin Makay to actually do the work, and occasionally get up from the chesterfield to preside over the ubiquitous slow fade at the end of songs.

John was standing in a different booth from Bug and me. His voice came over the headphones.

'Was the timing all right on that one? It felt a bit fast.'

'It didn't feel that tight,' I shouted back down one of the drum mikes. 'What did you think, Chris?'

'Yeah, it was okay, but we'll do bett—'

'No, no, leave it!! That was fuch'n grrate, leave it,' said the man in the know back at knobs HQ.

When we listened back, Chris, who hadn't been given the choice to work with a metronome ('you don't want any of that 80s click-track shit, you're a fuch'n drummer, not a fuch'n machine'), was all over the place, speeding up for the noisy sections, slowing down for the quiet bits; live, you can get away with it; on tape it just sounds amateurish.

'I thought you said the drums were fine, Geoff?'

'They are, they sound fuch'n grrate.'

I could see thin lines of smoke rising symmetrically from each of John's ears. As for the fiddle, well I just had to leave at that point.

The tracks were an absolute travesty, every single one of them, our first foray into a professional 24-track studio totally spoiled. John tore his hair out, travelling to and from Liverpool for days afterwards trying to superglue the wreck of the Titanic back together, but he was – to use the best expression ever to come out of Wigan – polishing a turd.

Re-arrange the following simple words: told, I, so, you.

This was no time for gloating, however. I could see all our hard work being flushed away in a few short weeks if those tracks ever saw the light of day. In such circumstances, Phil Tennant's fax was the distant sound of the cavalry bugle; an escape route out of a very tricky situation. But even then, it wasn't that simple.

'He's fuch'n crrapp, The Levellers are fuch'n crap, he's shit.'

The laughable element was that Geoff genuinely believed himself to be a better producer than an experienced professional who had done nothing else but work in studios since he was 15. These were clearly the signs of a lunatic, somebody who thought he could design a Tornado Jet Fighter having put together a Spitfire Airfix kit, and even then the stickers were upside down.

I was annoyed that John let me be the bearer of bad news; he didn't want to spoil his 'special relationship'.

'Listen Geoff,' I said, 'the band want to compromise. We still want to release the single, but we can't turn down Phil's offer. We'll pay for the session with him, and then decide afterwards which is the best version to put out. But we still want to stay with Probe.'

This statement was true, although with some in-built deception (hardly an unfamiliar sensation for Geoff, let's be honest). We knew damn well Phil's version, even if he wore earplugs and boxing gloves, would piss all over The Pink Museum stuff, but the fact remained that Probe was still our only release outlet. We had to be careful not to burn the bridge down completely. Geoff reluctantly agreed, though by this time, he had undoubtedly cast me as Probic Enemy No.1.

No matter, the bottom line was that the path was now clear for us to work with Phil, although the possible release of the Pink Museum recordings hung over us like a particularly pregnant storm cloud.

In the meantime, we had to keep up appearances with Probe and Geoff booked us as support on a few Half Man Half Biscuit dates. Now, we had always prided ourselves on being able to turn on any crowd, but the mind-numbingly moronic beery Biscuit-lads were clearly the exception. Manchester University was a disaster, my bass amp packed in and half the gig had to be performed acoustically by John and Janet. We actually managed to play a full set at Liverpool Poly, but the response was no better.

Next came Newcastle University, which became an instant Tansads legend. I can't remember the exact reason, but we had no engineer that night. Shit. The Biscuits had spent so long 'soundchecking' (i.e. four blokes twiddling away to their hearts' content playing completely different, totally unrelated sounds, for *hours*), that the doors had opened by the time it was our turn. The house engineer then refused to turn the disco off and promptly disappeared, leaving Geoff Davis standing bemused behind a thousand knobs, attempting to soundcheck a band during a disco whilst eating a pizza.

When we emerged to play, the few people in the room soon ran out as a howling gale of feedback swept through the hall, a cocktail of bass hum from the drum mikes mixed with high-pitch torture from the vocal mikes. The band stumbled its way through one song, there was a momentary lull when we stopped, so we started another, triggering an encore of white noise. That was enough. Off we stomped, never to return.

One lasting impression of that night remains. Amid total sonic and emotional mayhem, there was a vision of calm. Dom, whose accordion was a major source of the trouble, stood like a stubborn oak tree in a tornado, a hitherto unseen smile beaming across his face. Our anarchist friend had his wildest dreams of destruction fulfilled at last: the sound of the band falling to pieces. And he was basking in the rain of absolute chaos.

His favourite ever Tansads gig by a mile.

Time for totally irrelevant mention of The Smiths and a bit of rare praise for Geoff Davis. The one person Morrissey has stuck with from the early days until the present (at least, as I write this) is Mike Hinc, his agent. By some bizarre quirk of coincidence, Hinc also booked for the Biscuits. Geoff bent Mike's ear to see us live, and soon we got a slot at the Mean Fiddler in London, supporting the Biscuits. When it was cancelled at the last minute (can't remember why, maybe the Tranmere Rovers left back's cat had died or something), Hinc arranged for us to support The Oyster Band instead (now, they were folk rockers). The gig was on a Friday the 13th.

Once again, we took a crowd with us from Wigan to the Big Smoke and buoyed by their support, we played a stormer, going down well with the Oysters' crowd, with the band themselves, with the venue and most importantly with a bespectacled, pony-tailed little fellow in a bobble hat called Geoff Meall, one of Mike's junior agents. It didn't become apparent for several months, but we had just made one of the most important contacts, if not *the* most important contact, in the band's whole career.

One final point. Verve came to the show and even paid to get in. I think they were recording locally. Simon spotted them coming in, and leaving straight after we'd finished. Just thought I'd mention it, no great earth-shattering conclusions. I'm sure we'd have done the same, Wigan against the world and all that.

HOME IS WHERE THE HEAT IS

Lads, lads, can you imagine being married to a girl who's into bands and football, knows her Satie from her Sartre, dons a fabulous pair of monties, wears tight black leather trousers, and still does the cooking?

Yeah, me too, frequently.

The truth was that Alison didn't particularly like music, not really, not the way I did. She tolerated it and saw life beyond it. Incredible. By the time I found all this out, however, it was too late, as I'd only gone and fallen in love with the woman.

Jump forward six and a half years.

The idea of having a husband for a pop star had metamorphosed into the mechanics of him (nearly) becoming one. My average week: Monday to Friday, nine till five: office. Two or three evenings: gig, straight from work, usually. One evening, sometimes two, sometimes Sunday afternoon: rehearsal. One evening every second or third week: band meeting. Saturday and occasional Tuesday evening: covering the Wigan matches for the local paper, with away games in places such as Swansea, Exeter, Northampton. Then there was my songwriting and hours of solitary strumming at a time.

'What about me?' came the timid voice from the sofa.

With only our two ginger toms, Thompson and Bob (named after Wigan players) for company, Alison became a rock-'n'-roll/football widow.

'I'm trying to make something of my life here, I don't need grief. It's not as if I'm down the pub every night getting pissed. I'm working for the future, for our future!'

Even rows were usually interrupted by a telephone call from John or Damian about the band. But nothing was going to stand in the way of ambition. I knew what I wanted and, if Alison loved me, she would respect my drive.

The main source of tension was the fact that Alison didn't actually like either the band itself, or the lifestyle associated with it. She never took an active interest, rarely came to gigs, and generally didn't show me outward support. The flip side was that I never encouraged her involvement. Why? I don't know. Music was like having a mistress without being unfaithful. It was driving a wedge between us.

'You never tell me what you're doing,' she would complain. 'You tell John about things before you'll tell me.'

'That's because you don't like the band. You're not interested.'

'I'm interested in you.'

'Yes but my life is the band.'

'Tell me about the band, then.'

'Yeah, but talking about the band bores you silly.'

We would go round in circles, argue about arguing. I suppose something had to give eventually.

'GET OUT OF MY HOUSE!!'

Alison was in the bath. We were rowing, probably about the lid on the toothpaste tube or something. I splashed a palmful of water onto her face. She hates water on her face. I smugly stomped down the stairs, content in the knowledge I had ended the argument in the ascendancy. I was about to reach the bottom when an aquatic commotion upstairs was followed by excruciating pain in the calf area.

'AAAAAAHHHHHHH!'

I looked down and saw the (now decidedly sorry-looking) bathroom scales – a wedding present ironically, sorry Jon – lying by my ankles.

'DOES THAT HURT!?'

No need for the sarcasm, darling.

There were other rows, usually sparked off by the most inane domestic trifles. She threw a glass at me. I smashed a door in her face. And as the months wore on, our light of tenderness grew dimmer, smothered in a darkness of self-perpetuating tension and petty recriminations. The more we rowed, the less we remembered why we loved each other.

'I'll just go if that's what you want!'

'Good!'

So I did.

I finally lost the plot on December 30th.

'I'm leaving Alison,' I told a work colleague.

'Why? You two are made for each other?'

'I can't bear the rows and the constant fighting.'

I told Alison in the morning that I would pack my bags when I came home after work that day. At lunchtime, I went to the barber's. When I got home, I had hoped she wouldn't be there but, of course, she was, sat on the floor listening to music. She never listens to music.

'Your hair looks nice.'

'I'm going.'

She got up and put her arms round me.

'Don't, please don't, don't leave me, please.'

I shrugged her off, picked up my bag and my acoustic.

'Bye.'

I stayed at John's over New Year, then found a berth in the spare room at Gina's, one of the other journalists on the paper. I took some time off work. I thought about nothing else but Alison. I tried not to, but I couldn't take my mind off her.

One morning my acoustic fell and smashed onto Gina's concrete floor (it still bears the scar). Karma? Three weeks after I had left, I got a cold and the cold developed into flu, and I poured out that much sweat Gina had to give me a new mattress. Alison came to see me. She brought me some orange juice.

'I'm going away for the weekend, can you look after the cats? I'll be back late Sunday.'

'Of course.'

I couldn't go and sleep upstairs, not yet. I stayed on the sofa-bed in the living room all weekend, recovering. Being at home drained away the tension.

'You're still here,' she said on Sunday night.

There was little surprise in her voice.

'Do you mind?'

It took months, years probably, for the wound to heal; the threat of another separation hung in the air for ages.

ORDER YOUR BMWS

We hired the damp underground haven that was Splash rehearsal studios – conveniently nestled between Wigan's Police Station and Magistrates Court, it's a wonder they didn't smell anything illegal – for a whole week (but only after booking the time off work of course) in order to work with Phil Tennant. No more lugging, no more folding leads . . . we could just stop playing and go home at the end of the day.

Gosh.

And it wasn't even called rehearsing any more, we were now in pre-production, thank you very much. But a week for a whole song? We had never done more than a few hours for most of the set. What on earth were we going to do for all that time?

Our room was next to Verve's, which on the down side meant enduring hours of their shapeless, decibel-defying jamming, but on the plus side, their din reinforced our feeling of superiority. Tennant couldn't believe the muffled sonic boom from next door belonged to a signed band.

'Indie flash in the pan, you wait,' he said.

Our two paths had begun taking very different directions. The 'greatest unsigned band' in Britain was fast turning into the most hyped new sensation in Britain. While we played second support to the 16 year-old soon-to-be-Supergrass incarnation, The Jennifers, at an empty New Cross Venue in London, Verve's shows in the capital had every music journalist in the land ejaculating on to paper.

The *NME*'s Roger Morton, December 7th: 'They're the blinding flash merchants of architectural guitaring, an accident in a chemical factory, like God falling down an escalator.'

You what?

We were not altogether ignored by the *NME* – that treat would come later – but we were a curio to be kept at arm's length. What little we did get was down largely to **Stuart Maconie**. He came 'home' one weekend and spoke to me, John and Shrub (with whom he was once in a band called The Young Mark Twains, incidentally). The photographer snapped us all clinging onto the giant mill wheel outside Wigan Technical College, and under the headline 'Pram Heirs' (at least we avoided the Pier word), the interview appeared in the February 15th issue:

STUART MACONIE – Stuart's was a classic route into music journalism – an enthusiast who started by sending in reviews of gigs and gradually working his way into full-time employment with the *NME*. He progressed to *Q* magazine and then onto TV and radio work, where he currently hosts Radio 5 Live's *The Treatment* on Saturday mornings.

'The Tansads regularly sell out venues a whole posse of media darlings couldn't half fill . . .'

It would be the last positive press we received in the *NME*, once Stuart's 'patronage' had run its course. Once he moved onto to bigger and better things, there was nobody left to pick up the baton.

Unlike Verve, whose adulation in the media was beginning to really piss me off. I tried not to let it show when Wigan's two most famous up and coming bass players met in the Splash corridor:

'Hi Simon, how you doin'?'

'Hi, Ed, how's it going?'

'Great, great, we're doing pre-production with Phil Tennant on a new single. You?'

'Yeah, brilliant. The single's out on the 9th, it's called 'All In The Mind'. Dead happy with it. Then we're out with Ride on tour. Just getting it together now.'

'Excellent, I'll make sure you get plenty of coverage for it all.'

'Cheers, take it easy.'

Well, how did you expect me to behave?

When their single came out (produced by Stone Roses knob-twiddler Paul Schroeder, bastards), it was all too much for me. I began a one-man backlash.

First, a tirade against the danger of hype under the (I thought, anyway) utterly clever headline: 'With *NME* like this, who needs friends?' Then my review for the single (which I really like now, by the way):

'The whole shebang points upwards in a reverb-dipped swirl, but fails to grab you – a bit nebulous for my liking. No doubt this will be interpreted as small town paper trying to hold its sons back, but that is nonsense. I hope Verve are gigantic.' – Liar – 'All I'm saying is I don't like the record.'

The vitriol was thinly disguised, not that it mattered anyway. The days of my evangelical newsprint rantings were numbered. It was obvious something was wrong. Work, music, Alison. One of them just had to go. The latter wasn't plausible, we had just proved that, and I certainly wasn't about to jack in the band. That left one option. And actually it was Alison who planted the seed in my head, though she vehemently denies it now.

'If you're that unhappy, leave work,' she said, not long after I had moved back in.

Working with Phil was the catalyst I needed to finally take the plunge. He had given me a glimpse of the future, and I liked what I saw. During our pre-production week (when we turned up loud enough to drown out Verve), Phil took 'Up the Revolution' and 'John John' apart, spending a day on the drums and bass alone. The songs didn't change all that much in essence but it was like dismantling a car, polishing every last nut until you can see your reflection in it, and then rebuilding it all from scratch. The effect was astonishing, especially in comparison to Geoff Davis' comical bumbling.

After that, the demo just had to sound great and the next stop was Square One Studios, Bury, where during a lull in the recording session, John and I had a competition to see who could touch a beam dangling from the ceiling. I won (a small victory), he crippled his back, and was forced to use

Shrub's keyboard stand as a zimmer frame for the rest our time in the studio. We cancelled one show scheduled for the following week and John played another, sat *à la* Val Doonican.

And then there was the case of the missing bass drum beat . . .

'You fucking do.'

'I fucking do not!'

'You fucking do, I was listening, because I play to them.'

'Fuck off, I -'

'I know what I'm fucking playing.'

Demonstration on bass: boom boom-boom, boom boom-boom.

'Only sometimes, you play, 'boom boom' on its own. Listen to it on the playback. How can I play to the bass drum beat if you keep changing it?'

'I'm doing exactly what I've always done.

'Yeah, precisely, and it's always sounded shit.'

'ALL RIGHT GIRLS, CALM DOWN!'

The rhythm section was at odds for the recording of 'John John', in the first hour of our first session with Phil Tennant. Bug soon agreed, however, to play the same pattern for the whole song and I apologised for being a prickly bastard. In other words, when he missed his bass drum beats for the next take, I just shut up, and nobody was any the wiser, and the song ended up sounding great.

'That's a take,' said Phil, leaning back. 'And order your BMWs now.'

For the first time since leaving school, not only did I know precisely what I wanted, but Phil had shown it was possible to achieve it. In a blinding flash, I made one of the single most important decisions of my life.

Being a journalist was all very well. It was a good job. I had my music column, I got free tickets to gigs, to the theatre, and I got free CDs and new cars to test-drive. And I was paid to watch my favourite footie team, **Wigan Athletic**, home and away. I mixed with the players, I knew the manager, the staff, and the fans always wanted to talk to me. I was a local personality of sorts. Hardly a big fish in a little pond, but definitely one who could splash about with plenty of aplomb. And I was paid a decent enough wage too, after fiddling my expenses.

But it wasn't enough, and in between the good bits, there was still too much nine-to-five dross to yawn through. Work was certainly not what I yearned for. It wasn't what I dreamt about at night or what kept me awake when I wasn't dreaming.

My passion, my obsession, my drug, was music. I would play guitar for

WIGAN ATHLETIC – Just think, if The 'Sads had made it, I could have been The Latics' one and only celebrity fan. Apart that is, from John Finch, who won *Stars in their Eyes* as Marti Pellow a few years back. I actually managed to get 'Shandyland' played on the stadium PA before a match once, a Leyland DAF Cup Preliminary Round game against Huddersfield with an attendance of 1,000.

hours on end, writing songs, playing songs and recording songs on my four-track. The fact that it was such a transient career was totally irrelevant, I wasn't thinking about pension benefits. Rather, I was listening to my instincts. If you only get one opportunity in life, this, I had just convinced myself, was it. I wasn't naive enough to believe that just because a producer whose CV included such luminaries as The Waterboys, The Cure, and – gasp – Belinda Carlisle was demoing a couple of tracks with us meant instant stardom, although it would clearly do us no harm. It was more that meeting Phil, somebody whose entire existence was music, had taught me that unless I devoted myself completely, I could never be successful.

The following day I handed in my notice at work.

FLOATING ON AIR

I remember the date clearly, March 1st 1992.

'I envy your courage,' said Malcolm Hindle, my editor at the paper. 'I've always wanted to write, but, well, I've never got round to it, really.'

Managing Director Mark Ashley was less sympathetic, though he too, grudgingly, wished me luck in a roundabout way. A loud, large Yorkshireman I had nicknamed Fat Bradford, he insisted to my embarrassment on hauling me in front of everybody and choosing Relevant Anecdote No 53 from his Book of Public Speaking.

'When I was a reporter at the *Yorkshire Evening Post*,' he bawled, subtle as a town crier, a journalist by the name of Mark announced he was quitting the job for music. "You'll never make it, it's a mug's game," said the editor. Do you know what the lad's surname was? Knopfler.'

I was beginning to regret this.

'Well I'm not falling into that trap. You're a bastard, Jones, leaving us like this. I'm really in the shit now for replacing you.'

From Ashley, this was about as close as you got to praise, though to be mentioned in the same breath as Dire Straits did my image no good. Over the next four weeks, as I saw out my time at the paper, I got sick, and flattered, of people asking me if I would still speak to them when I was famous. It only contributed to the growing wave of excitement building up inside me.

A month down the line and I was a fully-fledged musician, with a wife, a mortgage . . . and an income of zero.

ALISON says, *'It's a wonder I didn't boot him out. First of all he made me sell Mary, our beloved green Beetle. She had been his car at first, but I'd paid as many bills as he had, more probably. Too expensive he said, but I still think it was because you couldn't fit enough guitar amps in the back. Then, he went and bought a Fiat Uno which I didn't want (plenty of room in the back – coincidence?) thanks to my two thousand pound bank loan, then he leaves me, changes his mind and comes back, and then leaves work.'*

How brilliant did that feel? If it had come to a choice at that time, I would have opted for music before Alison. If she loved me, I reasoned, she would support me and that takes a special kind of love. I was giving up a well-paid job to do something I believed in and enjoyed, while Alison was facing the prospect of keeping both of us on her less than brilliant wage earned from a job she hated.

But all artists need ego to fuel their self-belief. If there's a pot of gold at the end of the rainbow, this is not always a problem. You may be a selfish sod, but at least you're a rich one. Unsuccessful artists, on the other hand, or struggling ones, are just broke and selfish, an altogether less attractive combination. But I had to follow my instincts. How could I ever live with myself if I didn't?

As it turned out, it was only a fortnight or so after handing in my resignation that the band got a deal. I had the satisfaction of being able to hold my head up high in the office for two glorious weeks, my leap into the unknown being vindicated almost at once.

'Such joy!' François Grandchamp, President of French record label Musidisc was delirious. 'I have never seen such joy on one stage!'

The Phil Tennant connection had worked. On returning to London with the Bury demo, he had tapped a couple of contacts and, on the strength of his recommendation, Label Manager Jeremy Thomas and François made the journey to our next gig, a Hunt Saboteurs Benefit at Manchester University Burlington Rooms.

It was hardly the way I had dreamt it would happen, but things rarely work out as you expect. Unlike Verve, we had to make do with a solitary French outfit nobody had heard of. However, Musidisc were still a proper record company, and we were certainly not going to turn them away.

They had recently opened a London office in an attempt to blood new British talent, something we found out to our peril they were hopelessly ill equipped to do. But we were starstruck, and no one else with money had shown such an interest before. They had released the first moderately successful Levellers LP *A Weapon Called the Word* (produced by Phil Tennant, hence the connection), which is well suspect, but this had led to the band signing to China Records and breaking B.I.G. T.I.M.E. This gave us hope.

I will never forget the incongruity of that evening. Here was this elegant, mild-mannered, middle-aged French aristocrat, accompanied by a public school spiv in an ankle length leather coat, standing amongst a hundred moshing, Northern, sweaty animal-rights campaigners.

The gig was slow to start. But once the first few numbers were played, the sheer energy radiated from the stage and soon the room was alive.

Phil called us back a couple of days later with the good news. Musidisc wanted to sign us. They wanted us to go into the studio and record a single straight away, before contracts were signed.

'Go ahead, record the single and we'll negotiate the deal as we go,' said Jeremy Thomas, and although, on the face of it, we were going into another 24-track studio without any formal agreement, we knew Musidisc were no Probe Plus.

ALISON says, *'Of course, he expected me not only to keep a roof over our heads and food in our mouths, but also to pay back the car loan and put petrol in the car for him to go practising and playing gigs. Then he would get upset when I shouted at him. He said I humiliated him in front of all of his friends. I don't know how I tolerated it. Or how we stayed together.'*

Yes, they were far more subtle.

Phil had already pencilled in a date. This time it wasn't a hovel in Bury for a weekend, but a £500-per-day residential studio in Wales for five days. Julian Cope was finishing something off so we couldn't fit in until the following month.

Julian Cope!

Life had been turned upside down in a matter of days. The fact that Shrub left didn't really register.

'I've stopped enjoying myself,' he said. 'I'm fed up with John. He used to be my friend but now he's just a selfish shit.'

Fine.

The brutal truth was that the band would operate perfectly well in his absence. Cudo took over on keyboards, which he was able to combine with the percussion and vocals, and ultimately, one less member was one less wage. It was a shame because Shrub was a mate, but at least he can proudly boast of having been founder member of the Ex-Tansads Club.

I didn't care. I was floating on air.

Look at me now, all you doubters, look at me now.

CONTRACT KILLER

Contracts are an absolute spaghetti bolognese of bullshit and double-speak, divided into clauses and sub-clauses and featuring strange phrases like *heretounder*, *effectuate said option period* and *expiration of term*. We enlisted the help of David Irving from **Seddons Solicitors**, of London *and* Prague. Cost: a cool £1,800 for around a day's work. We saw him once more after the negotiations had taken place, when he pulled up in his brand new Porsche at a set of traffic lights in London, alongside our clapped-out big red van. 'Nuff said.

SEDDONS SOLICITORS – Seddons had printed sugar cubes. Nice.

There are actually two agreements to be made, the recording deal itself and the publishing agreement. The former, as the name suggests, covers the recording and release of songs, the latter is about copyright and ownership of songs. Record companies advance you money to live off. This is a loan, not against any individual, but returnable via your royalties. At least if you don't sell anything, you're not left with a debt more than the Gross National Product of Brazil.

RECORDING DEAL – The Railway Children contract with Virgin was, and I quote, 'for the World together with any part of the universe which may from time to time be visited or occupied by man'. Still, their advance was £450,000, and if you add up every subsequent advance on their recording and publishing contracts, it made a cool £2,327,250.

RECORDING DEAL. Our royalty rate was 12% for the UK and France, and 9% for the rest of the world. Pretty standard. But that doesn't mean that we got 12% of the price a customer pays in a shop nor what the shop pays for any given album. Oh, no. Deduct the distribution company's fee, the production costs, the packaging costs, the songwriter's royalty, the tax, VAT, the A&R department's charlie (oops), and a thousand other spurious nibbles of the cherry, and now take 12% from what's left. Something in the range of 50p per CD. It's a racket, basically. When you see a band being dropped owing £200,000, all it means is that they haven't managed to pay back their advances using this arcane calculation. The company hasn't actually lost that amount, it just seems that way. They'll still be in profit.

Our recording deal was potentially worth £69,800 over three years. The deal was divided into three option periods of 12 months, each time Musidisc having the legal right to drop us. Together it was the biggest package they had ever offered, but it was still peanuts in comparison to Verve's – the gossip saying it was in the region of £300,000. The money, though, does not all go to the band. £38,000 was what was referred to as Marketing Commitment, to be spent on promotional activities that included Tour Support and money to cover gigging losses. Sounds OK, I suppose, but what that really meant was that we had to justify all our marketing requests and Musidisc, at their discretion, had the power to refuse them (which they did, regularly).

That left £31,800. Quick calculation. Divide that by three for the number of years it covered, then by 52 weeks of the year, then by eight members and you get £25.48 each per week. And that amount was for everything, including wages.

PUBLISHING. You don't have to sign a publishing deal, but you'd be foolish not to. The publisher's job is essentially to promote your songs. They may take a cut of royalties but don't worry about that, because they also pay advances. In other words, when you're offered money, you take it and you run. Very fast.

We got £15,000 and we ran.

Had we been a democratic band where everybody was credited for songwriting, the advance could just have been added to the wages pot. But we weren't that kind of band. John wrote the songs (and didn't we know it!) with help from Robert. I had 'Gelignite' in the set and on the shortlist for the LP. Therefore, John got the majority of the publishing advance, though admitedly a lot of it went back into the band kitty (and didn't we know it), Robert a proportion, and me a smaller portion, £200 for the first year I think.

Only one more thing to explain. The Performing Rights Society (PRS) is the company that actually collects royalties from radio, TV and film companies and live venues every time your material is broadcast or performed. The PRS pays money directly to songwriters but, in order to join, you have to have had three published works released commercially. Only John and Robert qualified. The rewards were not great at this stage of our career but, one minor hit and the division would really bite. It's easy to see where and when the bitterness creeps into bands.

The first rule of thumb for any band about to get a contract is never sign a recording and publishing deal with the same company, because you are then totally at their mercy.

What did we do? Guessed it in one.

But there was a reason. Honest. Musidisc advanced us £4,000 more if we stuck with them on both counts and, believe me, that made a difference. Still, the only way we could afford to sign the deal, even with the extra money, was by robbing Peter to pay Paul.

This involved negotiating to have the majority of our advances – £18,600 – paid in the first year, which only left £6,000, then £7,200 in the next two years.

Average gig fees at the time were around £150 (break-even, roughly), but a year down the line, after a successful album and the big Musidisc push (ha ha), we were banking on them having risen dramatically. We settled on £30 a week each, which added up to £12,480, leaving £6,120 for everything else.

Absolute financial suicide, but it was our only chance. Our original budget had been for a £90,000 advance. OK, that was pushing it to a point, but we had expected more than the initial £5,000 they offered. £5,000? We should have walked away there and then.

'Don't go near them,' Levellers' manager Phil Nelson told Damian.

'I would advise the band not to sign,' was David Irving's advice, 'but we all know you will. Won't you?'

And that, ladeezngenelmen, in a nutshell, is what this whole darn book's about. The contract killer never misses the musician, it's just a question of whether you've managed to become rich enough to buy a bulletproof vest when he does.

OK, let's assume there exists an aspiring pop star who has the bollocks to say 'Fuck off, you greedy corporate bastard' to the only record company prepared to offer terms. What then? Well, he or she may be lucky, lucky, lucky. There may be a second chance. But what if the offer of a second company does not match the first? What then? And what if there are no other takers? What if you have to spend the rest of your life thinking up anagrams of Pete Best?

It's bad enough being ripped off by the wankers but, believe me, it's far worse not being ripped off by them. So we signed, naturally, and as of June 1st 1992 (even though the donkeys dated the contract 1991) we were officially full-time professional musicians.

PRESS-GANGED

The next day, before the ink had even dried on the contract, the *Wigan Evening Post*'s music correspondent Dave Barnett published the following story.

Rising stars of pop world sign super record deal
Success on the line

Wigan's rising stars The Tansads have signed a half-million pound worldwide record deal. The pop-folksters have signed on the dotted line with London-based independent label Musidisc. Tansads manager Damian Liptrot said: 'The group is at pains to point out that the days when they will be seen cruising the streets in a stretch-limo are still some way in the future, but no matter how massive we become, we will always be known as a Northern band.'

The paper hit the streets around 3.00 p.m. At 3:15 p.m. the phone rang.

'Ed, it's Malcolm here.'

My old editor at the *Wigan Reporter*.

'Hi Malc, how's it going?'

'You're a bit of a one, aren't you?'

'Why, what have I done now?'

'Going behind my back like that with the exclusive on your big news. Don't you remember your old friends now you've hit the big time?'

'I'm sorry?'

'Giving *The Post* the half a million story.'

'*Post*? Half a million?'

'Come on, don't play the innocent, Jonesey boy.'

'Honestly Malc, I haven't the faintest idea what you're talking about. We've just signed a deal, but it's certainly not worth half a million. I wish it was, believe me. I think someone, somewhere may have got the wrong end of the stick.'

'Oh.' Shakespearean pause. 'Well what is it worth then?'

'I don't really want to put a figure on it, to be honest. I've no idea what Damian is playing at, but I need to talk to him first and I won't be able to until tonight because he's at work.'

'The thing is we've got to have something today. It's deadline at 5 p.m., as you know.'

'Look, I don't mind confirming all the details about the deal, but I really can't tell you a figure. If you must, quote me as denying it's £500,000, but I owe it to the others to keep it confidential.'

'Fair enough, mate. Off the record, though?'

'Off the record, it's actually difficult to say exactly, because some of the amounts aren't fixed. But over the three years, it's probably worth between £45,000 and £70,000. Not quite half a million, anyway.'

And that's where we left it and Malcolm said he could use what I'd given him. In Journalese, off the record is not just a cliché, it really does mean a verbal promise not to publish. Malcolm was the one who taught me about its importance.

That evening, Damian was taken to task by a decidedly unhappy John and me.

'Look, I'm sorry, I didn't mean this to happen, I thought they'd get the joke.'

The press release had read: 'The deal is worth closer to £500,000 than the magic million.'

Very clever of course, only Dave Barnett didn't quite get it. And neither did we.

'Damian, it sounds like we've signed for half a million.'

'Yes but it doesn't say you have.'

'That's clearly not what Dave Barnett thought.'

Pop stars not a day old and already we had lost our sense of humour.

Two days later, on the Thursday afternoon, the phone rang. It was John.

'Ed, have you seen *The Reporter*?'

'No, why?'

'You said you didn't tell them any figures'

'I didn't.'

'Well how the hell have they written an article saying we've signed a deal worth £45,000?'

DISC THREE

June 1992 – December 1992

BUG BEER

'Who's nicked my beer? Who's nicked my fuckin' beer? There were four cans of Grolsch in the fridge and now there's one! Who's nicked my fuckin' beer?'

Bug was not a content drummer. He had just finished a hard day's recording and now somebody had nicked his beer.

'Who's nicked my fuckin' beer?'

We never did find out the identity of the phantom beer nicker.

Later that night, with his alcohol levels back at a satisfactory high, we watched the completely unfunny *Uncle Buck*, starring John Candy, on the video. It was made even less funny by the fact that Bug laughed hysterically throughout, and punctuated every scene with:

'Watch this, watch this, this bit's fucking hilarious, HAHAHAHAHA!'

Two points:

1) Drummers. Either happy or sad.

2) Beer. Very precious when the nearest shop is six miles away.

GOING IN LOCO DOWN IN . . . LLANHENNOCK

Loco Studios in Llanhennock, Carleon, near Newport, is, according to Kemp's International Music Book, 'a residential studio in beautiful Welsh border countryside, with a spacious daylight control room, live room, normal acoustic room, and iso booths, with full catering and accommodation'.

What it doesn't say is that it is run by a dead ringer for Harold from *Neighbours* called Nick Smith. Alongside an extensive technical inventory, he includes a lists of former clients: The Verve (of course), Oasis, The Stone Roses, Ash, The Stereo MCs, 60ft Dolls, Julian Cope, The Saw Doctors, Jethro Tull (is that a boast?), The Mission, Shed Seven, and many more including Queen Elizabeth (who the fuck are they?). But there is no mention of The Tansads.

Bastard!

We recorded TWO full albums at your place. We must have spent tens of thousands of pounds with you. You said we were one of the best bands you had EVER had in. Do you say that to all the girls? Well, Harold, you can take your Lexicon 480L with LARC, ATC SCM200s, and Yamaha NS10Ms and shove them up your antipodean arse.

Thank you.

LOCO – The Saw Doctors derived great pleasure in erasing the last ten minutes from the majority of the pirated videos in the TV room. Thanks.

It's true that **Loco** is a haven as there are no neighbours and you're miles from the main road (and the pub), so essentially you can do anything you want and get away with it.

And most bands do. Allegedly.

We, however, were far too sensible to be particularly naughty by rock-'n'-roll standards and our intoxicants were either legal or obtainable at all good Amsterdam coffee houses. We said 'please' and 'thank you' for our food and I even spoke to the mad gardener Alan. He finished his day by lunchtime and most bands probably never even realised he existed. I thought he was great fun, though, and I made a point of speaking to him. He was one of those blokes who always had to go one better.

'In a band are you? I used to play marbles with Mick Jagger, you know. Like football, do you? I was League of Wales top scorer in '71-'72, you know. Like a pint do you? I've had six a day since 1912 and I can still run a mile in four minutes.'

Guaranteed to cheer the parts other gardeners can't reach.

We recorded the album in stages. Five days in April had been spent doing the single – 'Brian Kant' – and now we had three weeks in two chunks of ten days lined up for the rest; 13 songs to be trimmed to 12 on the final cut.

We never found out the actual cost, but the full recording budget for the LP was around £20,000. Phil's method of work was the traditional way. Drums and bass first for all the songs, then guitars, keyboards, and so on.

I knew the songs inside out, so we could, in theory (i.e. if Geoff Davis was behind the mixing desk), have done them in one take. But parts were analysed, sounds were changed and we did five, ten, fifteen takes per track at least, to the point where the performances actually started dipping. I've got a fairly decent sense of timing, but I managed to get behind the rhythm, ahead of it, inside it, through it, under it. I did everything but shag the bloody thing.

But it was good for me. Phil pushed me to new heights of achievement and I began to learn how to feel the part rather than think about notation. Simply, to relax under pressure. There's a definite art to it.

The disadvantage was that once Bug and I had done our bits (about ten days in) there was, literally, nothing left for us to do (although Bug did sing some backing vocals). And vice versa for the singers, who were idle for the first two or three weeks almost, then had to cram everything in at the end.

I basically just sat and played guitar, wrote songs, read, went for walks, practised my football juggling, drove to the bank for the wages, and did the accounts.

For everybody apart from John and Phil, Loco was one long working (sort of) holiday. I remember some tricky phone calls home.

'Hi, love, what have you being doing today?'

Oh, you know, lying in the sun, playing football, reading, while you've been slogging your guts out at work to keep me.

'Oh, you know, working in the studio, practising my parts, it's intense but it's rewarding.'

After all the tension of chasing a deal, negotiating contracts, and leaving work, not to mention domestic troubles, it was hard not to wallow in the artificial decadence of the studio life. This was the plus side of not being the songwriter. I could mooch around and have a great time listening to the album take shape. It sounded so good: part pop, part rock, part grunge, part folk; part borrowed, part unique. It was definitely us.

The Tansads.

But as much as I would have preferred to be at the cutting edge, twiddling a few knobs and changing arrangements of songs, I wasn't. As simple as that. But as 'Gelignite' was in the final batch of songs for the album, my soul was at rest. And then . . .

'We're not going to have time for 'Gelignite.'

Phil seemed a little sheepish. It was our last day at Loco. I remember it well, June 25th. I had felt the time ticking away as the song remained untouched since the drums and bass had been put down in the first few days, but a mixture of fear and pride forbade me from bringing the subject up.

'We're having two extra days in London. We'll finish it there.'

'OK.'

There wasn't time to worry about that now. The small matter of a lifetime ambition had just bullied its way into my consciousness. For so long just a circle round a date on the calendar, now it was merely 24 hours away.

The Tansads were playing Glastonbury.

MORNING GLORY

It was only the acoustic stage. And it was at 11.00 am on the Friday morning. But we were on the posters and we were in the programme, and I've still got the official car park and backstage passes to prove it.

IT WAS GLASTONBURY!

At around 5 a.m. that morning, with the dawn mist clinging to the ground like dry ice and the dew sparkling in the waking sunlight, the vale of Avalon certainly is the stuff of fairy tales.

Our fairy godmother had come in the shape of agent Geoff Meall who with one giant wave of his magic wand had managed to book the most glamorous gig of our lives . . . ever.

It had been a mad 24 hours. A posse of girlfriends, wives, and friends had descended upon Loco on the last night all set for Glastonbury and when there's eight of you in the band, plus management, plus crew, and you get a guest each, that amounts to a fair few people. Of course, being The Tansads, we couldn't just go the 50 or 60 miles from Gwent to Avon like ordinary bands would have planned it.

Oh no.

We had to go to Glastonbury via Cambridge.

Oh yes.

We were going to The Rubber Ball; a student extravaganza in the middle of nowhere sponsored by Durex.

Of course.

'It's too good to turn down,' Damian assured us.

Hmmm. A room full of ballgowned and tuxedoed chinless students clutching handfuls of the sponsors' wares, too pissed to even realise there was a band on anyway, is not particularly career-enhancing at the best of times. And we were supporting River City People.

It certainly wasn't too good to turn down, especially when it finishes in the early hours of the morning and you have to be 200 miles away at 9 a.m. for the greatest gig of your life and the red van with all the equipment, and half the band inside is liable to collapse at any time.

Miraculously, chugging along at 50 mph, the convoy of four cars and said dodgy van rode heroically through the night, and bar a few unsavoury noises emanating from the Iveco's undercarriage, we all arrived in one piece on a diet of adrenaline and bleary-eyed bewilderment at around six-thirty am.

GLASTONBURY!

Luckily for us, 1992 was one of the hottest on record. Advantage: no re-enactment of the Somme required. Disadvantage: a distinct fragrance of stale urine come the second morning.

It could hardly be said that we were in the lap of luxury. But the fenced off area behind the acoustic stage at least had its own private Portaloo, a bar, and more importantly, a tap. That helped.

The acoustic bit is a misnomer. It refers to the nature of some of the acts, rather than the lack of a PA, which, thankfully, was satisfactorily large and loud. But 9 a.m. was no time to be lugging heavy gear about, especially without sleep.

It goes without saying that we would have dearly wished to be on one of the two main stages and a later time but there was not even a whisper of a complaint from the camp. How could there be? We knew we'd be back and anyway, spare a thought for Cindy Stratton who was on at 10.30 a.m.

The important aspect, time-slot egos notwithstanding, was just being there. You can take your Reading, Phoenix, V90s, and Ts in the Park, but Glastonbury is the still the festival to play and be at. Three generations of fans, bands – and me – can't be wrong.

I mean, headliners at Reading can get anything up to £200,000 to perform, and The Verve were rumoured to have got £800,000 for their two performances at V98, but the main players at Glastonbury can only expect between £70,000 and £100,000.

Why do it, then?

Because it's the best.

I don't actually remember that much about the show itself, apart from the sound being awful on stage, and a crowd of around 1,000, many of whom wore Tansads T-shirts and sang the words. Sang the words! At 11 a.m. on the first day, away from the main stage, I think that's called a decent gig.

Our manager Damian had given a lift to Stuart Maconie and his *NME* colleague Andrew Collins. They also stayed in Damian's oversized tent, and seemed to enjoy our backstage luxury. I'm sure they felt impelled, therefore, to mention our performance in their Glastonbury round-up for the paper, although it has to be said, it was a mere footnote:

'Further up the hill, we find the Acoustic Tent where the use of a PA belies the Luddite affectations. Hooray, then, for Wigan's Tansads for braving this hot outpost.'

GLASTONBURY – On the Friday The Tansads played, the headliners were as follows – Main Stage: Carter USM and Shakespear's Sister; NME Stage: Primal Scream and The Orb; Acoustic Stage: Baba Yaga and Nan Vernon.

Ah well.

From The Tansads' point of view, Glastonbury was already over before things had really started. We weren't complaining, however. The sun was beating down, and we had earned our passage to the world's most famous rock festival. I floated around for the rest of the day on autopilot, fuelled in no small measure by the smugness of the back-stage pass wearer and the copious amounts of free Red Stripe.

That night, in the bizarre delirium of sunstroke, alcohol, and tiredness, I sat outside the tent watching with amusement the faces of the gatecrashers as they scrambled over the perimeter fence and dodged the SS searchlights, only to find themselves in a secure enclosed compound. Laugh? You bet.

THE LEVELLERS – Jeremy Thomas was first to spot their potential and signed the band to the fledgling Musidisc UK, with their Phil Tennant-produced debut album going on to sell around 40,000. There's no denying they were (are?) something of a phenomenon, enjoying consistent success despite a hate-hate relationship with the media; bassist Jeremy Cunningham once famously sent a turd through the post to the *NME*. Funnily enough, François Grandchamp once described Cunningham as being the smelliest person he had ever met.

We stayed until **The Levellers** had finished their set on the Saturday night, watched by 60,000 and more.

Wow.

There were people as far as the eye could see in every direction, stretching right up the famous hill in front of the main stage. This was a former Musidisc band?

A glimpse of the future, perhaps.

DON'T BE A KANT

Selling singles is all-out nuclear warfare with no code of combat. Musidisc tried to take part armed only with a Swiss army knife and a copy of the Geneva Convention. And we wondered why our record never even made it into the shops.

The rules when issuing singles have changed in recent times and free gifts, be it postcards, personalised yo-yos or whatever, have been banned. There are still dozens of marketing scams (legal or otherwise) to increase sales, however. The name of the game seems to involve the throwing away of obscene amounts of money, as singles simply do not make a profit. End of story. It is purely an advertising medium to sell albums.

The charts are not an accurate reflection of the number of records sold. For a start, only certain outlets ("chart return shops") qualify for inclusion. Naturally, record companies focus their attention on these, and give thousands of copies to retailers, which are then sold cheaply. They also provide copious amounts of promotional material, such as posters, display boxes, giant cutaways of the lead singer, dangly mobiles, limited edition, specially remixed, repackaged boxed sets, and so on. All that is pretty well documented.

But there are less well-known practices. Individual deals are struck between company and shop: take ten, five, three, or two copies of New Band X's single, depending on how hard it is being pushed, and pay only for one. Sailing even closer to the wind, record companies often hire out hit squads, whereby shops are targeted by a special sales strike force who provide extra marketing material and gifts of records and videos for the staff (but only for their personal use, of course), and generally shower them with attention. And definitely over the line are buying teams, people hired literally to go and purchase their own records back from chart return outlets.

Selling singles is a sophisticated marketing jungle and the system is rife with corruption. Unfortunately, we had a record company in Musidisc that had no money, and an unsophisticated marketing strategy and knew none of the tricks. Great. But there's always radio, isn't there? Not quite.

Daytime Radio 1 is still the most influential for sales and, along with all regional and independent stations, they have a playlist. There are three playlists at Radio 1. The A list is the pot of gold, guaranteeing around thirty plays a week; the B list ensures fifteen plays a week; and the As-Featured list is the reserve basket where you will get the occasional play.

And to get on a playlist? Well, that's where your radio plugger comes in. Nestling under large music biz water lilies by night, this rare pony-tailed, black leather clad creature can be spotted slithering through daytime radio station lobbies on the way in and out of producers' arses. DJs, in the main, are producers' puppets, and pluggers buzz round production offices like flies round shit, promoting their wares. Those who curry the best favour get the best results. And it costs. Basically, the more you pay (average: £1,000 a month, but it can go much, much higher), the more chance you get of having a playlisted single. Around 200 singles are released each week, a fraction of which make it through. What were our chances?

Naturally, we were not yet educated in all these shenanigans at this stage and we thought the single had a chance. It came out on July 6th, and was definitely the wrong choice. The original plan was to put out 'John John' or 'Up the Revolution'. But while Musidisc preferred the former, we wanted the latter, and in the spirit of compromise we issued the catchy 'Brian Kant', a rehearsal-room piss-take based upon the combed-over hairstyle championed by the *Playaway* presenter. Nobody, however, got the joke (again) and it simply reaffirmed in our minds the industry's prejudices against anything outside of London.

There were three versions, 7-inch, 12-inch and CD. Musidisc press officer Sheila achieved the sum total of no reviews in the music inkies (not even a slag off), while our go-ahead company insisted on charging full price. Conundrum: 15-year old pop fan hears great new song on radio, goes to buy song, but finds CD is not in shop and has to order it at a cost of £4.29. Pop fan only has £2.50 pocket money. Madonna single is out in the same week, that's all right too, costs only £1.99, and there are dozens of copies under a massive poster and lifesize puppet of the dame herself. What does pop fan do?

On our insistence, we did actually manage to make Musidisc budge slightly on this issue. It was to be the first and only time. We waived our right to any royalties (ha, ha) on sales of the 7-inch, they agreed to give copies away to retailers. Jeremy Thomas thought of the brilliant ploy of producing a sticker heralding the great news: 'Don't be a Kant,' it read, 'pay no more than 99p'.

The problem was that this was the 1990s. Vinyl was dead. It sold about six copies, although that was more than the 12-inch version, priced at a bargain £3.99.

The 'Brian Kant' sales campaign was summed up when Damian set up a dreaded in-store record signing at Alan's Records, Wigan. In a straight steal from ***This is Spinal Tap*** (though Damian declined to play the role of Arty Fufkin), we stood around like lemons in an empty (home town, remember) record shop for a FULL HOUR. The only 'fan' who turned up was a spotty, bespectacled teenager too shy to come and talk to us. He flicked through a few records before departing, leaving us to the sniggers of the staff.

THIS IS SPINAL TAP – The film, satirising the life and times of a heavy metal band, featured, among many others, such classic lines as "Turn it up to eleven", "The bigger the cushion, the harder the pushin'" and "Sexism? What's wrong with being sexy?"

In amongst all this doom and gloom, there was a small ray of sunshine. Some DJs do sometimes get the chance to play the occasional track outside the playlist, but they are few and far between. Our plugger (one of the rare times anybody associated with Musidisc actually seemed able to do what they were paid for) was called Tony Byrne or Tony the Tongue as he became (semi-)affectionately known. Credit where it's due, he could lick a posterior good and proper.

Unsurprisingly, 'Brian Kant' didn't get playlisted but, surprisingly Tony managed to get it on the Steve Wright afternoon show on Radio 1, and we got plays and even a few sessions on loads of regionals.

Then one day Tony phoned up and sounded really pleased with himself.

'I've lined up something really special,' he began. 'It's an acoustic session on a Saturday morning show on Greater London Radio called "Round at Chris's and his Missus". It's absolutely mad, and it's got great figures. The DJ loves the single and wants you on. His name is Chris Evans.'

Tony was right. The show was crazy. The DJ loved the single. Chris Evans was a natural behind the mike. As we arrived, the girl sent from the studio to his flat to empty the contents of his Hoover was currently on air reeling off her discoveries.

I can't remember why it was chosen (because it was good?) but we performed 'Gelignite', then Evans played the single before phoning up the real Brian Cant and broadcasting the call live.

'Did you know there was a song written about you?

'I do now.'

'What do you think?'

'Can I have the royalties?'

Ho, ho, ho.

When we finished, Evans took off his headphones and came and spoke to us.

'You lot are brilliant,' he said. 'I'm from Warrington myself, just down the road from you, and I can understand what you're about. I love your attitude. You must keep in touch, any time you're in town, call me up. Make sure you do, I mean it.'

Chris Evans soon left GLR, and began presenting a Sunday afternoon programme on Radio 1. He then presented *The Big Breakfast* on Channel 4, became Radio 1's breakfast DJ, and went on not only to front Virgin Radio's breakfast show but to own the whole damn station. He is responsible for breaking some of the biggest names around today, such as Kula Shaker, Space, **Ocean Colour Scene**, (the odious) Divine Comedy, as well as transforming Texas from sad 80s has-beens to arena-filling megastars. He is probably one of the most powerful, if not *the* most powerful man in pop show biz.

OCEAN COLOUR SCENE – With the recent revelation concerning singer Simon Fowler's homosexuality, and his subsequent declaration that it was one of the worst days ever, it remains to be seen whether the outing will affect the commercial success of a band whose core following comes from traditional, checkshirt-wearing 'lads' with sensibilities more akin to *Loaded* and *Razzle* than *Boyz*.

'You must keep in touch,' he said.

Apart from a couple of newsletters, to my knowledge he never received any more communication from The Tansads, not in 1992, not in 1993, not ever.

Why? I truly, hand on heart, couldn't possibly say.

A VOICE FROM THE PAST – A new single by The Galley Slaves, a band featuring my former Lancaster University and Mysterons cohort Pete Ryan, is described by Steve Lamacq in the *NME* as 'twisted but imaginative'. Lamacq first came across the band, he reveals, when he saw them at the Hammersmith Clarendon some months previously. Their support band that night were recent Glastonbury headliners and flavour of '92, Carter The Unstoppable Sex Machine. Pete, I know how you feel.

SLEEPWALKING

The small of my back is beginning to ache. My right shoulder too. I have exhausted every conceivable position: slouched (legs together and apart)', foetal left, foetal right; upright (head down, left, and right), arms folded, arms down and behind the head'; legs up, down, and crossed.

Nothing works.

The thrill of hiring a real McCoy customised rock-'n'-roll gold-coloured splitter van, with twelve seats, a video, tinted windows, curtains, wall to wall carpet, and all the gear stashed in the back clearly went to our heads. The seats may be fairly comfortable for the first four hours but, as I was soon learning, less so for the next thirty.

Accommodation?

Pah! We'll sleep in the van, we've paid enough for the damn thing (£300 for two days to be precise, almost twice our fee for the Peterborough and Hull gigs, but hey, we're a signed band now).

Now that reality has crept up on us, sleeping together as a band suddenly seems less than idyllic. John and Janet decamped into the back aeons ago, where at least their sleeping bags found a flat surface among the guitar cases and drum boxes. That leaves a modicum of extra room in the front, but of the remaining ten, only two can sleep. Terry, who can settle anywhere, any time, if he's in the mood (and he is) and Bug, whose alcoholic oblivion has metamorphosed into the loudest, most stubborn and irrepressible snoring I have ever heard.

Most of us try to ignore it and pretend it isn't happening. Not engineer Dave Fillingham. He insists on adding to the noise by carrying out his own monologue set against the soundtrack of Bug's snoring.

'Fucking 'ell! Shut up Bug, you pissed cunt.'

Snore. Snore. Snore.

'This is stupid. Shut the fucker up, somebody.'

A few more uncomfortable minutes crawl by.

Snore. Snore. Snore.

Then Dave shifts position heavily on his seat, wriggling and bouncing, shaking the van in the process. Nothing.

Snore. Snore. Snore.

'Shut up, for fuck's sake, shut the fuck up!'

Snore. Snore. Snore.

And then it happens.

Bug is slouched on the bench seat at the back, next to Cudo, who's also a fully-paid-up member of the wide-awake club. For a moment, perfect silence. Bliss. Then the distant rumble of the big one is heard. It gathers momentum and . . .

WHAM!

The snore gushes out like a 30-foot tidal wave, taking Bug with it on the follow-through and he lands on top of a startled Cudo.

'FUCKIN' ELL, THAT'S IT! THIS IS FUCKIN' RIDICULOUS!! I'M GETTING OUT OF HERE!!!'

Cudo explodes into life, sweeping down the centre aisle and leaving the drunken drummer (who doesn't wake up) to collapse on the floor.

The only way out is over the vacant driver's seat. But in the darkness Cudo forgets to outmanoeuvre the television, which hangs down, and his head cracks sickeningly against the wooden casing. The thud is followed by the dark, terrifying howl of agony. The door flies open and a cursing Cudo disappears into the murky depths of the car park. A Siberian blizzard (remember, this is Humberside in August) blows in from outside.

'Shut the fucking door!' shouts Dave.

I lean forward and do as instructed but, seconds later it swings violently open once again as Cudo has obviously decided exterior discomforts outweigh even those indoors. He is still audibly agitated, however, and I say nothing.

He sits on the driver's seat, in front of me, and begins rolling a joint furiously as if the future of the world depends on it. Maybe it does. Or at least, Bug's future. Anyway, he opens the window and nobody, not even Dave, says anything. The man is obviously possessed, so I decide that feigning unconsciousness is the safest option.

As I lie with one eye open in case he pounces, I watch as he starts to calm down, though I can still detect some under-the-breath cursing. And then I realise. Silence. Cudo's suffering has not been in vain. The snoring has stopped and I can sleep.

THE GREENHOUSE EFFECT

The Greenhouse couldn't have contrasted more with Loco Studios. Based in a converted warehouse off City Road in East London, the studio, although brilliantly equipped, felt cramped and suffocating. There was nowhere to escape to and play guitar in peace, nowhere to go and hide, and it's in a particularly bleak part of the City as well.

There was one studio on the ground floor (current occupants Kingmaker – now *they* were shit) and another one for us on the top floor. In between was a huge, cold (in every sense) communal living room. Accommodation was a borrowed terraced house (Musidisc-arranged) up the road in Islington.

It was an ordeal from start to finish. The Greenhouse effect made me question my presence (again) in the band. I was within an inch of leaving.

The trouble really started shortly after returning from Glastonbury when the rough mixes from Loco were digested. Jeremy Thomas, well-known judge of rock music, was less than enamoured, although he did offer some advice.

ALISON says, *'The bastard, he's shaved his hair off. The stupid, selfish sod. How could he do it? How could he do that to me? He looks disgusting. He's just turned into one of them. He's started talking like them and now he wants to look like them. That's it as far as I'm concerned, I don't want him in my house any more.'*

'Can't you write a song like that one by what's their name, you know? The uhh, B52s, that's it, you know the one, "'Love Something", "Love Shack".'

There were no obvious singles on the LP, he said, and he thought the balance between the singers was too heavily in favour of Andrew.

Changes must be made, and alas, the by-product of the Stalinist purge was my burgeoning songwriting career.

Ten songs had already been recorded, which left two 'vacancies' on the LP, due to be filled by one of John's songs, 'Stone The Crows', which was far better than some of the guff that eventually made it on there, and 'Gelignite', my song. Phil never even mentioned the subject, and that hurt especially after our conversation at Loco. John, though, did at least have the decency to broach it.

'Sorry, Ed, 'Gelignite's not going to make it. But it's hard for me too, you know, 'Stone The Crows' has been dropped as well.'

I felt like smacking the patronising cunt in the gob. Instead I turned the other cheek and watched in silent torture as two half-completed Janet songs, 'Camelot' and 'Chip Pan Ocean', got cobbled together and became late additions to the album. The fact that 'Camelot' was undoubtedly the naffest, most sugary slice of meaningless, pompous twaddle we ever produced only served to rub copious quantities of salt into the wound. And I'm not being bitter. It was shit.

Geoff Meall has a little party game whenever he has friends round and the atmosphere needs slightly lifting.

The rules to Guess the Crappest Lyric in the World are simple. Take one

Ed Jones: Bass How Low Can You Go? (Picture by Sean Staunton)

The Voice of the Mysterons: May 1986 at The Priory Hotel, Lancaster and the maiden voyage on the 'unsinkable' SS Pop Star. (Picture by Alison Jones)

Perambulators Are Go: Hey, hey, we're The Tansads … (Picture by Alison Jones)

Are You Being Verved? A young Richard Ashcroft reaches for the stars.
(Picture by Sean Staunton)

The Beautiful Game: A reminder to Paul Heaton not to give up the day job. (Picture by Sean Staunton)

Morning Glory: Hello Glastonbury … (Picture by Sean Staunton)

The Voice of a Generation: Andrew displays the emotion within 'Camelot' …
(Picture by Sean Staunton)

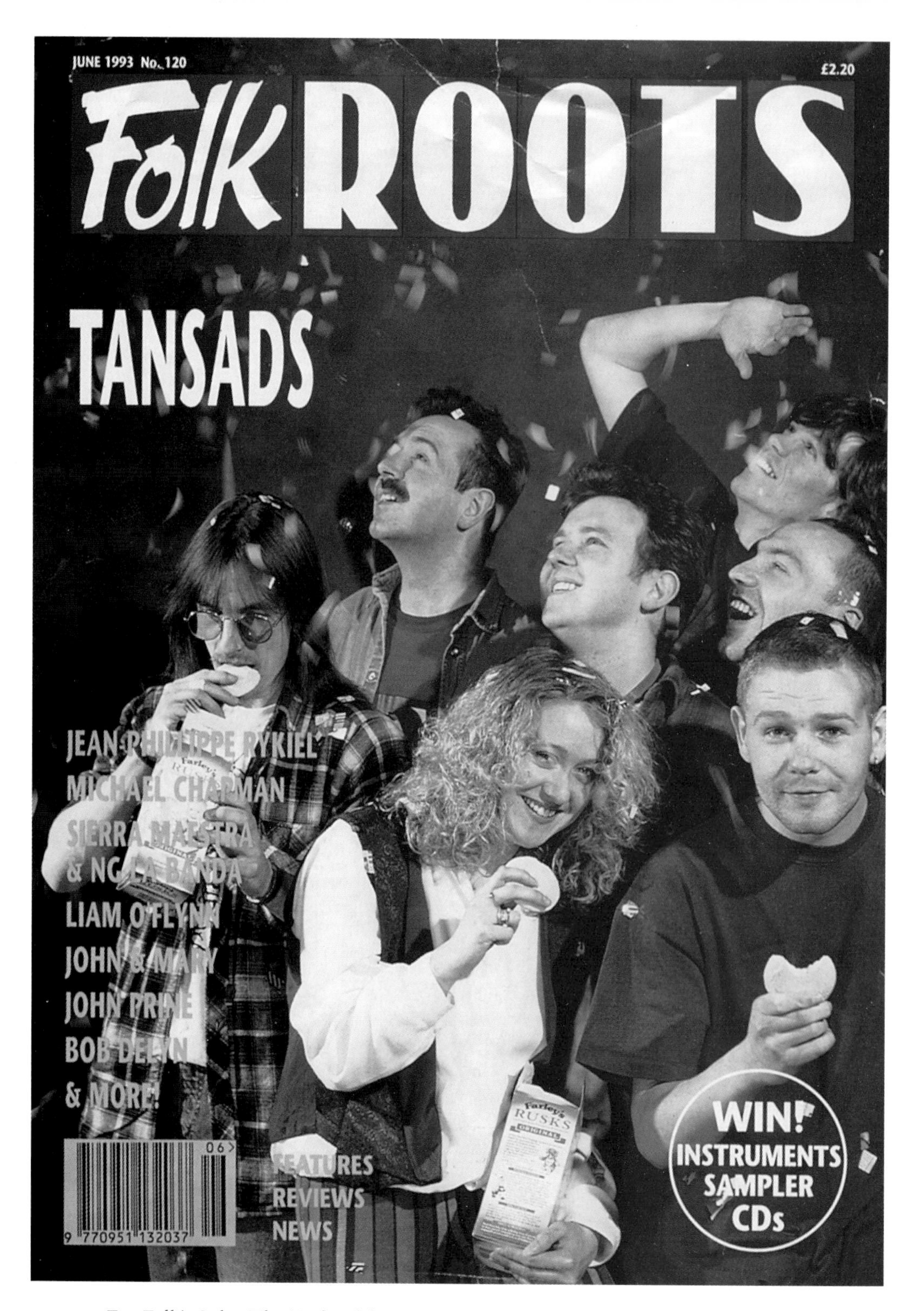

For Folk's Sake: The 'Sads celebrate.

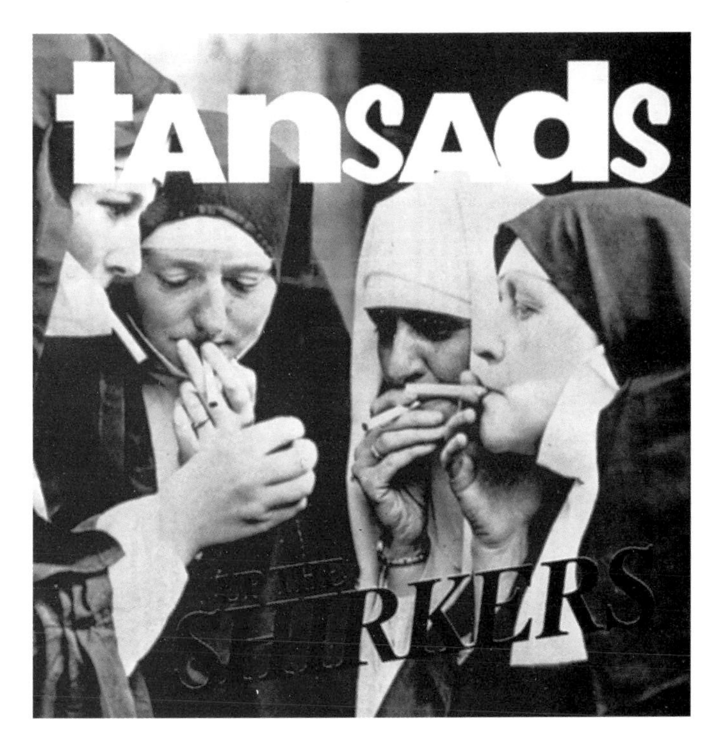

The Greatest Album in the World … Never: Kicking the Habit. (Reproduced with the kind permission of Castle Music Ltd)

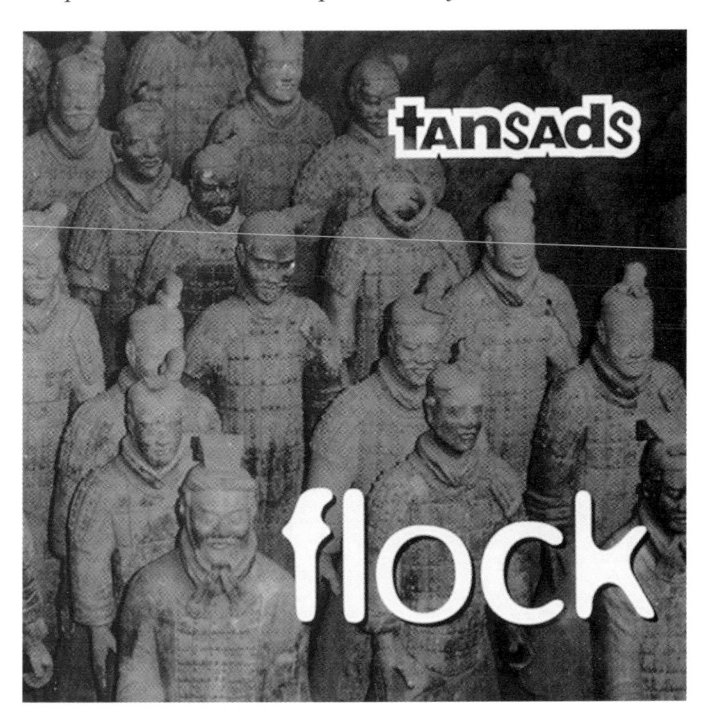

The Greatest Album in the World … Never Part 2: Stiff Little Figures. (Reproduced with the kind permission of Castle Music Ltd)

The Tansads. And I wonder why we never made it … (Picture by Nick Fairhurst)

copy of 'Camelot', place it carefully in the CD player, pick up remote control, and press play. Listen to pleasant acoustic guitar, accordion and staccato keyboard intro, while ensuring your index finger hovers over the pause button. The singing starts:

'*Going down, going down,*
Going down to Camelot.
Some people say it's there—'

Slam finger down. Now, allow your guests to complete the couplet.

'The temperature is hot!'

No.

'I couldn't give a jot.'

No, that's in the next verse.

Guessed it by now? Release finger from the pause button, listen and enjoy.

'. . . *Some people say it's not.*'

Cringe. I don't know whether to laugh or cry.

My heart wasn't really in it as we recorded. John was running out of patience with me as I struggled to learn the bassline. The notation was easy enough, but I couldn't perfect the feel. This time, I couldn't relax under pressure. Worse, I couldn't even hear where I was going wrong. We (or should that be they) were going for a clean sound all round, the drums for both new songs were written on the computer, and the bass plugged straight into the desk. In other words, I was in the control room, no headphones, just old-fashioned eye contact. I could sense John's growing frustration.

'Try again,' said Phil, after another take.

'That any better?'

'It's definitely improved, we're getting there, try once—'

'Look, we haven't got time for this, I could play it straight away.'

John's presence was a huge distraction.

'Give me a chance, for God's sake,' I urged, 'I'm trying.'

But it was no good.

The combination of a lack of confidence, the bitterness churning round in my stomach, and the tension in the room was overwhelming.

John took the bass from me.

'Look, do you mind? We need to press on. I'll stick something down and if we've got time, we can give it another go.'

Yeah, right.

The swine banged it in first take, of course, while I watched from the couch, brimming with hatred and humiliation. I eventually mastered the thing for the live set, but it's the one song on the album on which I don't feature. For that I should be grateful.

I didn't go back to The Greenhouse for the final mix. I mean, why torture myself further? 'The omission of 'Gelignite' was a huge personal blow. After all the sacrifice, all the work, all the rows at home, and the self-induced poverty, I desperately needed something in return. I knew it wouldn't be financial, but had I only been able to hold up the album, point to my name on the sleeve and say 'Look, I know it's a struggle, but that's why I'm doing it.' That would have made all the difference.

The only reason I didn't leave there and then was sheer bloody-mindedness. I didn't want anybody being able to point the finger and say I'd not given it everything. I'm no quitter. That's always been my problem.

MONEY'S TOO TIGHT TO MENTION

One of the first entries in my newly started diary, dated September 1st:

Jeremy said the following phrase to Simon today: 'I'm holding the cigar, but I'm not smoking it.' Our fate lies in this person's hands. I think we should be worried. We have 22p in the bank.

ARISTA LA VISTA

Can your whole world change in a day? Of course it can. The stunning Sainsbury's checkout girl who happens to serve the editor of *Vogue* magazine or the 16-year-old backstreet football wizard spotted by Alex Ferguson. How about the ramshackle Wigan eight-piece band sharing a pint of the black stuff with the top cat from Whitney Houston's label?

WHAT!?

Oh yes. Talk about out of the blue. The mood in the camp was pretty positive although the single had flopped badly. The dark clouds that had been circling my head had almost all been swept away by the fact that we were in the midst of what was basically a successful tour. Somehow, the Deputy President of A&R for Arista in New York had heard some of our material, including 'Brian Kant'. He called Musidisc and requested a meeting.

'They're not in London? No problem. Where? How far is that? I'll be there tonight.'

When they're interested, they're certainly interested. Within hours of hearing about the phone call, we were sitting opposite the man and his grey-haired girlfriend at the Tudor House in the town centre of Wigan.

Richard Swerrett was an early 30-something college boy type, very polite, very warm, and the most amazing thing about him was we didn't have to explain anything.

'I love it. I love the band. I think you would do really well in the States. The regional thing's irrelevant. The themes are universal and that's what I like. And I like the different sides to the band. Long term, that's important.'

'Why does somebody who lives 3,000 miles away get it, when people who live 300 miles away don't?' asked John.

Stripped away of British hang-ups over credibility, class, North-South divides and what length the other A&R guy's pony-tail is, Swerrett was simply taking us at face value. It all made perfect sense to him.

'What we're looking for is to release something in the States, and bring the band over, probably aimed at the college circuit. Then go from there. But we're looking for the definitive song. We need that. We need a great debut single.'

He had wanted to see the band live but, as there were no shows booked for a couple of weeks, we plumped for take-away pizzas and a camcorder-recorded video of our last Mill date. At least he got the idea.

'That's the one!' he shouted. 'The whole crowd came alive when that tune started. What's that song called?'

'"Cobbly Back Yard".'

'"Cobbly Back Yard"? You guys are weird over here. We just put grass in our back yards, doesn't hurt as much when you fall.'

We saw him and his girlfriend back onto the last train to London, and he was gone. The next day, Jeremy rang to say he had, as promised, gone in to discuss the situation with him.

This was getting serious.

I began to think of bands from the British Isles that made it in the US before coming home and conquering domestic shores: The Cranberries,

RADIOHEAD – The breakthrough came with the single 'Creep' which reached number 34 in the US charts before storming to number 7 in the UK. Their albums, *Pablo Honey* (1992), *The Bends* (1995) and *OK Computer* (1997) reached chart positions of 25, 6 and 1 respectively. Nothing much to be so melancholy about really...

Radiohead, and Bush. It is an accepted, if slightly unconventional route. Maybe this was the way ahead. Britain had not bitten initially, or at least not very hard. Not only would a licensing deal with Arista point the way for the long-term future, but a short-term injection of cash would do a world of good. And, if it worked over there, maybe big fish Arista would buy out little tiddler Musidisc over here.

So, can a day change your life? Of course. Not for us, unfortunately. The Arista interest withered away and Musidisc called a month or so later to tell us that, although they were still keen, we were being put on 'long-term hold'. They wanted to wait for something to happen in the UK first. In other words, they were letting us down gently.

Still felt the bump, though.

AT THE RACES

If you were an *NME* journalist and received two press releases, one from Sheila at Musidisc, and one from the agency that handles The Stone Roses, The Manic Street Preachers, James, Paul Weller, The Levellers, and a hundred others, which are you more likely to read?

Even Jeremy Thomas knew the answer to that one.

More surprising was that he was able to do something about it. Phillip Hall, the man behind Hall or Nothing PR, and heavily involved in managing The Manics was a friend. He travelled to see us at a Citadel gig and his very presence was enough to convince Simon Moran, whose SJM company was big then but is now the single biggest promotion outfit in the UK, to come along as well.

This was potentially our most important gig . . . ever. And it went well. The following week, Phillip phoned Jeremy to say he would take us on. The week after that, Geoff Meall rang to say that Simon Moran was also interested, would begin considering us for support gigs and was keen to promote our next Mill at the Pier show. That's the thing about the music industry — when it happens, it happens. We were ready for lift-off . . .

We met Phil again a few weeks later in his office in Shepherd's Bush, London. Unlike Moran, who literally did not speak a single word to anybody at the Citadel, Hall was very warm.

'I like the band, I wouldn't consider working with you if I didn't. Jeremy has not got much money to play with, but that's fine. I still think we can build things slowly, the potential is there.'

John, Damian, and I sat there lapping it up.

The very fact we were here in this office, having this conversation, was a massive vindication of the struggles we had endured because Hall didn't back losers. One glance at the office walls was ample illustration. Throughout there were framed magazine front covers of his acts. Bands didn't chose him, he chose them.

'It's clear you've had problems with the *NME* and *Melody Maker*, but what has gone before doesn't necessarily matter. All we need is one person. That's what happened with The Levellers. The key is to find a more focused angle. From what I can make out, Andrew is your strongest asset. I suggest we push him hard as the frontman.'

YES, YES! But I'm not volunteering to tell Janet.

'The thing is he's not really up for doing interviews', John said. 'The brains behind the band is me really, I'm the songwriter.'

That annoyed me.

'It tends to be John and me who do the talking.' I tried to redress some balance. 'Is that going to pose an image problem?'

'Maybe, maybe not. A bit of mystery has never hurt any profile, we'll work round it.'

We spoke for over an hour. He wanted to know about the personalities in the group, the relationship with Musidisc, and our own hopes and aspirations. Everything.

'Well, we'll just have to see how things develop. I suggest we try and tag onto the current Levellers thing. It's not exactly who the band is, but I reckon that's going to be the way to get press. Initially, at any rate.'

The meeting with Phillip Hall had thrown up as many questions as it had provided answers. Would Hall or Nothing be able to improve our profile? How would John broach the subject of putting Andrew forward as a frontman to Janet? Was it wise being lumped in as a crusty band when clearly that was only half the story?

But to be involved with somebody like Hall was such an immense leap forward that we simply had to trust his judgement. Jeremy agreed to pay £400 a month, less than half the amount a major label might be expected to fork out. Horses for courses, I suppose.

It's a pity we proved to be a donkey.

GUARDIAN AGENT

TOILETS – Some of the rooms such as the Portsmouth Wedgwood Rooms and Liverpool Lomax are actually quite palatial but because of their size (200 – 300 capacity) they get lumped in with the dives. The theory is that bands rise up a gigging level with every release and tour. So from the Toilets you would move onto 500 – 1,000 capacity halls (London Astoria, Wolverhampton Wulfrun) then onto the 2000 – 3000 venues (Glasgow Barrowland, Brixton Academy) before finally reaching bona fide pop star status with a shorter 10,000 – 12,000 arena tour. In some cases, this does happen…

Touring was our forte. We had played over a hundred gigs, built up a following, and released an album and a single, but after two and a half years, we still hadn't managed to break onto level one of the pro circuit, the gloriously and aptly titled Toilets.

You had to have a recognised industry agent. Nobody really told us that. Without such an agent, the pro scene is a closed shop and without a deal and/or some big A&R noises, you can't get an agent. For once, however, fortune smiled on The 'Sads.

Until Geoff Meall arrived, we were still relying on Damian and Dave Evans for bookings, along with Tony Russell, an enthusiastic part-timer we had picked up around the Probe era. The luck element in netting Geoff was in the timing. He had recently moved from CMA to The Agency, a much bigger company, as a junior booker and needed to build himself a roster of acts. We were desperate for a higher profile tour to support the album in the New Year.

Sure enough, as soon as Geoff rang up on our behalf, hitherto barricaded Toilet doors miraculously opened: Bath Moles, Leeds Duchess, Tunbridge Wells Forum (which was actually a converted Victorian public convenience), and every other indie mecca in the land.

Geoff took 15% of our fees but that was a small price to pay. Our name was now on a roster which included The Beastie Boys, Public Enemy, The Beautiful South, and The Pogues, not to mention more dinosaurs than you could find in Jurassic Park: Pink Floyd, Status Quo, Deep Purple, The Moody Blues, Uriah Heep, Yes, Nazareth, Rush, Camel, and Blue Oyster Cult, amongst others.

The money we got was at best £100, at worst a percentage of the door takings. But we weren't really bothered because suddenly the tour had a more than proper ring to it.

The Toilet to top all Toilets was the legendary Camden Falcon. *Everybody* had played there, so when Geoff got us a pre-tour warm-up date on November 12th, we jumped at the chance to up our London profile.

Scandalously, the place has since been done up to include things like a stage upon which you can fit more than a guitar stand, a dressing room, and somewhere punters can stand without their shoes sticking to the floor. But no such luxury existed then. The rising damp met the falling damp in the middle of the wall and you could see it through the white sheet that attempted to cover it up. To cap off a great evening, we had a crowd of five people and we were paid £28. Bottom line: about £200 in the red.

Thanks, Geoff.

DOM AND DOM-ER

Précis of the conversation between accordion player-cum-black cloud machine Dominic Lowe, and fraught bass player-cum-human resources director Ed Jones. Date: Friday December 4th, 1992. Location: Uncle Dom's Cabin, Wordsworth Avenue, leafy Wigan suburbia. Agenda: signing of Tansads partnership agreement. Anticipated length of conversation: 15 minutes. Actual Length of conversation: 180 minutes.

'What is it?'

'It's an agreement to say we're in business.'

'Why do we need it?'

'It's the law. We have to present accounts.'

'Why do I have to sign it?'

'Because you're in the band.'

'What if I don't sign it?'

'You can't not sign it, your name's on the record contract.'

'I don't want to be in a partnership.'

'But you're in the band.'

'I'm not in the partnership.'

'The band is the partnership.'

'Why?'

'It's just a device. It means nobody's personally liable. We share profits, and we are equally liable for losses.'

'So if the band goes bust, I'll have to pay.'

'In theory. Yes, but—'

'So you want me to be liable for decisions taken by you.'

'What do you mean, decisions taken by me?'

'By you, by John, whoever. You decide where the money goes, not me.'

'Do you want to become involved? Is that what you're saying?'

'No.'

'No what?'

'No, I don't want to become involved.'

'Well what *do* you want?'

'I don't know.'

'Are you saying nobody can make any decisions?'

'I don't know.'

'Well, somebody's got to make the decisions. Otherwise there'd be no band.'

'I don't trust you or John.'

'Well in that case, get involved.'

'I don't want to.'

'Dom, do you want to be in the band?'

'Not particularly.'

'Well leave, then.'

'I don't want to.'

'So what are you saying? You don't want to be in the band, but you don't want to leave it. You don't trust anybody, but you don't want to get involved.'

'Something like that.'

An impasse had been reached.

'Listen, do what you want. You either sign it or you leave, the choice is pretty simple. I've wasted enough time arguing. We're supposed to be on the same side. Phone me up when you've made up your mind.'

Telephone call from Dom, Sunday December 6th:

'It's Dom.'

'Hi, Dom'

'I'm not signing it.'

'Fine. Bye, Dom.'

At least Bug was mature about it when John and I went round to his flat with the partnership agreement the next morning.

'I want to leave. I've thought long and hard. It's not the agreement as such, but it has made me think about the future. I love drumming, I love the band, but I can't hack everything that goes with it. I'm not enjoying it any more, and I can't see things improving.'

Dom was dispensable. His cynical scowls looked good on stage, but they came at a price to everybody else's wellbeing. Bug was a different story, however. He could be a moody git but, musically, he was the rock on which we stood.

This was a bombshell.

'Don't try and convince me otherwise, you'd be wasting your breath. But don't worry, I'll not let you down. I've got a place at Manchester University in September, and I'll stay until then if you need me and I'll do the tours and anything.'

No need, mate. I made a quick telephone call to Guy Keegan, drummer with The Railway Children, later that same Sunday.

'Guy? It's Ed Jones here, from The Tansads. We met when I was at the *Wigan Reporter*? I was wondering . . .'

Guy didn't take much convincing. He had the talent and experience to have joined any band in the country. He'd lived the rock-'n'-roll cliché, stretch-limo in New York included, and he was – is – a great, great drummer. But The Railies were no more. He had a young family, his life was in Wigan and, Verve aside we were the only signed band for miles. As far as he was concerned, you don't get opportunities like this landing on your doorstep every day of the week, albeit for £30 a week.

Guy's transition into Tansad-dom was incredibly smooth. From the first practice, he was totally dedicated. His drumming was tight, he didn't overplay, and (are you sitting down?) *invited* criticism. It was still hard work teaching him a full set, but his arrival was a blessing in disguise. We were back to a seven-piece, new life was injected into old songs, and there was a huge spirit of rejuvenation. As a band, a new desire was born.

BOXING CLEVER

If you want a sign that says 'serious pro, don't mess', look no further than flight cases. These large boxes on casters with metallic trim, solid padlock, foam-cushioned interior, and (most importantly) the name of the band stencilled on the side, are just about as clear a calling card as you could wish to leave.

Three reasons.

One. They're so expensive nobody else but bands with money to burn can afford them.

Two. They are, it has to be said, the safest way to transport valuable instruments about the country, i.e. you obviously do travel around the country, i.e. you're not a tin-pot local band.

Three. Sad musicians think they are very sexy.

For months now, we had been taunted at Splash rehearsal studios (where most of the gear was stored) by the presence of flight cases belonging to The Railway Children and the *nouveau riche* Verve. Our own storage material consisted of a ramshackle collection of individual guitar and drum cases, old suitcases and wooden crates.

The demise of The Railway Children, therefore, couldn't have been better timed for us. We were able to bring Guy on board but far more importantly, they were forced to sell their precious flight cases. I think we paid in the region of £300 to £400, probably a tenth of what they cost new. Some of them weren't in the best of nick but, after a bit of spit and polish, and once we had replaced their name with ours, we were instantly transformed into a proper, signed touring band. The historic first flight-cased gig was support to The Cardiacs at the Clapham Grand in London, December 16th.

So, not only did we now have The Railies' drummer on board, we owned half their gear. Back in 1985, shortly after Alison and I had met, she told me one of her classmates, Lorraine, was the sister of Gary Newby, singer and lead guitarist with a new band from Wigan called The Railway Children. I bought the debut single 'A Gentle Sound', genuinely liked it, and was an avid supporter thereafter. I was very disappointed Newby failed to turn up both times I had interviewed the band for the paper but, as I was a fan, I forgave him.

There was no escaping me now, however, because he needed my money to pay for the flight cases. We met one day at Splash.

I was still a bit nervous.

We duly negotiated a price, but I hadn't brought the band chequebook with me.

'Give me your address, I'll drop the cheque off.'

'No, it's all right, you can leave it here.'

'I'd rather give it to you in person and get a receipt.'

'I want you to leave the cheque here.'

'I'd rather not. This is between us, I'll phone you and we can make an arrangement to meet somewhere if that's better.'

'No, I'd rather not.'

The message was clear. Newby was a pop star who didn't give out his phone number while I wasn't a pop star and therefore didn't get pop stars' phone numbers.

Today, Gary Newby is a graphic designer.

A CLASS ACT

Is it a coincidence that both my sister Lucy and I married into tight-knit working class families?

Probably not.

Given our rather disenfranchised upbringing, we were both drawn towards something we'd never had. There are too many fundamental similarities between Alison's and Lucy's husband Ray's background for it to be an accident. Both families immediately embraced us, without any need for ceremony or questions. Alison and Ray had made their choice, and that was all that mattered.

In complete contrast, Alison and Ray went through a painful initiation with Mum. It's not that they were deemed unsuitable necessarily but, instead of unconditional approval, we had to fight to justify our decision.

The great traditional institution of marriage was almost a rebellion for me in that sense. Mum was worried that I was selling myself short somehow. Not because of who Alison was, but because I had put being with her, staying in the North and this silly pop music business before a real career.

The dichotomy couldn't have been more clearly illustrated than in the Kettle clan, where Burt and Margaret's entire brood had turned into no-good rock-'n'-rollers. They may have been driven into submission by years of guitar amps, drum kits in the parlour, and being taken for granted but, ultimately, there was a deep-rooted pride in what their boys were achieving, especially when we began getting attention and regular (albeit nepotistic) coverage in the *Wigan Reporter.*

Unlike me.

Alison's parents were never overjoyed about my lack of income, although they never complained to my face. But Mum simply couldn't come to terms with the band and I remember very clearly a particular conversation on Christmas Day that year. We were gigging throughout the festive period, so Alison and I stayed at home. I called to wish her all the best and was really positive explaining about all the good things that were happening; the agent, the tour, the new album, Simon Moran, *Hall or Nothing*, Guy. We were on the crest of a wave and going places, I said.

'I didn't realise you still played the guitar,' she replied.

No word of a lie.

I'm not really criticising Mum. Or maybe I am. I don't know if her reluctance to support me came from the inability to believe her son could really be creative, or from a fundamental lack of knowledge and therefore fear of rock music, or, simply, that plain old worry that I was wasting my life away. It was probably all three.

But I do remember being extremely frustrated and downhearted that we could never get beyond the 'When are you going to get a proper job?' line. It was saddening that Mum showed no interest in something that meant everything to me. She could even have faked it. But no.

'Act your class' was the implication, 'not your shoe size'.

DISC FOUR

January 1993 – March 1994

A DAY IN THE LIFE

January 16th 1993. Can you believe it's 15 years?

I hate today. I always feel guilty if I don't think about him all the time. I hate telling people what day it is. Not because I don't want to, but just because it ends up being really awkward, no one ever knows what to say. Then I get frustrated because people think I'm acting strange for no reason. So I tell them. And it's really awkward. So I still end up acting strange all day. Only this time people feel sorry for me. Which I hate. It's the same every year. Then I go to bed again and forget about it for 364 days.

DOING THE CANNES-CANNES

Flight cases double up as great beds. They do anyway at 5.00 a.m., in the deserted departure lounge of Gatwick Airport, when you've been awake since 7.00 am the previous day, driven halfway across the country, unloaded a van full of equipment, played a sweaty gig, loaded the van back up, driven the other half of the country and been directed to the wrong terminal.

On the way to The Princess Charlotte in Leicester, **Johnnie Walker** had played 'Up the Revolution' on Radio 1. Again.

God, that felt great. How was it for you?

Listening to it on the radio, it just *had* to be a hit. No question. The gig, however, was crap. Sixty or so people in the dingy back room of a city-centre pub. But that was behind us now. Because, get this, we, The Tansads, were on our way to Cannes for MIDEM, the music industry's equivalent of the Film Festival.

While Musidisc were a no-mark company in the UK, in their native land, their reputation was such that they hired the swanky Hotel Martinez on the glitzy yacht-strewn seafront for a showcase of their three main acts. Them being The 'Sads, The Tender Trap and the American band Shoulders. The purpose was to sell their wares to the global market. Ahem.

We landed at Nice Airport at lunchtime on February 24th, the dismal English January replaced by the warm glow of the Mediterranean sunshine. Press officer Sheila was there to greet us, tanned and gushing as ever, with the obligatory Ab Fab double peck for the chosen few, of which – alas – I was one.

'Sweetie,' *mwa-mwa*, 'how are you?'

JOHNNIE WALKER – At the time of writing the BBC disc jockey is in court charged with supplying cocaine. Walker, 54, is accused of supplying the drug to the *News of the World* undercover reporter Mazher Mahmood at a London hotel during one of the newspaper's infamous 'stings'. The story appeared on the front cover where the *News of the World* suggested that the DJ was also involved in prostitution. Walker, of Maida Vale, west London, is also accused of possessing cocaine on the same date in April this year. Our thoughts are with you, Johnnie...

The bonhomie disguised, as ever, the fact that she was way out of her depth.

She spoke no French – perfect for a Paris-based record company – and the coach driver knew no English and the mixture of emergency semaphore and scraps of paper with hotel names on them was not working terribly well.

After a drive round La Napoule for the third time, an up-market Torquay-ish suburbia but a shanty town by Côte d'Azur standards, it was just becoming too painful to bear. Sheila was really struggling.

'Look, you stupid man, Hostellerie du Golf, La Napoule, ici, oui?'

'*Ben, ouais, La Napoule. La Napoule, La Napoule mais où à La Napoule, c'est pas petit, huh? Mais j'vous d'mande.*'

'Yes, that's right, La Napoule. Now we're getting somewhere. Near the river I think they said.'

'*Oh, merde, c'est pas vrai, enfin.*'

Reluctantly, I stepped forward.

'Sheila, I speak French, do you want me to help a bit?'

'Oh, please, this bloke's getting really narky. I don't fucking know where the hotel is, that's why we hired a fucking coach driver, isn't it?'

I leant forward innocently.

'*Monsieur, je parle français, je peux traduire.*'

The storm hit me full in the face.

'*Ah, bien, putain de merde, c'est un bordel ici, j'm'en fous de ce festival de con! Moi il faut qu'je sois à Nice dans une demi-heure, putain. Je ne sais pas oû il est votre merdier putain d'un hôtel enfin.*'

The others screamed from the back.

'What's he saying, what's he saying?!'

'He says, whore of shit, he hates this fucking crap festival, he doesn't know where the fucking shitty brothel of a hotel is and he's due back in Nice in half an hour.'

The sight and sound of 20 foreigners doubled up with laughter was not exactly the right tonic for the now inconsolable coach driver. He threatened to kick us out there and then.

'I think they're laughing at my translations,' I proffered, unconvincingly.

We did eventually find our way but the incident had set the tone for the visit.

The opulence of the Hotel Martinez was in stark contrast to the dishevelled, penniless band that had just entered its marbled portals. Jeremy looked in his element though, and introduced us to a procession of overbearing shiny happy people.

'Craig is a big fan, he is looking to release the album in Australia. He wants to know how the band gets its inspiration. Klaus handles distribution in Germany, could be important, I'd like you to *bond*. Per is head of A&R for EMI Denmark. Very interesting development on that score, if you could just chat to him for a bit.'

And so on.

We had floated through the day so far on a cocktail of no food and lack of sleep, photographed and interviewed into a bizarre oblivion, even autopilot was beginning to get dizzy. But an interview by the pool for Austrian TV transported us deep into the realms of the surreal.

'*What* is your music?'

The reporter was a middle-aged, balding, slightly overweight man, wearing inappropriately ill fitting youthful clothes.

'Do you watch Austrian TV, yes?'

'Of course we do.'

How could we not?

'We do the music show, yes, very good, very big. You talk now. In German ja?'

Whatever drivel emanated from our mouths was provoking the same goofy grin on his face.

'We play the music of British peasants', said John.

Then the Austrian started waving at us.

'Make like this, make like this, yes?'

The novelty of being treated like stars on the doorstep of the rich and famous was wearing a little thin. Our measly salary had already been long since spent, and with typical forethought and consideration, Jeremy had forgotten to give us the generous sustenance allowance we had had to fight for: about £10.00 in a town where a cup of coffee costs £4.00.

'I was wondering,' he began, 'whether you chaps would spend an hour leafleting for tomorrow night round the town.'

Excuse me?

'Jeremy, you take the biscuit.' I was off again. 'We've been on the go since yesterday morning, we've hardly eaten or slept in that time, you've flown us out to this place, we've spent the afternoon parading round like performing monkeys, and now you want us to leaflet around a town we've never been to before for a gig we're not being paid for.'

'Yes.'

We had had to battle for everything with Musidisc. They hadn't wanted us to bring our own instruments, any crew members, a sound engineer, or Damian (*Simon* paid for his flight, for goodness' sake), and they didn't want to give us any money for food, and nor had they planned any transport for us despite the hotel being five kilometres from the venue.

Yet they still expected a professional show with all the trimmings.

Musidisc thought we were being prima donnas. Our patience was only tempered by the fact that The Levellers had played the same gig when with Musidisc, and their career had since gone ballistic.

But we made a stand. We didn't do the leafleting.

However, things did improve the next day, which François described as 'his proudest moment in 15 years of show business'.

He must have had some career.

There was an awful lot of hanging around, but at least we were fed, watered and given a big, comfortable dressing room. The gig was wild. It was full, but an industry crowd is the worst kind: standing motionless, clapping not an accepted means of communication. John managed to convince Andrew to take his shirt off for the show. With his skinhead and pleated pony-tail, John Lennon shades and a pair of combat trousers, he looked fearsome. I just remember going crazy, over-compensating for the lack of response from the floor, careering round the stage like a lunatic. By MIDEM standards, apparently, we had gone down a storm.

We had more sycophantic introductions afterwards with faceless record executives, and optimistic promises were made about 'Brian Kant' being a potential hit in the US and a rosy future involving Rolls Royces in swimming pools.

The worst offender, though, was Terry Staunton of the *NME*. He had been paid to introduce us on stage, and sounded really impressed in the bar afterwards, where Jeremy had opened a tab, probably worth about ten times our food allowance.

'I didn't realise how good you lot were. All my preconceptions have been shattered. I thought you were like The Levellers, but that was really different. There was danger, and real power.'

Staunton was by this time pretty merry.

'Fantastic. I think we've turned a corner tonight as far the paper goes, I know we've not been that interested up until now. But that'll change.'

Never heard from the twat again, needless to say.

Apart from massaging Musidisc's ego, and wasting more than we earned in a year, Midem failed to achieve anything. Jeremy claimed we had *tweaked* our profile up a few notches, but there were very few tangible results. 'Brian Kant' was never released in the States, we never did get distributed in Germany, or enjoy cult success on Austrian TV, or become huge in rural Armenia. If our standing within the industry had improved, we saw very little evidence of it.

I did get to see some *huge* yachts, though.

SHIRKING RESPONSIBILITY

'Up The Revolution' is released, and Gillian Porter from Hall or Nothing gets it reviewed by Gina Morris in the *NME*:

'It's the way he sings 'going up me own arse' in a rather common Northern accent that first grabbed me. After that it was the way they managed to combine Chumbawamba, The Levellers and Kate Bush in a get together round the campfire at midnight that made me turn it off.'

Mind you, Superchunk's 'The Question Is How Fast' tastes far worse lashings of vitriol: 'After six listens it begins to grow on you. Then again, if you sit long enough, so does mould.'

At least we are considered important enough to slag off.

Tony the Tongue achieves the Radio 1 As-Featured playlist, a quite astonishing result. He also secures an acoustic session on Johnnie Walker's Radio 1 show. On a weekend show playlists don't apply, and Walker likes the song so much he plays it twice in one afternoon, again the following week and our session is broadcast the week after that. When we have finished the interview with Walker at Broadcasting House, we spot Steve Wright, then DJ for the afternoon show, in the neighbouring studio.

'Tony,' John asks, 'is there any chance we could just say hello to Steve, thank him for playing 'Brian Kant' the other month?'

'Of course, of course, come through. I'll go and see if he can come out.'

Guy, Janet, John, and I duly follow. But suddenly sweat begins dripping from Tony's pony-tail.

'What are you doing?'

'I'm sorry?'

'*What* are you doing?'

'Steve Wright? Thank him? Just agreed?'

'But, but, but, you can't, you can't *all* come.'

'Pardon?'

'No more than two, man. You can't hassle stars.'

The album is released on February 8th. Our original title, *Chips, Peace and Gravy* is deemed 'too parochial' by Jeremy, so we call it *Up the Shirkers*, which isn't the least bit parochial, and will translate perfectly into German.

Simon is paid (eventually, £1,000) for designing a cover that features a terrific picture of nuns on a fag break. Once again Hall or Nothing do the business.

Johnny Black in *Q* gives it three stars (out of five):

Q – Also on three stars that month were Joan Baez and Jesus Jones. Stiff Little Fingers got two for their new album *Fly the Flag*, while Banarama's reunion record and *Chippendales: The Album* (eh?) both got one. Four stars went to releases by Dinosaur Jnr, Ian McNabb and The The, while no-one got five. Interviewed in their questionnaire that month was Billy Bragg, who asked if he was afraid of failure said, 'No, I think runaway success can be more destructive.' Oh, for the chance to find out.

'They combine Poguesy energy with the innocent tunefulness of mid-60s pop, but they add wah-wah guitars, soaring harmonies and a hippy-politik stance which separates them from the pack.'

Rock CD magazine also gives us three stars:

'The band show no fear in incorporating funky guitars and grown-up harmonies to the often anthemic songs.'

'There isn't a dull track', say *Hifi World*.

Adam Sweeting in *The Guardian* tries to be polite, but finishes with 'time to dust off that useful cliché, worthy but dull.'

Oh well, can't win them all. But we get four stars in *Hit CD*, though the prediction, alas, is a little off target: 'It's highly likely The Tansads will become millionaires.'

Select also come up with a dodgy prognosis: 'Urban folk that'll sell shitloads.'

'Bloody brilliant' is Reading University paper *Spark*'s succinct appraisal.

Then Dave Jennings reviews the album in the *Melody Maker:*

'Another stale slice of life with the crusties (Northern folkie division) . . . It's all polished, crafted and arranged with care, so much so that it's possible to enjoy, say 'John John', which actually generates some semblance of urgency, or the pretty 'Camelot', just as long as you ignore John Kettle's appalling lyrics.

'Unfortunately that takes a lot of willpower. There is something unhealthily compelling about rubbish that stinks as bad as say 'Chip Pan Ocean', or 'Brian Kant', puddles of wet whimsy like The Beautiful South taking a rustic ramble, after taking drugs that seriously damage the intelligence. Hey nonny NO.'

Ooops.

'He was the only person I could find to do it', explains Gillian. I maintain, however, that it's better to be slated than ignored.

The 'crusty factor' is a double-edged sword, evidently. Riding along in the Levellers slipstream is all very well, but some of their mud is flying off and sticking to us. And it doesn't always smell that good. OK, we have a gigantically improved profile, but at what price? We are now 'anarcho-Celtic urban folkies', whatever that means.

Gillian says not to worry.

'If that is the device that gets you noticed and established, go with it. Once you've achieved your status, then change.'

We bow, a little tentatively, to her superior knowledge and watch as the Musidisc promotional machine once again shoots itself in the foot.

'We can't budge on the price,' says Jeremy.

Shirkers CDs will cost £15 a copy, a good £3 to £4 more than average (remember, we are talking a few years ago). Result? Fans write to us to complain some shops are having difficulty even ordering the thing. Generally, figures are very poor, an improvement on *Shandyland*, but given the difference in budgets, and the media profile, the sales are pathetic.

We do at least make the *NME* indie charts this time.

The first week, it enters at 13 (though the pillocks list it as *Shandyland*), it stays there for the second week (with the correct name), dips to 18 the next week, then dies a death. In the trade magazine *Music Week*, it registers at 20 in the indie chart for a single week. We also make the *Folk Roots* chart, in at 12, then down to 14. Alan's in Wigan says *Shirkers* has the most expensive dealer price they have ever come across. If it weren't for the fact they knew we had a local following, they wouldn't have touched the thing.

Being No1 in the Alan's chart, then, is something of a hollow victory.

MAKING PLANS FOR NIGEL

The Tansads had been in existence as a gigging outfit for three years now. We had an album out and our name was coming to prominence with 'Up The Revolution', with Geoff the agent, Hall or Nothing, SJM, MIDEM, Tony The Tongue, Radio 1, with a placing in the indie charts, with big adverts in *Q, Select, NME, Melody Maker,* and with (dare I admit it) the likes of Jeremy Thomas schmoozing round industry parties boasting about 'this marvellous bunch *I've* unearthed, *destined for greatness*, I tell you'.

The key thing was to ensure a foothold while our name was still fresh and we were still a curiosity. This window of opportunity tends to last around six months. After that, once the industry has chewed you up and spat you out, it's very unlikely to fancy another bite. Nothing is cast in stone, the exceptions give everybody hope but, generally, if you don't get your teeth into a solid, tangible bit of success during this period, you will struggle to make an impression again. To all intents and purposes, we had just been born, and therefore had roughly until the end of the summer to make a significant mark. Six months and counting . . .

Decisions had to be made.

Damian, our manager, had to go. We met at John's house on February 14th.

'Damian, we're very worried about the situation.'

'We feel we're missing out on so many opportunities because you don't have time to spend on the band.'

'Calls are taking days to get answered.'

'Geoff and Jeremy say they can never get hold of you.'

'We feel you're not concentrating on the right areas.'

'You're answering letters from fans. You're still talking to local gig promoters. Somebody else should be doing that.'

'You're sending T-shirts to Red Rose Radio. Why?'

'You worry about when we need to play Wigan next when we need to push ourselves in London.'

'You're still concerned too much about the past, maintaining links.'

'We need to be looking at the big picture.'

'We need a London baseball bat.'

'Someone to knock Musidisc into shape, to make sure Geoff's on the case, to feed Hall or Nothing with stories.'

'We're worried it's becoming too much for you.'

'We think you need a helping hand.'

'Mistakes are being made.'

'You never even told the promoter at Amersham we had cancelled.'

'This is an important time.'

'We're struggling to keep up as it is.'

'We need to be ready if we break.'

'We can't afford not to be prepared.'

'We're looking at professional management.'

'But we don't want you to leave.'

'It's no reflection on your abilities.'

Sorry, mate.

Luckily for us, Damian was mature and intelligent enough to read the writing on the wall. He knew Jeremy Thomas had little respect for him. He knew he didn't have the contacts in London or the time to forge them. He knew ultimately if it came to a *him or us* situation that he was dispensable. He didn't really have a choice. If he wanted to remain involved, he had not only to step down but be positive about doing so, and help us find a new manager.

We told him he would still have a vital role to play as buffer between the new man (or woman) and us but over the ensuing months he gradually became an increasingly peripheral figure.

'The band forgot who they were, got their priorities all mixed up around this time,' Damian later told me. 'You forgot everything that had got you success in the first place.'

He's probably right. After all, he got the band T-shirt on *Brookside*. On two different characters. Firstly, Owen Daniels as he announced to his wife that he was leaving. Then, it was to be seen on the body of bad boy Darren Murphy, who burned down the local school, nearly killing Jacqui Dixon in the process, vandalised Ron Dixon's shop, and also mugged Julia Brogan. An errant husband and an arsonist. Talk about role models.

But we had to progress. If this involved treading on a few trusted, and trusting, toes, then so be it; success, unfortunately, comes from ruthlessness.

The search for a manager took around two months. Jeremy was beside himself with excitement. He genuinely felt Damian had been a millstone round our necks and busied himself canvassing for potential interest.

Not wanting a Musidisc puppet, we sent out feelers of our own and after dozens of rumours including Simon Moran himself and Martin Hall (brother of Phillip and manager of Manic Street Preachers), the list was dwindled down to four.

Pete Hawkins was involved with the maverick 80s psychobilly nutters King Kurt and had recently got a band called 5.30 signed to major label East West.

Jeff Abbott had secured Liverpool's The Real People a deal with Columbia (now Sony), the band more than anybody else upon which Noel Gallagher has said he modelled himself (apart from some bunch called The Beatles, that is).

Matrine McDonnagh managed James and was probably the most heavy-weight contender.

Lastly, Nigel Morton, former manager of New Model Army, had overseen their rise from £10-a-night indie hopefuls to £50,000 festival headliners and EMI black sheep.

Unfortunately, the Martine McDonnagh interest died very quickly. I never met Jeff Abbott but John spoke to him on the phone and the word was that he was running a carpet shop in North Wales. The combination of shag pile and Mold was hardly the stuff of dream manifestos, let's be honest, and he was never truly in the frame.

We met Pete Hawkins at a gig in London, and although he was very positive, he was also Jeremy's choice, which put the mockers on that.

In the end, it was a matter of simple psychology.

Nigel Morton had shown the greatest amount of enthusiasm. By far. He travelled up to Wigan to see us, he enthused about the material, he was sympathetic to the Damian situation, and he would definitely not be in Jeremy's pocket. Put simply, he was on our wavelength.

And there was this as well.

Cross my heart and hope to die, on the life of my son, I swear that he spoke the following words as we all sat in John and Janet's living room on that fateful Sunday, February 28th 1993:

'You can pay me when you're famous. I don't want a contract. All I need is a letter of agreement to formalise the deal. If the band doesn't make money, I will have failed, so I don't want my share until the band can afford to pay me.'

Got that? No money. No cut.

Oh dear.

It is difficult for me to explain quite how big a mistake **Nigel Morton** was. Let me try. If I said there is one person more than any other on this planet who wrecked my dreams of being a pop star, then it is him.

NIGEL MORTON – One of the things The Tansads never achieved was to support The Levellers. There was much talk of it at one point and although it would have confirmed our crusty label, it may also have been the making of us, as it was for The Levs when they supported New Model Army. It was only much later that we found out the real reason we never got the tour: Morton had been such a cunt to them that they vowed never to have anything to do with him again. Figures.

'Why did you part company with New Model Army, Nigel?'

'Well, I'm going to level with you here . . .'

We heard about alcoholism, a nervous breakdown, a bad car accident, a divorce, and blaring rows with front man Justin Sullivan (or Slade The Leveller as he ridiculously used to call himself).

I'm sorry, but I simply have to say it again. Oh dear.

You really have to wonder about our sanity in appointing Morton. It's not even as if he hid all these things from us. Quite the opposite. And, unlike when we signed to Musidisc, we did have a choice this time. To his eternal credit, John was probably the one member of the band who had serious reservations (guess who persuaded him to go with the majority?).

I wasn't alone in making the decision then but it still ranks as one of the worst I've ever made, right up there with breaking up the songwriting partnership with Dave. It was one that displayed a complete, terrifying lack of wisdom.

Morton proceeded to destroy virtually every relationship we had within the industry. Worse, though, was that we believed in him and had faith that there was a method somewhere in his madness. By the time we came to our senses and sacked him six months down the line, that window of opportunity had been locked tightly and boarded up.

Scapegoat?

You bet. Every time. The inescapable fact remains that Morton is the one to blame. I cannot think of a single benefit derived from having him on board.

His opening salvo was to ditch Hall or Nothing. Ironically, he told us of his decision as we drove away from the most tangible result they had organised for us, a cover-picture session for *Folk Roots*.

Much as I was suspicious of it, the folky element of the band was undeniable, and to achieve such status in the bible of the genre was a huge result. So much so that there was outrage in certain traditional quarters that the magazine had devoted so much space to a band who were capable of mimicking Metallica or Nirvana, never mind Fairport Convention.

'They're a luxury we can ill afford,' said Morton, 'We'll just use Sheila at Musidisc, and push her. If you get the basics right, the press looks after itself.'

I can't believe we let him do that.

Next, Morton antagonised Geoff Meall virtually to breaking point. We had asked him to push Geoff, see if something could happen, see if we could up our fees at all. Little did we know what was really going on.

'If I wasn't there, he often left rude messages with the receptionists', Geoff recalls, 'and was incredibly aggressive on the phone. He kept refusing shows because he thought the Toilets should be paying more, but the fees were a reflection of the band's pulling power. He questioned everything I did.'

Oh, God.

Morton was an agent himself, but he assured us that he was not after that job as well. However, he said he would be if Geoff failed to live up to expectation, and stupidly, we just took his side, blaming our low fees on Geoff. It only transpired several months later, in early September, exactly what damage had been done. John and I met up with Geoff at Euston Station, on our way home from a meeting with Musidisc. It was the first time we had really sat down with him, away from managers and record companies.

'Why can't we be playing more shows?'

'What do you mean?'

'Well, we don't seem to have been building on the first tour.'

'But you asked me not to.'

'What?'

'You asked me to only book shows that were going to make money.'

'When?'

'Nigel told me . . . '

'Ahhh . . .'

Next was Morton's expressed intention to pummel Musidisc into dropping us. He argued that eventually they would decide we weren't worth the bother any more, and release us from the contract. He started off politely enough, I think, but when he didn't get anywhere, a maelstrom of (usually faxed) aggression began sweeping through their Holland Park offices in the lead up to our contract renewal date in May. When this didn't quite have the desired effect either, he tried the cold shoulder routine, and refused point blank to speak to anybody from Musidisc.

The plan backfired badly. Obviously.

Not only did Musidisc pick up their option for a second year, but what little goodwill had existed between us evaporated in a matter of weeks. Morton had awoken the beast in François.

'I seriously considered putting you on long-term hold,' he later told us, the nightmare banishment-under-contract that is the ultimate threat to all signed bands.

Finally, Morton went a bridge too far.

First of all, the promised letter of agreement metamorphosed into a fully blown management contract. 'If you can't fit it on a side of A4 it's not worth having' turned into 'I've taken legal advice, and it's better to get everything formalised in advance.'

Then, the mutually beneficial protection clause we had agreed upon for a six-month notice being required by either party was conspicuous by its absence. An oversight, he assured us.

Next, he billed us £1,300 for services rendered, including **commission** on the low-paid gigs even Geoff didn't bother with.

Talk about a kick in the teeth.

'What happened to 'pay us when you're rich', Nigel?'

COMMISSION – While there is no hard and fast rule, managers usually charge between 15% and 25% (you can guess at which end of the scale Morton was). This didn't include other expenses such as his phone bill and travel costs. The idea, though, is that the manager increases your income to such a degree that you are far better off even after his deductions. Fine. In our case, however, the manager was threatening to bankrupt his clients before they got the chance to pay him...

'What are you talking about?'

His word against ours.

'Don't worry about it, you can pay me in instalments. I've got to eat, you know.'

And now for the *pièce de résistance.*

He decided to charge interest if the debt climbed over an agreed ceiling.

Can you believe that?

Well, that was it, we would no longer be making plans for Nigel. We hadn't signed the letter of agreement (thankfully), so our only Achilles heel was the debt, the bulk of which remained unpaid. I volunteered to speak to him, and for once I had no qualms about sacking a member of the team.

'Nigel, it's Ed. Listen, I've got some bad news . . .'

Morton had obviously bitten off more than he could chew. His master plan had been to seduce us, forge a deal with a major, get us out of the Musidisc contract and then sit upon a money-making machine. But he had no luck with the majors, he realised Musidisc would be too tough a nut to crack, and then changed his tune because he realised he hadn't backed the right horse. The only thing he was successful at was destroying our career.

But at least we never finished paying off his stupid bill.

LOITERING WITH INTENT

'Where the fuck have you been, wankers?'

The welcoming party caught me offguard.

'Easy, Terry.'

'Easy my arse. We've been fucking working our bollocks off here while you've been upstairs getting pissed. It's always the fucking same with you lot.'

'We've been TALKING,' barked John.

'I bet you have.'

'What's that suppose to mean?'

'Well, while you've been *talking*, we've been *working*.'

'Look, there's some important people up there, who could make a difference. We needed to be with them.'

'What, the whole fucking lot of you?'

The source of Terry's grief was that he, along with new roadie/guitar tech

Andy and Marc the sound engineer, were left to negotiate the load-out of death. Any bands who have played the New Cross Venue in London SE14 will know what I'm taking about. On the way in there's a lift; on the way out, because it's a late club and the lift is in a public area, you have to use the back steps. And we're not just talking a few steps.

The stage was two storeys up in an old warehouse, and there were hundreds of the damn things, together with interminable corridors, steep gradients, puddles and dog-shit. Each journey takes forever.

When you're a seven-piece band with £18,000 of equipment (I'd just filled in the inventory for the insurance company) to lug and one flight case in particular weighs more than a Mini, I suppose Terry did have a point. The unwritten rule after shows, though, was that the crew would pack everything away while we recovered (as proper pop stars *cannot* be seen tidying up), only emerging to help when the crowd have dispersed.

But not tonight.

The *NME* are here, Musidisc are here, Hall or Nothing are here.

'You fucking turn up now the fucking work's nearly done, don't you? What a fucking coincidence.'

'Look Terry,' John was aroused, 'We're the band. There's some people up there who could change the future. You're the crew. Crews load gear.'

Place the following words into a more recognizable order: rag, bull, a, to, red, a.

'I'm not hanging around you cunts to hear that sort of bullshit,' grunted Terry as he stepped into the Transit.

'Andy, start the fucking engine, we're going.'

The Transit roared off into the night, leaving us shamefaced amid a haze of diesel fumes.

'Ed, keys.'

Andrew, probably.

I reached into one pocket, then another.

'Sorry. John, must have them.'

'Our kid?'

Rustle, rustle.

'Robert? Cudo? WHO'S GOT THE MINIBUS KEYS?'

We looked at each other.

And then I remembered. I'd put them on the dashboard of the Transit. They were currently driving away at pace on their way back home. Terry had been gone a good couple of minutes, but he might still be in the one-way system. I legged it up the hill, past the front door of the venue and onto the high street. Like a Green Cross Code Man on speed, I looked frantically from side to side. Nothing.

Panic.

I started running. I didn't even know if it was the right direction, or for that matter, why I was doing it. If ever one incident summed up my whole life this was it. I was sprinting through the streets of East London at 2.30 a.m. on a freezing cold January night, chasing a van which was probably travelling the opposite way, driven by somebody who would quite happily run me over.

Eventually, I came to a standstill, and my head drooped between my knees amid excessive panting.

'Jonesey, what the fuck are you doing?'

'Terry, I thought you'd gone.'

'I should have been. We took a wrong turning.'

A miracle.

I must have been half a mile from the venue. When I unearthed the keys from under a mound of crisp packets and discarded cans of pop, Terry and Andy burst out laughing.

'If I'd known they were there, we'd have definitely driven on!'

The following week the *NME* failed to change our future. The review written by Roger Morton (never trust a man in a brown suede suit) read:

'Wigan's Tansads indulge in a cross between knees up raggle-taggle and Peacenik Merrydown philosophising. Its visual equivalent is the old bloke sitting outside the 7-11 in an old RAF coat with cake mix in his hair. Sexy, eh?'

Our first proper tour of the Toilets, however, was a moderate success. After trying to get a gig there for five years, we finally played the Leeds Duchess; we crammed onto the stage of the **Hull Adelphi** (a terraced house transformed into a cathedral of indie); played to 40 people at Glasgow's King Tut's (no McGee that night, he'd be at Tut's six weeks later watching some band from Manchester); played to just nine at the Edinburgh Venue (though two thirds of them danced); and Kidderminster Market Tavern (sharing a pre-gig curry with a fledging Radiohead).

If we hadn't exactly conquered the Toilets, at least we weren't loitering suspiciously outside any more. It was difficult to reconcile these infested shitholes as something to aspire to, but then rock-'n'-roll is full of contradictions. Every promoter bar none had been impressed with the band, if not

HULL ADELPHI – Some of the bands who have graduated into the Top 40 and once played the Adelphi: The Bluetones, Carter USM, Cast, Cranberries, Chumbawamba, Cornershop, Del Amitri, Dodgy, The Farm, Happy Mondays, PJ Harvey, The Housemartins, Inspiral Carpets, The Las, The Levellers, Manic Street Preachers, Mansun, Oasis, Radiohead, The Shamen, Shed 7, Skunk Anansie, Super Furry Animals, Supergrass and Travis.

always with the number of punters we had pulled, so at least there was something.

'We have to be patient,' said agent Geoff. 'It's a start.'

NOBODY'S HERO

Whenever a name band plans a tour, record companies compete in a frenzied auction to land the prized support slot. This is known as the buy-on and can cost as much as £30,000 for a really big arena tour. The average, however, is somewhere around £3,000 to £5,000. It makes sense, I suppose, a captive audience, and from a credibility point of view, there is nothing better than to be seen touring with a fashionable name. The band themselves get a token £50 or £100, but that's not the point as this is what tour support budgets are for.

You actually have to pay in order to get ripped off. Great.

There are exceptions, though, as we found out. Simon Moran was definitely developing into the sort of person you want on your side. Keen to propel our name forward, he convinced Russell Emmanuel, manager of punk legends **Stiff Little Fingers**, to waive the £1,500 buy-on for their five-night 'St Patrick's Tour', which kicked off on March 15th at Leeds Poly (now Metro University), before calling in at Newcastle Mayfair, Glasgow Barrowland, Manchester Academy, and Bristol University Colston Hall.

STIFF LITTLE FINGERS – Taking their name from a line in a Vibrators' b-side, the group began life as a Clash covers band. Taken under the wing of journalist Gordon Ogilvie (who subsequently became involved in the songwriting), SLF began to rely on original material, releasing their incendiary 1978 debut single, 'Suspect Device' on the self-financed Rigid Digits label. Wound tight, both lyrically and musically, with the frustration and anger of living in battle-torn Belfast, the record introduced the band as one of the most visceral and compelling punk bands since The Sex Pistols.

SLF would not have ranked highly in our own top ten bands to support, their retro-punk cabaret hardly the stuff of cutting edge, and we were a bit fearful that old punks would never die and bottle/gob us off stage for not being hard enough. But we weren't complaining. This was the first fruit of our association with Moran, our first big venue tour, and we would be playing to 10,000 people over the five nights, by far the greatest collective audience of our lives.

For me, the dates were made even sweeter by the presence on bass for SLF of all-time hero Bruce Foxton (rumours of a Jam reunion were rife in the *NME* around this time). We would make a huge loss of course, but Musidisc were paying from the tour support budget. Or rather, they would be lending us the money from our ever-increasing debt.

We cut corners as much as we could, but expenditure was still going to top £2,500 after the hiring of a splitter van, of Marc the sound engineer, accommodation, crew costs, £5.00 a day for food (such excess) and most importantly from my point of view, an experienced tour manager with the confidence-inspiring name of Noddy.

As we set off for Leeds, there was an air of satisfied anticipation in the van. For once, worries about money, managers, record distribution, vehicle hire and a hundred other distractions were put on hold. This one was all about *us*, and about how *we* could perform, the tension focused, as it should, on our ability to turn a cold, uninterested crowd.

There is a lightness in our step when we unload the gear into the venue. As we sit on our flight cases watching the SLF crew setting up, front man Jake Burns comes over and introduces himself.

'How ya doing, I'm Jake,' the Belfast brogue not eroded by years of international touring. 'We'll try and make sure you get plenty of time, everything's going smoothly so far, so we should be OK. If you want anything, just ask. I hope you enjoy yourselves this week, I've heard you're something special on stage.'

This was totally unexpected. A small gesture that alters my whole attitude towards the tour. I suddenly feel confident that we belong at this level.

'Thanks, brilliant,' I say, a little overcome. I try and make conversation. 'Uuuh, do you know how tickets are going for tonight?'

'Not great. I think it might be a bit quiet. But tomorrow's sold out, and Glasgow as well for St Paddy's Night, so those'll be good nights for sure.'

Burns turns away and joins Foxton, who has just walked in. Old Brucie looks just the same. His skin is still terrible, he's got that same crappy Chris Waddle haircut, and he's wearing the sort of glasses last seen on 1980s DJs. And I'm way taller than he is.

As SLF soundcheck 'Smithers-Jones' with Foxton on vocals (one of the few non-Weller Jam tracks), I wonder absent-mindedly if, as another bass-playing songwriter, he suffers the same frustrations I do. I'll ask him later. Maybe.

Then it's our turn. The stage is tiny and illusions of grandeur take an immediate tumble as I stand in a one foot square gap, the edge of Cudo's keyboard poking me in the leg and Guy's crash cymbal between my shoulder blades. The on-stage mix is dreadful, as all I can hear are the drums and Janet's voice. But Marc says out front it sounds great.

The room is a third full when we go on, and there's more atmosphere on Mars. Space constraints mean we can't even leap about as usual, and the gig feels all wrong. There are a lot more people in when we finish, and a few clap, some even semi-enthusiastically. But mostly we are ignored.

Never mind. I think, at least there was no abuse, and no flying bottles.

'Excellent, really excellent! That was fantastic. I've never heard our support get a response like that.'

SLF manager Russell Emmanuell is the spitting image of Danny De Vito.

The Mayfair couldn't be more different from the Leeds venue. It's an old oblong Victorian ballroom far wider than it is deep, satisfactorily decrepit, and the stage is so vast that we can't use all the space provided. Maybe it's something about the further North you travel, but the vibe is brilliant even before we come on.

For a start, it's packed (the bar being in the same room helps, let's face facts), and the stage time is later. But the instant we walk on, you can feel people are in the mood to party.

'Brian Kant' starts with just groovy drums and percussion, almost a Latin feel. It's the perfect way to grab attention. When the band kicks in, there's an amazing buzz across the stage. We really go for it. 'Eye of the Average' is a truly original hybrid, a folky tune set to pounding grunge guitar, sat on a plinth of thunderous bass and drums. Andrew's nasal aggression belts out my favourite John lyric:

> I've been doing bugger all, wondering about wondering,
> I believe in irony, I believe in doing the ironing.

Starting with a deep keyboard drone, it explodes into life, and the four of us at the front leap into a synchronised pogo (it wasn't choreographed, honest, it just evolved that way).

The Geordies respond.

Adrenaline pumps through our veins as the show builds. The space of 'Right On' adds dynamic, even the hateful 'Big Wednesday' sounds half decent. Then the final flourish. 'English Rover' is a twee thing on record, but live its 2/4 jig is pure mosh-pit fodder; 'Up The Revolution', with heads-down go-for-it Clash thrash and a chorus as catchy as 'flu in a lift', rouses the crowd even further; and for dessert, the grandiose 'I Know I Can', which grows to its frenzied climax before disintegrating into white noise.

Wow.

The band has never sounded so tight, so powerful, never felt so committed on stage, and never performed with such energy. As we leave, the hands are raised above the head right to the back of the hall, and as far as I can see on either side of the stage.

A truly unbelievable, but deserved response.

The change-over is lightning-fast (no, we don't have to come and move our instruments off the stage like lemons), and the crowd starts chanting.

'Fingers!'

Clap-clap-clap.

'Fingers!'

Clap-clap-clap.

The whole building shakes. I have to go and watch. SLF roar on to the tune of 'The Dambusters' March, and all hell breaks loose as the spirit of '77 erupts on Tyneside.

The journey to Glasgow is sweet. The band is relaxed, joking with each other, and all the tension and worry has evaporated. Playing the Barrowland was a personal ambition fulfilled. The venue is a rock-'n'-roll legend and, after Newcastle, we are dying to get back on stage for a repeat prescription. It's everything I expect, another huge old ballroom converted into the perfect music cathedral: massive stage, with sprung floor which literally bounces up and down.

As we wait for SLF to set up, Simon and I start kicking a football to each other at the back of the room, using the pillars as goals. A couple of fearsome looking bouncers trot over.

'Oh shit, Sime, better put the ball away,' I mutter, but we have spotted them too late.

'Fancy a game boys, Scots v. Sassenachs?'

Culloden is re-enacted for a few glorious minutes, only this time the English get their come-uppance. Just as well I suppose, given the size of the opposition.

Fire regulations have reduced the Barrowland's capacity to 1,900. The place has held twice that in its day, but it still looks like an awesome number of people. It is virtually full as we come on. There has been a second support and, as the lights dim, the crowd expects SLF. Instead they get an English band gatecrashing a Glaswegian party on St Patrick's Night.

Oh dear.

To make matters worse, a side show has developed in the mosh pit. A couple of glasses are chucked on the stage. We fear the worst, and the first few songs are a bit nervy. But, after two or three numbers, we seem to have been accepted, especially when Andrew introduces 'English Rover' as an anti-England anthem. Then as we race through a wild 'Up the Revolution', it becomes clear we are beginning to talk their language. By the end they shout for more.

After two such highs, there had to be a down. The next night was Manchester where the crowd is generally more reticent but, as we are playing near home, at least we have some support. Bristol is quieter still, a good show and a decent response for a support band but nothing like the madness of Newcastle and Glasgow.

Overall, the tour has been amazing. We have proved we can perform on a big stage, and confirmed in our own minds that the band is good enough to succeed. The response we received generally was overwhelming, and the number of people who have signed on the mailing list at the **merchandising** stall (not to mention buying T-shirts) is massively encouraging.

MERCHANDISING – This is a highly lucrative area for bands, especially if they handle their own merchandising. We charged £10 a T-shirt, which was a relatively low mark-up of 100%. On the SLF tour, Simon had to up the price to £12 to match the price they charged, and he brought in around £120 a night, £10 of which went to him. The Fingers merchandising guy was on a wage (probably around £80 a day) and a percentage. Their average nightly takings were around £3,000.

Why couldn't it be like this all the time?

When Fingers have finished their set on the final night, Janet and I are volunteered as ambassadors. I knock on the dressing room door. Danny De Vito opens it.

'Oh, hi, Russell,' I stammer, 'I, uh, we just popped in to say goodbye, and thank you for the gigs. We really enjoyed them.'

Jake Burns calls from the back of the room for us to come in, and he stands up to shake our hands.

'You were great, honest, really great,' he said. 'Most of our support bands get booed off. I've never seen our people respond like that'.

I spot Bruce Foxton slouched in an armchair.

'You can come again,' says Jake with a smile, finally.

'That would be great, brilliant. Thanks a lot,' says Janet.

Danny De Vito reaches over to a nearby table. He grabs a couple of bottles of Jack Daniels and a handful of T-shirts.

'Here, mementos from the tour. This is no bullshit. We were impressed with the band, and we'd love to work with you again. I'll speak to Jeremy next week, and you must keep in touch. If ever you want any help, any advice, whatever, give me a call. I'm always willing to help.'

We were about to leave but I couldn't go just yet. I had to do it. It was now or never.

'Bruce,' I heave the words out of my mouth with a pulley, 'Bruce, what's all this about a Jam reunion I keep reading in the *NME*? Is it true?'

There's an awkward silence for a second.

'Fuck off!' he says, not even a hint of a smile on his face.

I laugh nervously, pick up the T-shirts and the JD and run.

THE COURT JESTER

One of the greatest rock-'n'-roll myths (which by now I hope to have well and truly dispelled) is that there is money to be made from being in bands. Universal fantasy dictates that if you're signed, you're loaded. I lost count of the amount of times people said to me, 'In a band? Drinks are on you then.'

I wish.

The painful truth was that we were broke with a capital *Brr*. The suicidal tendencies so readily displayed in signing the Musidisc contract were becoming clearer by the month. The halcyon first year, in which we needed to succeed to simply break even had come to an end, and much to everybody's chagrin (especially Morton's), Musidisc had decided to carry over the Chinese torture into a second term.

What this meant in real terms was that, because of the way the contract was structured (cast your eye back over the chapter entitled 'Contract Killer' if you've forgotten), the advances for the second year totalled the paltry sum of £6,000, less than a third of the first year. The outlook for the next twelve months looked very grim.

ALISON says, *'The only good thing about him being in a band was that it sounded quite glamorous when I talked about him at work, in my office full of accountants. Especially as they all thought he was the best looking one by far. Mind you, there wasn't a lot of competition, let's be honest. At least it made me forget about all the bad things and made it tolerable. For a while, anyway.'*

We owed for everything.

Rehearsals, van hire, equipment, agency fees, Morton, friends, ourselves. And we were running out of lenders. We discovered Simon's pit of generosity did, in fact, have a bottom when he was made redundant. Net amount 'borrowed' from him: £9,000. Others helped where they could; I, for one, dipped into a fast dwindling savings account (Alison loved that), but the quicksand of debt was relentless. Our wages fell to £20 a week and the reality was that we were all kept by wives, girlfriends, parents, and in John and Janet's case, Wigan Council.

In the end, we had no option but to start relying on that most flexible of all friends, Mr Visa. This was an incredibly dangerous game to play, especially as we were at the mercy of Musidisc, who displayed their customary lack of class by continually stalling on their contractual instalments, and repeatedly refusing our ever-more-desperate requests for tour support.

'It's our money, you owe it to us.'

'It is money for touring, not paying wages.'

How could we not harbour resentment when the hand that fed us kept closing up, teasing, and cajoling us with the crumbs in its clenched fist?

The ultimate irony, however, was that our turnover was so high the band was forced to become VAT-registered and be turned into a limited company to protect individuals from total financial ruin. I had a house in my name, and The Tansads were not, repeat not, going to get that as well.

We became the poorest company directors in history.

To cap it all, the Council sent bailiffs round to collect my poll tax arrears. We settled on £1 a week or something.

My overriding memory of this period is of utter, energy-draining humiliation, the gradual erosion of personal dignity, and a dark rage, festering in my psyche like mould. How on earth were we expected to hold our heads up in such circumstances, never mind perform shows or be creative?

And then it came. When I bent down to pick up the mail on April 6th, the intriguingly shaped buff envelope with a Liverpool Crown Court postmark caught my eye. I opened it up and just laughed out loud. Clearly, the myth of the signed band extended to certain quarters of the industry. Geoff Davis from Probe Plus in Liverpool, no doubt assuming we were dripping with wads after releasing such a high profile platter, slapped us with a writ for the Pink Museum sessions. Rock-'n'-roll legend has it that 'where there's a hit there's a writ', only in our case there wasn't even a hit, just a letter *s* in front of the word.

I'm sure Davis thought that, now we were famous pop stars, we would just pay him off. He must have received the shock of his life when he found out we were all on Legal Aid, as he was. It was almost worth going through all the crap just to see the look of confused horror on his face when his solicitor explained to him that this might not be as easy as was first anticipated.

Anyway, the bottom line was that the git now reckoned we owed him money. £2,708.38 to be precise. But his case was shot with more holes than a watering can.

This, remember, was the same Geoff Davis who hadn't given us a penny for *Shandyland*, even though it sold over 2,000 copies. The same Geoff Davis who instigated (allegedly, don't sue me again, please) his own independent distribution of the record and gave us just 75 copies of the album instead of the promised 750. This was the same album that Simon did all the artwork for at his own expense, that we paid a press plugger to promote, and for which we paid for the cassette versions, many of which were sold by him.

He now had the temerity to claim we verbally agreed to record an album with him and that, in breach of this agreement, we then saddled off to record a session organised and paid for by 'Music Disc' (he couldn't even get their name right). The session he was referring to was the Square One recording with Phil Tennant which we had paid for ourselves, and which was used in order to secure the Musidisc deal, so he was wrong there again.

But the cheeky sod was also claiming production fees of over £900 when all he did was sit on his arse for the whole session, get off his head on weed and let John and engineer Colin MacKay do the work.

In our naiveté, we had assumed that Geoff would have the wisdom to see that if he didn't chase up the Pink Museum money, we would lay the *Shandyland* ghost to rest and call it quits. But no, he was either desperate (probably), greedy (possibly), or both.

What a fool.

We decided to issue a counter-claim. We were advised that as the cost of actually taking the matter to court would be more than the sum in dispute, and that, even if there was a positive ruling nobody would be able to afford to pay anyway ('You can't take a sock off a bare leg', as they say in Wigan), it might convince him to drop the case.

So an out-of-court meeting was organised at the offices of Mace and Jones, in Water Street, Liverpool. John, Damian and I, along with our solicitor Peter Howard arrived in convivial mood, confident a satisfactory stalemate would be achieved.

But Geoff had other ideas.

'You Jones, you're a fuch'n starstruck cunt. You never thought Probe was good enough did you, you fuch'n cunt?'

Hey, hold on. Why pick on me?

He was a man possessed, and about as much in a mood for compromise as the day Hitler discovered Poland in his school atlas.

I was remarkably calm, I seem to remember; unusual for me, as I'm usually game for a slanging match. I turned to Peter Howard:

'Is there any point carrying on this conversation if this is the guy's attitude?'

'Gentlemen, gentlemen,' intervened Geoff's solicitor, 'shall we try and make this a little more civilised?'

Order was restored but to no avail, as Geoff wasn't backing down. So we left, with a proverbial 'See you in court' ringing in our ears.

Over the ensuing weeks, we (or rather Damian, he worked like a Trojan on our defence) had to hoe through more form-filling, more report-writing, until eventually, a few months down the line, after more laborious solicitorial exchanges, Davis finally accepted what we had known the day we received the summons, and the whole thing petered out into a pathetic, painful anticlimax.

And Ed Jones was off the Probe Christmas card list.

BLOWIN' IN THE WIND

Wolverhampton Polytechnic (as it was called then), May 7th 1993. Simon, a man without a girlfriend, stands behind The Tansads' merchandising stall, in a lonely corridor. Trade is very, very quiet. A beautiful female student sidles along and picks up a T-shirt.

'How much?'

'Ten pounds.'

'Can't afford it. I like it, though. Can I have it if I give you a blow job?'

'Sorry.'

He later told me, 'I thought you would shout if I gave away a T-shirt.'

Some people just have no sense of priorities, have they?

PULP FRICTION

The ultimate gauge of all pop success is television. To grab the attention of the nation for a glorious few minutes – what better boost for your average enormo-ego?

Even on a postmodernist diet of MTV and the digital explosion, the pinnacle of achievement is still Auntie Beeb's good old *Top Of The Pops*. Other contenders come and go – I remember *Rock Goes To College*, *The Old Grey Whistle Test*, *The Tube*, and these days (at least at the time of writing) we have *TFI Friday* and *Later With Jools Holland* – but the benchmark is still *TOTP*, more facelifts per annum than Joan Collins notwithstanding.

Guy made it on there with The Railway Children once. He says the studio is minuscule, but proof of its status if ever you needed it, was that Virgin Records provided the band with numbered car park spaces after they appeared and 'Every Beat Of The Heart' was in the Top 40.

Alas, Guy reminiscing about the past is about as close as I ever got. Our zenith was a show on BBC2 hosted by former Fairground Attraction singer Eddi Reader, called *No Stilettos*. Don't knock it. We may not have been talking eight million *TOTP* viewers or whatever, but it was still national TV, watched by significantly more people than most of our concerts lumped together. And, importantly, in a financial drought, it was a temporary oasis, £1,200 finding its way nicely into our bank account for both original broadcast and later repeat, thank you very much. And, for probably the only time ever, having loads of members actually went in our favour, as the BBC pay fees per person.

BBC – Musicians must be part of the Musicians' Union in order to be paid the union-negotiated agreed rate of £90 a session per person. So in order for us to do the show, Musidisc had to fork out for seven MU memberships, which set them back around £500. I'm sure Jeremy made us pay for it from Tour Support, though.

It was another Tony the Tongue special. Musidisc had no right employing somebody so efficient. Unfortunately, *Stilettos* turned out to be his swan song as, sadly for us and no doubt highly sensibly for him, he moved on to pastures new shortly afterwards.

Set in the disused Cottier's church just outside Glasgow city centre, the show was essentially a vehicle for Reader to plug her own material. Following performances from her and her band, 'friends' from the wonderful world of showbiz were invited each week to share a moment of musical intimacy in front of an extravagant backdrop of stained glass and wooden gargoyles.

We travelled up to the glamorous Dumbarton Travelodge on the Tuesday night, recorded the show on Wednesday, April 7th, and the historical first network broadcast was transmitted on May 24th.

Reader's close personal friends that week were The Dubliners, with vocals by Shane McGowan, but to make up the numbers, she also brought along a few unknowns: The Tanzoids (as she introduced us), solo Canadian singer-songwriter (and soon-to-be million album seller) Ani Di Franco, and some bunch from Sheffield called Pulp (pre-big-time of course, though you wouldn't have guessed from the attitude).

The theory was that each act would get a soundcheck and camera rehearsal before performing in reverse order of billing in the evening, in front of an audience. There were two stages, the acts being staggered so that as one rehearsed, another could be setting up, and so on. The schedule was tight, with no room for error.

Or so we were told.

Having moved a veritable galaxy in order to honour the 9.00 a.m. call, our credulity received its first test when we had to wait for two hours outside the venue for anything to happen. It received a further jolt when

Pulp's Jarvis Cocker, who had clearly failed to wake up on time, rudely told us to move our splitter van because *he* was rehearsing first and wanted to be nearer the front door.

We watched Mr Pulp's patience being stretched further as he was told that the band had been scripted to appear on the small stage with Ani Di Franco (stained glass and gargoyle factor merely silly as opposed to ridiculous, but easily large enough to fit the band on), while nobodies 'The Tanzoids' were on the main stage with the big boys.

I'll skweam and skweam and skweam.

'But,' responds producer, 'it won't affect your broadcast. It simply makes it more practical for us during the change-overs. You'll still get the same exposure, and it means there'll be more time to rehearse.'

But Mr Pulp decides to take his ball home.

'Either we're on the main stage, or we don't play,' he says.

'Well, seeing as you put it that way . . .'

Definitely a case of Pulp Friction, (War of the Roses Division), as, having screwed up the entire day's schedule, the net result of Yorkshire's tantrum is that Lancashire's camera rehearsal time is scrapped.

Actually, the petulance was all to no avail as it turned out, because even Mr Pulp hadn't bargained for Shane McGowan being so pissed he – literally – couldn't stand up.

As soaks of considerably more experience, The Dubliners could at least achieve vertical status without serious threat to life or limb, though not without their guitars acting as finely-tuned stabilisers, choreography borrowed from *Thunderbirds*, and that nagging fear in the back of your mind that they could topple over like dominoes at any moment.

Their rehearsal allocation was already well exhausted by the time they had negotiated the tricky descent from the upstairs bar and battled through the equally challenging ascent of Mount Main Stage. So by the time they eventually managed to muster some vaguely co-ordinated stab at The Pogues' 'Irish Rover', Pulp's rehearsal time was also (sadly) more or less used up too because Shane could only remember one verse, and even then he got all the words wrong.

Miraculously, when it came to their actual performance, The Dubliners got it (sort of) all right on the night, probably something to do with having been through the same charade every day for the past 30 years.

Of course, as they always do, and despite our enforced total lack of preparation and the entire day spent sitting around getting bored and frustrated, things fell into place for show time, although not without some fraught moments.

Conducted by a nervous-looking floor manager, a bemused audience were herded into the room, and then encouraged to whoop and clap to – ha ha – check sound levels and camera angles. The truth of it was that the performances themselves were totally stilted. Every band stopped mid-song and then started again, the audience certainly didn't clap, but naturally, when it was edited together, the illusion of a gig was slickly maintained, and all the bands appeared to be greeted enthusiastically.

Ah, the spontaneous magic of television.

I don't imagine **Pulp** remember any of this. Since their rise to megastardom, *No Stilettos* has probably blended into hundreds of televisual memories. Pulp were arseholes that day, no question.

Maybe, though, that's what it takes to make it.

PULP – Another testament to persistence, as the band formed in 1981 as Arabacus Pulp became an overnight sensation 13 years later with the success of the album *His 'n' Hers* (no. 7), followed by the number two smash-hit single, 'Common People'. Beating up Michael Jackson at the Brit Awards was clearly a great career boost as the band's next two LPs, *Different Class* (1995) and *This is Hardcore* (1998), both went to numero uno.

ROVER AND OUT

Our network televisual debut was a natural progression in the band's ever-increasing profile. The name was now in the public domain more than ever, and in that sense, *Stilettos* was timed to perfection. All we needed was a killer summer single to surf the crest.

Ah, I knew there'd be a catch.

We, or rather, Jeremy, chose 'English Rover', a nasty little mock-folky nonsense. I hated the song. Sheila did miraculously manage to get it reviewed in the *NME*, her one success for us (if that is the correct term). I suspect, however, that it was probably less to do with her powers of persuasion than our nemesis Paul Moody spotting another chance to exercise his collection of contrite one-sentence put-downs:

'Having consulted the best minds of a generation as to the reasons why The Tansads are putting out records, I find, to my disbelief, that it is because someone somewhere ACTUALLY BELIEVED THEY WERE GOOD. Sad to say, were 'The English Rover' a young child, the NSPCC would consider it a hopeless case.'

Unnecessarily, mercilessly cruel, of course, but it was a terrible – and lazy – choice for a single. Playing right into the knockers' hands, it fortified all media prejudices about us being folk-rockers, Levellers clones, crusties, anarcho-Celtic urban warriors, or whatever drivel they were chucking at us that particular week.

Yet the head of steam Hall or Nothing had built up for us was not quite exhausted and, if ever there was an opportunity to appease the critics (while they were still there), it would have been to surprise or confuse them by taking a risk.

My favourite track on the album was 'Music Down', a broody, rocking beast, five minutes long, wild and subtle together, totally unsuitable single material, AND THEREFORE THE ONLY POSSIBLE CHOICE. Nobody agreed, but there was plenty of other stuff on there that was not so obviously fiddle-de-dee, poor man's Pogues.

Mind you, you could also say that it was totally irrelevant what we put out. This, our third single with Musidisc, did at least prove our record company were world-beaters at one thing: a quite unparalleled, breathtaking capacity for incompetence, dwarfing even their own spectacular previous efforts.

This is the background to the release of 'English Rover'.

François Grandchamp (or Frank Bigfield as he shall henceforth be known) suffered from the retarded notion that a song should become a 'radio hit' before actually hitting the shops.

Oh, dear me.

Even if a new band has a major indie hit, scrapes the edge of the Top 40, and has more press than Paul Gascoigne, it struggles to get on a playlist, as we have already seen. But to rely on a plugger attempting to convince radio producers they should choose an unknown song by an unknown band which isn't even in the shops ahead of, say, the new single by Michael Jackson, is just plain dense.

For all Tony the Tongue's miracle working on 'Up the Revolution', the track had stood little chance because the only way you could buy this CD-only release was (in the overwhelming majority of cases) by ordering it at the full cost of £4.29.

However, 'Revolution' enjoyed a highly polished and sophisticated sales and marketing campaign compared to 'Rover'.

It was Jeremy's idea to record a new song to follow up 'Revolution', and initially he wanted it to be the live favourite 'I Know I Can'. The week before we were due to record everything was in place but we were still awaiting final confirmation. Phil Tennant had travelled to Wigan for pre-production and his time was booked; we had Loco Studio on hold; we had booked vans ready to drive down, and there were countless other arrangements made involving childminders, cat-minders and cancelled milk bottles.

'Jeremy, you can't keep us dangling like this.'

'Why not? What else are you doing next week?'

The arrogance of the man. John gives him an ultimatum of 6.00 p.m., or else we refuse to record.

Yeah, right.

John grudgingly dials the familiar number when Jezzer hasn't called by zero hour.

'Oh, didn't I tell you? I have to get clearance from François. He's not contactable for two days.'

The bastard, he knew all along. So we wait, whereupon – surprise, surprise – the plug is pulled on the recording. Having organised everything, we then have to unorganise it all again, profuse apologies being forwarded to all concerned and I'm becoming really popular with the van-hire company.

Next, Jeremy decides he wants to pursue the retrograde step of re-issuing 'Brian Kant'. Anything to do with the fact there are still loads of copies in the cupboard? We convince him it's a stupid idea.

Then he wants 'Camelot'. Then he changes his mind again, and plumps for 'English Rover'.

'But I think it'll need a bit of tweaking. Why don't we do a partial re-record and remix?'

So, Loco is rebooked for two days, as is Phil, who then has to come back up to Wigan to work on the track and, as for the van hire company, well, they just love me by this stage.

Then, on the day we are due to travel, we receive a call from Harold at the studio to say Jeremy has still not confirmed in writing that he will pay for the session. In other words, don't bother to travel until he does.

Frantic use of the telephone later, Harold finally gets his fax, and the session can go ahead. But then we discover the negotiated price is so low, that Loco cannot provide any food and are only allowing house engineer **Tim Lewis** to work on the track because he likes us and wants to.

Eventually, we do manage to get to South Wales, and have to face a much-aggrieved Harold, who has obviously agreed to the session against his better judgement.

The song sounds exactly as crap when we finish it as it did when we had started. On the day of departure, Harold, clearly regretting his decision to give us the green light, refuses to release the master tapes because Jeremy has still not paid him. We have to leave them behind.

TIM LEWIS – House engineers are the uncelebrated stars of every studio session. A good engineer can be the making or breaking of a record. They must have patience and technical wizardry in equal measures and Tim certainly had that. In our case, he also wrote all our string arrangements. Julian Cope always insists on using him when he goes to Loco, and actually invited him to join his band at one stage as a synth player, which Tim did under the stage name of Thighpaulsandra.

Jeremy then asks us for five tracks in total for the single, until Damian informs him that four songs is the maximum you're allowed by official compilers Gallup to qualify for the singles chart. Remember: Jeremy, record company executive; Damian, college lecturer.

Just defies belief, doesn't it?

It doesn't stop there, however, as there is a pressing fault in the French factory, so that 'English Rover' doesn't actually appear on 'English Rover' and has to be re-pressed, delaying the release (for what it's worth) until July 5th.

Needless to say, Frank Bigfield's 'radio hit' fails to materialise, after Tony the Tongue's replacement Russell Fraser achieves no plays anywhere (we suddenly realise how good his predecessor was).

Musidisc, meanwhile, don't even get round to sending out the postcards we produce to alert the 'fan base' that there is some new material available.

Result?

'English Rover' goes into the annals of rock history as the poorest selling commercially available single of all time (probably). I don't think Tansads' stronghold *Alan's Records* in Wigan even ordered one.

There were other gems.

A French tour was organised on our behalf, to coincide with the high profile Gallic release (ha ha) of *Up The Shirkers*. Fine, great, progress at last. We drew up a budget to get us over there, involving the hire of a rock-'n'-roll sleeper coach (wa-hey!), by far the cheapest way to accommodate us, a sound engineer, our paltry £10-a-gig crew of three, and something like £5 a day for food for everybody. In order to minimise expenditure, I (as a parleur of le Français) reluctantly agree to take on the stressful task of tour managing, but ask for a (scandalous) fee of £20 a show (for the record, any self-respecting professional tour manager wouldn't get out of bed for less than £80 a day). Cost in total: around £6,000, to come out of tour support.

By normal industry standards, this is absolute rock-bottom, cheapo, basic, *My Mum's Tour* stuff.

'You can have £2,500.'

'£2,500? Are you serious?'

'Deadly.'

'We would have to take no sound engineer, merchandising seller, lighting engineer, tour manager, just one crew member, and have no food.'

'Fine. Your choice.'

Even if we spent all our gig fees on sustaining the tour, we would still be £1,000 out of pocket. The French tour is off.

Next there was quibbling about tour support when the issue of a Pogues buy-on slot came up. We became involved in a pathetic scramble whereby we were offered the tour for a buy-on of £2,500, then Frank Bigfield decided he wanted his American act Shoulders to do it and offered £3,000, before we were all usurped by stablemates The New Cranes, who offered £4,500, apparently from their own pocket.

What else?

Well, Musidisc kindly sent us into the red when they failed to accept we had become VAT-registered, and refused to forward the (reclaimable) extra money on our advances.

'We only pay what is on the contract,' said Bigfield. After much stressful negotiation, the money eventually arrived, three and a half months late.

Finally on the cock-up front (for now), having initially agreed, Musidisc, who had just opened an office through a licensee in America, refused to pay for us to appear at a mega-profile extremely-difficult-to-secure showcase at the New York Seminar (a MIDEM for grown-ups).

Naturally, we were bitterly disappointed and secreted much bile towards our narrow-minded, tight-fisted, short-sighted paymasters. Only subsequently did we discover the (probable) real reason behind the decision. Musidisc's plan to release the album under the title *The English Rover* through their Stateside licensee fell through when the latter was discovered to have run off (allegedly) with the proceeds from the sale of 25,000 copies of The Levellers' first album!

I'm glad I can laugh about it now.

CAUGHT IN POSSESSION

A phone call between legendary Birmingham Toilets promoter Dave 'Lee' Travis (Jug of Ale, Pen and Wig, etc.) and Geoff Meall, agent, c/o The Agency, London EC1:

'Hi Dave, it's Geoff.

'Hi Geoff.'

'Dave, what did you think about the CD?'

'Which CD?'

'The Tansads.'

'Z'awright.'

'Well, how about a show? They'll pull.'

'Sorry.'

'Why not?'

'I don't do bands with moustaches.'

John eventually did shave off the offending facial hair but it was all too little too late. The damage had been done.

THE GREAT PRETENDERS

By taking up the second option period back in May, Musidisc had commissioned the follow up album to *Shirkers*. In the middle of impending financial ruin, then, we were contractually obliged to write 12 new songs.

For John, the problem was to produce under pressure. For me, the tension was created by not being under the sort of pressure he was, no matter how much I wanted to be.

I also hated rehearsing new material.

Watching him in the throes of artistic endeavour, conducting the orchestra, wrestling to compose his works, I was in agony. What annoyed me was the fact that he would bring half-completed sketches to rehearsals and use the band as a tool to write. It felt as though he was rubbing my nose in it, when I had to write and demo stuff before it was even considered.

Actually, what annoyed me even more was the fact he had every right to do so. Granted, I may never have liked them, but the songwriting politics had not changed from day one.

And that made me bitter.

Bitter that the band did not use more of my songs. Bitter because, in order to get anything played, I had to swallow my pride and contribute positively to the writing of *his* songs. Bitter because I relied on his generosity in letting me use his eight-track recorder. Bitter because I had no power over my destiny. Bitter that even after all the sacrifice, I still had to pay lip service to somebody else. Bitter, essentially, because I had got myself trapped in this situation.

I don't know which was worse: not having a song in the set or going through the ordeal of having something approved. Either way, it seemed to bring me untold misery. Even my one real escape, writing, even that wasn't safe any more. I would demo my stuff, try and mould it for the band, then expose myself to the ritual humiliation of playing it to John and hoping he liked something.

Talk about making a rod for my own back.

After all the suffering I'd gone through with 'Gelignite', you would think I might have learned. But no, not me. I opted for more self-inflicted trauma, and unfortunately, was handsomely rewarded for my troubles.

'Ship of Fools' didn't boast the most original of names but, after a lengthy campaign, it won its by-election in style and received the Kettle nod, just at the correct time to become a contender for the new album.

It was different from John's stuff, but sat quite comfortably alongside all the other new songs. In complete contrast to 'Gelignite', it was a breezy little pop song, based around a silly play on words set to a catchy tune and chain-saw guitars:

> It's the ruling of the waves,
> You must wave away the rules,
> 'Cos only wise men sail a ship of fools

Like its predecessor, it didn't quite come out as I would have wanted. John played it on the acoustic, not my preferred choice, the electric, and he decided Janet would be more suited to the vocals, which together made it lighter than I'd hoped. But I was not about to start complaining. Simply to get something else accepted was, in the context of my position in the band, a massive result.

Naturally, all this behind-the-scenes frippery could never be leaked into the public domain. A united front was essential. To the punters and to an industry keeping us in its 'one to watch' basket, Tansads Plc *appeared* to be happily careering along stardom superhighway during the summer of 1993.

And we did everything in our power to perpetuate the fantasy.

Like the microcosm of a big-name band, we showcased the new material at two sold-out nights in a small venue, as a treat for the fans. OK, OK, arena-size acts go back to their roots by booking Glasgow Barrowland for such exercises, but we made do with the trusty old 200-capacity St Helens Citadel, which I booked for two nights on July 22nd and 23rd.

It was still, *relatively speaking*, a dead rock-'n'-roll thing to do. We did everything by the book, cliché for cliché. We played for an hour and a half, twice as long as normal, got the gig going with the normal set, carefully dropped in a few first album rarities, the new stuff was then subtly incorporated into the mid-set lull, before we finished in grand style with all the hits.

Well, 'Revolution' and 'Rover'.

There was more. Geoff lined up a string of high profile dates to extend the myth further. The continuing association with Simon Moran saw us play with Liverpool hopefuls Pele, who were getting the big push from Polydor, as well as another support with Stiff Little Fingers at The Forum (or Town and Country, as it used to be known) in Kentish Town, London.

It was at the latter that I fell from the stage. There I was, ready to come in for that crucial first beat of 'Right On'. Just another bar to go, getting set, step back, and ooooooooooooooooooh!

I'm staring at the ceiling. A staggering pain in my coccyx as I look up and spot my shoe, prized away by Cudo's monitor speaker as I gracefully tripped over it, sitting alone in a spot where I should be standing, as if it were the only remnant of my spontaneously combusted body.

Oops.

We also played several small festivals around the country, and did four Heineken Big Top concerts (remember them? A touring three-day mini-festival throughout the summer – undoubtedly some kind of multinational tax dodge.) The set-up was excellent, but their choice of headliners was, to say the least, erratic: from the sublime, Manic Street Preachers (including the soon to be errant Richey) in Swansea, to the downright bizarre, Desmond Dekker in Preston.

The best show, however, was at the first Phoenix Festival in Stratford-upon-Avon, Mean Fiddler main man **Vince Power**'s answer to Glastonbury. We were in amongst the big boys again.

VINCE POWER – One of the most powerful men in rock. He started by opening the Mean Fiddler club in Harlesden and went on to run many other major venues in London, such as The Forum, The Powerhaus, The Garage and The Jazz Café. Phoenix Festival only lasted a couple of years, but Power also runs The Reading Festival and the Fleadh events which have taken place in London, Dublin and New York.

The great pretenders.

For those few minutes on stage that summer, even we could begin to believe our own extended lie. Lost in the thrill of playing, absorbed in the total concentration and physical dedication of performance, I remembered why I was involved in music. All the tension and all the worry evaporated and it was as if, through leaden clouds, the sun had just made an appearance.

Then, in the blink of an eye, it was gone again.

KISS AND DEL

'Hi, Ed, it's Cudo.'

'Hi, Paul, what's wrong? It's eleven in the morning and you're up.'

'I just wondered if you were in. Can I come round?'

Half an hour later, Cudo sat in my lounge and explained why he wanted to leave the band.

'I think I've made my mind up, but I wanted your advice.'

Cudo's gripe was with John. Surprise.

'I was really disappointed with the way the last record went. When I joined, I came in because of my interest in production. But I hardly got a chance on *Shirkers* and I know the new record will be no different.'

Another happy customer.

'Have you talked to him about it?'

'No, you know what he's like.'

'Yeah, but if you want to change something, your only chance is to discuss it. If you don't say anything, it definitely won't change.'

Cudo said he'd think about it, and decide whether to approach John with his worries. But it never happened. A couple of days later, he presented him with a *fait accompli* and that was the end of an era. The Ex-Tansads Club boasted another full member.

If I'd had my reforming way, we wouldn't have replaced Cudo. And not just for fiscal reasons. Perhaps it comes from being around in the 80s when music was massacred for a decade by man's nauseating discovery that he could make a black plastic box with a plug on it resemble a (very bad) string section of an orchestra, and that the dreadful people using said box assumed they had to play with it all the way through every song at its loudest volume.

I hate keyboards. With a vengeance. I always have, and I probably always will. If it were up to me, all keyboard players would be shot as they walk out of the music store carrying their Yamaha MX-what-nots, with their infernal machines being ritually trampled to smithereens by the taste police.

Alas, John wasn't as blinkered as me. My proposal was shot down in flames and the search was on for a new keyboard player.

It was a measure of how far we'd come, or rather, how much the illusion had grown, that news of a Tansads vacancy spread like wildfire within the musical fraternity of Wigan and *environs*. A lifetime on the dole seemed an attractive vocation compared to the employment benefits we had to offer, yet those two hypnotic little words 'signed band' were enough to send normally rational human beings into a zombie-like trance and queue up to hop on board our £30-a-week gravy train.

Well, Delbert, anyway.

Delbert, real name Lee Goulding, was about as different from Cudo as you could imagine. Come to think of it, there was nobody on the *planet* quite like Delbert. If Cudo was a grumpy old Collie, Delbert was an irrepressible kitten, who was either asleep or running round biting your ankles until you kicked him out of the way.

He had unparalleled enthusiasm but an attention span of about four seconds. He was also unbelievably gullible, and became the butt of all the jokes, practical and otherwise, mainly because he said things like 'I'll recognise it when it becomes familiar.'

Oh, and if you're wondering about the name, Lee became Leeroy became Delroy became Delbert, naturally.

The archives show Delbert's first rehearsal was on September 28th, and from that day onwards, an absolute breath of fresh air swept through the band. Similar to when Guy had joined, a new presence galvanised sagging limbs, and prevented us from dipping into autopilot mode just as we needed a lift, prior to our biggest – and arguably most important (again) – tour.

But that's enough compliments. He was still a keyboard player, after all.

HOTEL RICHMOND

I'm a great believer in key moments.

November 4th was a particularly awful gig. None of our travelling supporters could make it, and we ended up playing to about 20 uninterested souls in a deserted Kingston University Students' Union bar.

The mood in the van was still upbeat, however, as we'd played worse places for less money. Such temporary blips had become an accepted part of life on the road, and things generally were looking extremely promising.

We were playing in the North the next day, so I booked a Travelodge on the M1 and, as I was driving, I had mapped a route from Kingston through Richmond to the South Circular, then onto Hangar Lane and round to the motorway. It all seemed pretty straightforward, especially at this late hour.

Shortly after leaving the venue, the Iveco laboured up a long tree-lined hill. I dropped it down a gear, then another. The road bent to the left as we reached a junction at the summit.

Then it happened.

For a moment my body froze, but I managed to bring the van to a standstill. I stared motionless at the floodlit building opposite before opening the door and running down the street, my face wet with tears.

John came after me. He looked confused. Concerned.

'What's going on, Ed. Are you all right?'

I just couldn't help myself crying. I'm not usually so demonstrative. I'm English remember, and male. But the urge inside was too strong to control.

I hadn't seen the Richmond Gate Hotel since the day Dad told me he was going to die. Then it was just there in front of me, and 15 years of pain coursed through my veins. It wasn't remembering, it was *being there* again. Raw memory.

It gave me a serious jolt. A thousand feelings came flooding back to the surface about Dad, childhood, Mum, Alison. One of the things I had always found difficult to reconcile in my mind was the fact that circumstances had forced me to grow up far sooner than normal. I hadn't so much flown the nest as the nest collapsed and left me no option but to get those wings out and fly. I never chose to leave.

A part of me had always forced itself to compete with Dad's memory, to seek an impossible approval every time I made an important decision. Instead of truly living my own life, I wanted to mirror his, and the real tragedy, of course, is that he wasn't around to stop me.

When I first got into music, I convinced myself Dad was behind me. I doubt, however, whether he would really have been so supportive. But the point is I never knew him well enough to say for certain, which meant it was so easy for me to manipulate his memory. I *made* him believe in me.

That night, outside the Richmond Gate Hotel, I cried because I realised it didn't matter about Dad any more. Living the dream of music was *my* achievement. It was *my* life.

REASONS TO BE CHEERFUL

'Camelot' was "released" as our new single on October 18th. Sum total of sales, about 14. Honest. Sum total of radio plays and national press reviews, a very round number indeed.

On the plus side, however, I was now only one song credit away from being able to join the PRS after volunteering 'Gelignite' as a B-side (which we recorded in Steve's garage). Although this probably killed all hopes it had of ever making it onto an album, I still saw it as a small victory.

Despite this, we remained astonishingly upbeat. A quite ludicrous state of mind to adopt of course, but then hopelessly naive would-be pop stars tend to be, by definition, hopelessly naive.

Reasons to be cheerful, part 1.

Jeremy, towering administrative icon of efficiency that he is, parts company with Musidisc. Yeahhhhhh! Is it a jump or a push? That we don't know. However, as we are still managerless and nobody is left in the London office to run things, business is now conducted directly with Frank Bigfield.

'We have worked out that by buying a van now, we could save half our budget for the year by saving on the cost of hiring vehicles.'

'Okay.'

'Pardon?'

'Zat is fine. You have drawn ep an intelligent argument, becked ep by figurz. I accept.'

But what about the statutory opposition? The weeks of waiting? The begging and stealing from friends and families to pay the bills while you make your mind up?

Coincidence or beginners' luck that in John's and my first managerial meeting, we extricate an unprecedented £7,000 from Monsieur Bigfield, virtually the entire year's tour support allocation?

Conclusion: managers, who needs them?

Reasons to be cheerful, part 2.

We immediately go and blow £5,000 on an ex-Royal Mail Ford Iveco 65-12 Zeta Turbo long wheelbase 7.5-tonne van (with air brakes that go wushhhh) and spend the rest on converting it into our very own shiny rock-'n'-roll splitter bus. This is where your choice of associates comes to the fore. Roadie Andy was a welder by trade; Terry knew one end of a screwdriver from the other; Andrew was a former apprentice joiner; while Delbert's dad, Barry, fitted kitchens for a living (favourite saying: 'I'm always saying to our Lee, the music industry is just like the kitchen game').

With reclaimed coach seats, a camping heater and tinted glass, we were soon decked out for the road in style. Since the demise of John's red van not long after Glastonbury, we had spent well over a year chucking money down the drain hiring a Transit van and minibus for every show. Not only will it save us thousands of pounds, but we have our very own van to keep.

Reasons to be cheerful, part 3.

Big-time London managers Paul Crockford and Jolyon Burnham, express a genuine interest in us (following Jeremy's spadework, credit where it's – reluctantly – due). The bad news is that they made their money managing the ghastly Level 42. The good news is that they made their money, and now want to invest some of it in us after a vacancy appears on their roster.

They come to see us play twice, we meet up on two further occasions, and communicate several more times on the phone. They study the Musidisc contract in detail, and *still* seem interested.

'The contract is dreadful but, if we offer you something, we would work towards finding a major label to take you on, either to buy it out, or to pick you up when you are dropped. We think the band have an enormous amount of potential. But the main stumbling block is Musidisc, no question.'

Are Crockford and Burnham the cavalry, or do they just sound like characters from a dodgy American '70s cop show? We are in no position to know, of course, but once again, have to close our eyes and hope for the best. The mad thing however, is that having spent a lifetime attempting to get signed and release records, we now desperately *don't* want to do a new album and *pray* we are dropped the following spring.

Reasons to be cheerful, part 4.

Geoff books a 34-date UK marathon, our second Toilets circuit headline and we call it 'The Camelot Tour' on the glossy posters Simon designs. Geoff's policy of asking for a realistic fee (between £100 and £200) means that, despite our diminishing profile (thank you, Morton), promoters actually make money (unlike us), which means they'll have us back next time. Our average nightly pull is a highly credible 100 people, easily on a par with a host of media darlings, such as Verve.

Notoriously hard to please John Keenan at The Leeds Duchess raves about us:

'You're definitely one of the best bands I've had in all year, and that was certainly one of the liveliest shows. You're absolutely streets ahead of The Levellers musically. Don't worry, keep going, it'll happen for you.'

It's a similar story all over the country, although there are one or two obligatory lows. Playing to a farmer and his wife in Hereford is no fun, and neither is dragging my sister Lucy out to a half-empty wine bar in Brighton.

Wigan and St Helens are obvious highs, however, and a personal triumph is returning to a frenzied Sugar House in Lancaster, the very scene of my wide-eyed musical apprenticeship.

I've taken over Cudo's backing vocals duty. Although incredibly nervous at first, and sounding like a petrified cat in a wind tunnel, I'm assured it gets better, and the effort is worth it just to be able to pose on a stage behind a microphone stand.

Reasons to be cheerful, part 5.

The polarisation between our live work and dealings with the industry grows more extreme every month. One world is real, the other is clearly not. A rugged professionalism has been born out of touring, reflected by ever more confident performances.

A significant factor is in the growth of the fan base since the Stiff Little Fingers tour. We now have pockets of fans all round the country, none more so than in the West Midlands, where a group of young punks adopt us as *their* band, follow us everywhere and, led by a madman named Oz, turn every night into a celebration. We return the compliment by getting them into gigs for free, and witness such things as Oz inside a phone box – a post-modern Clark Kent for the millennium – throw up, subsequently search through the vomit, pick out a pill and swallow it for the second time that evening.

OZ (Mark Osbourne to his mum), toolmaker and recent father, Burntwood, West Midlands – *'I remember seeing The Tansads for the first time, you don't forget an experience like that. We started doing loads of shows, it was a buzz getting in for nothing, then getting the crowd going. Ed told me one day that I was as important as the band, because the gigs needed me. That blew me away. I'm not telling a lie when I say The Tansads changed my life.'*

Another Tansads posse, meanwhile, from Leigh, near Wigan, take up the challenge with the Midlanders to see who can attend the most concerts.

Hey, watch out, we're in danger of becoming a real band . . .

THE PROFESSIONALS

Remember, remember, the 11th of November. How could we forget?

It had been another storming night. The gig, at London's Highbury Garage, was a support to the Oyster Band. Our fans began the Mexican wave, and the room responded. After half an hour of pure energy and dedication, we went off to rapturous applause.

'I lurve zis barnd, I lurve zis barnd!!'

We had, it turned out, been *too* good.

Frank Bigfield insisted on coming to see us, which placed us in an awkward situation: we could hardly play crap on purpose. That's *exactly* what we should have done of course (what would disappointing 300 people for one evening be compared to being FREE from Musidisc?), but naturally, we were too professional to be professional.

'I remember now why I lurve zis barnd!! Zat was fantastic, what a barnd!! We *must* record ze new alburm. No more delays.'

And so it was we decamped to Loco studios, recording the album at the

beginning of the New Year, with a release date set for the summer.
Of course, this meant Musidisc taking up the third option period on the contract . . .

EGO-A-GO-GO

THE EGO RACE, a modern day morality play.

Dramatis Personae:
-Artistic Ego....................John Kettle
-Confused Ego................Ed Jones
-Deluded Ego..................Bob Kettle
-Knobs Ego......................Phil Tennant
-Where's Your Ego?......Andrew Kettle
-Lord Delbert...................Delbert
-Kegsy.............................Guy Keegan
-Queen.............................Janet Anderton

ACT I, SCENE 1: LORD DELBERT'S BEDROOM, DECEMBER 28TH 1993.

-Lord Delbert, Artistic and Confused practise material for forthcoming recording session.

Artistic: I've drawn up a provisional list for the new album. This is it.

-Crinkle of paper as Confused and Lord Delbert mull over the words on the page.

Lord Delbert: Great laaaak.

-Confused stares at the list without saying anything. Takes a deep breath.

Confused: What-uh, what about 'Ship of Fools'?

-Artistic seems genuinely taken aback.

Artistic: Oooh, uuh, I've decided I want a 12 song album. I'm sorry but I just can't fit it in.

Confused: How do you mean?

Artistic: Well, I – uh. Look, there's so much great new material, something has to make way.

Confused: I'm sorry, but, but, I, it's just not good enough.

Artistic: Good enough?

Confused: I, you – uh, you can't just dismiss me like this.

Artistic: Listen, I've got a responsibility to write the new album. You know what the situation is. I'm the songwriter. I've chosen the songs.

Confused: No, I'm sorry, this is wrong. *He shifts uncomfortably on the bed.* I slog my guts out for this band. I work harder than anybody, and you know it. I don't ask for much in return. I know you're the main writer. But I think I deserve a song on the album.

Artistic: Deserve?

Confused: Yes, deserve.

Artistic: I didn't realise you felt so strongly about this.

Confused: What? Do you think I get my kicks spending my days doing the accounts, negotiating with managers, paying the wages, working out VAT returns, sorting out contracts, booking hotels? For goodness sake. The band wouldn't operate without all these things. You're quite happy for me to make everything else happen. But when it comes to getting a cut of what really matters, it's a different story, isn't it?

Artistic: Queen's offered to help out, you know she has.

Confused: That's not the point.

Artistic: Well, if you can't cope with it. . .

Confused: I'm not saying I can't cope! I'm saying I just want something in return, I'm sick of being taken for granted. I'm not asking for much. One song, is that so much? You've got eleven, ELEVEN, not to mention all the rest from the last two albums. And you begrudge me one song?

-There's an awkward pause

Artistic: Alright. I'll put it to the band. See what they think. Is that fair?

Confused: Ok.

Lord Delbert: Great laaaak.

SCENE 2: CONFUSED'S KITCHEN, LATER. THE PHONE RINGS

Confused: Hello.

Artistic: Hi, it's me. I wanted to apologise. I've not been fair. I've thought about what you said, and it's true. I'm sorry. There's no need to vote on this. Maybe we'll have to make it a 15 song album, but I want you to have something on there, however many songs we do. Definitely.

ACT II, SCENE 1: SPLASH STUDIO

- The band are finishing a week of pre-production for the album with Knobs. Last night was the 'office party', and hard-drinking Confused is suffering, suffering bad. He attempts to down two bottles of orange Lucozade, but the contents perform an instant U-turn on entering his stomach, though thankfully he has made it to the toilet first.

Knobs: I insist on a twelve-song album. I don't think we have time to do anything longer. We have twenty-two days booked at Loco, that's all we're getting. I need two days a song ideally, I'm having to cut corners as it is. Twelve songs it has to be.

Confused: Uuuuuuh.

Artistic: Right, we'll just have to trim the list by three. The band can vote on it.

-Confused wonders to himself why democracy has suddenly entered the equation, before rushing back to the toilet for the next instalment of his isotonic yawn.

Artistic: I will write all the songs down, then everybody should pick their favourite 12. How much fairer could that be?

-Well, you could explain to everybody what you promised me the other day, for a start, and tell them how we agreed I deserved *a song in there on principle, muses Confused, but feels so weak he can't summon up the energy to speak. A nervous few minutes elapse as the ballot box surges into action. Then it's time.*

Artistic *(reading list, minus* 'Ship of Fools', *naturally)*: Well, that's it then.

SCENE 2: CHEZ CONFUSED, LATER.

-Still suffering from a bad head day, Confused sits alone writing in his diary: 'I feel betrayed. I feel completely and utterly deflated. Not a week ago, I was assured *there'd be no vote and I'd have a song on the LP. Now he's backed down from that, and* 'Ship of Fools' *is on the 'reserve list'. Democracy my arse, where is the justice in this? And as for the rest of them, what a bunch of ungrateful bastards.'*

ACT III, SCENE 1: LOCO STUDIO, JANUARY 10TH TO FEBRUARY 2ND 1994.

- As creativity flows around him, Confused gets bored sitting around like a spare part in the studio block one evening, so makes his way down to the living quarters. Deluded is playing pool with Where's Your? and they have clearly not heard Confused come in.

Deluded: Do you know what he's said to our kid, though?

Where's Your?: Hmm.

Deluded: About his song?

Where's Your?: Hmm.

-Confused stands as still as a statue, not daring to move.

Deluded: He does a few accounts so he says he should have a song on the album.

Where's Your?: Hmm.

Deluded: Who the fuck does he think he is? Me and our kid write the songs.

Where's Your?: Hmm.

-Confused starts crashing around in his bedroom to alert them to his presence. The pool room suddenly goes very quiet.

SCENE 2: THE NEXT DAY.

-Feeling misunderstood and still brimming with bitterness, Confused sits in one of the recording rooms strumming his acoustic. Artistic comes in.

Artistic: We need to record B-sides for the single. I wondered if you wanted to put anything on there.

-Confused is confused. Should he smack him round the head for proffering mere creative left-overs, or should he swallow his pride, get something recorded, and thus be able to join the PRS? He opts for the latter.

Confused: Ohh, uhh, thanks. Yes.

Artistic: There's not a lot of time, so I suggest something recorded live on the acoustic with Queen singing.

- Later that evening, Confused fulfils a dream. While the rest of the band are in the pub, he and Queen stay behind with Knobs and Lord Delbert to record 'I Don't Know' on *the 24-track, a ditty he knocked out in Cannes (how rock-'n'-roll is* that?*) The song is very low key, and retains a simple spontaneity, helped by a wonderfully haunting vocal. When they all troupe back from the pub, the moment of truth arrives. As the song plays, Confused shifts uncomfortably in his chair. Artistic listens, motionless. When the song finishes, he turns to Knobs.*

Artistic: That's an album track.

SCENE 3: THE NEXT DAY.

-In the control room, Artistic and Knobs lean over the desk. Confused sits on the sofa with Lord Delbert, Kegsy is pacing up and Down.

Knobs: I'm telling you, it's behind the beat.

Artistic: It's not, he's bang on. Listen to it with the click. *They listen.* Perfect.

Knobs: No, it's still not right. The feel isn't right.

Artistic: It is.

Knobs: No way.

Artistic: It's in time, he's swinging it, that's what I want.

Knobs: Well I'm not accepting that.

Kegsy: It felt fine to me, I must admit.

Artistic: You two. What do you think?

Lord Delbert: Great laaaak.

Confused: Yeah, uhh, well, I, it sounds OK. But—

Artistic: We're not doing that again, there's nothing wrong with it.

Knobs: I'm not having this. If I say I want something doing again, I want it doing again.

Artistic: But it won't get any better! We're wasting our time. Everybody apart from you agrees. And anyway, *I* want to keep it.

Knobs: Right. If you want to produce your own record, fine.

- Knobs storms out. After a DAY of arguments, recriminations, negotiations, pointed fingers and conciliatory handshakes, Knobs finally returns to the action. But honestly, what a palaver!

SCENE 4: LATER THAT WEEK, IN THE ISOLATION BOOTH.

- Confused stands like a proper rock star, headphones perched on one ear and a microphone dangling tantalisingly in front of his mouth. All is quiet. . .

Confused: BREEEEEEAAAAK YOUR HEARRRRTT OF AYYYYYON!!

-All goes quiet again. . .

Confused: BREEEEEEAAAK YOUR HEARRRRTT OF AYYYYYON, AYYYYYON MAAAAAAAAAN!!

-Quiet once more.

Confused: Was that any better?

-Through the glass, Confused can see Knobs and Artistic sat behind the desk in the control room, talking. He waits for an answer. Come on, put me out my misery, chaps. . . Knobs leans forward and presses the talk-back switch.

Knobs: Ok, come in.

-Confused frees himself from his electronic chains, and joins the others.

Artistic: I think we're going to leave it.

Knobs: It's not the singing as such.

Artistic: Your voice just jars with the others

Knobs: The singing's fine, it's in tune and everything.

Confused: Look, don't worry. We tried.

-If you listen very carefully to the backing vocals on 'Iron Man', *and one or two other songs on the album, you can hear Confused's dulcet tones. But you have to listen VERY carefully. 'Deep into the mix' I believe is the industry jargon.*

SCENE 5: LATER.

- Confused sits at the kitchen table, doing the accounts, or something equally creative, artistic comes up the stairs, Lord Delbert is making toast. The conversation below actually takes place over two hours.

Artistic: I've been hearing rumours.

Confused: Rumours?

Artistic: Yes, rumours.

Confused: About?

Artistic: What you think of me, mainly. That you're blaming me for not having a song on the album.

Confused: What?

Artistic: Come on.

Confused: Crap.

Artistic: You sure?

Confused: Of course.

Artistic: That's not what I heard.

-One of those dramatic pauses again.

Confused: Well, yes. I suppose I am.

Artistic: Look, there's no future for you as a songwriter in this band.

Confused: I know that, I'm not completely stupid—

Artistic: So do something about it.

Confused: How do you mean?

Artistic: If you want a band, start one. That's what I did.

Confused: But this is my band.

Artistic: No it's not. You know things can never change.

Lord Delbert: (*munch munch*) Great (*munch*) laaaak.

- *Soliloquy, much later.*

Confused: Is this the beginning of the end? I have been left in no doubt as to where I stand as a writer in this band: absolutely nowhere. If I was in his position, I would treat me differently, of course. But at least he has been honest. Maybe this is the jolt to finally knock some sense into me, and get me out of this crazy situation. Whatever, I better get used to the fact I'm not going to have a song on the album. But starting a band? Well, yes, I suppose he's right. Maybe I should just get off my arse and do it. Oh, I don't know. . .

SCENE 6, THE NEXT MORNING.

- *Confused saunters into the control room, where Knobs and Artistic have been discussing the day's agenda.*

Confused: Morning.

Knobs: Morning. How do you feel about starting 'Ship of Fools' in a minute?

- *Confused starts running around the room in ever diminishing circles, rips his shirt off, beats his chest, and begins screaming like a Tibetan shaman.*

The End

After the most difficult birth imaginable, 'Ship of Fools' had finally been born. I can't quite describe the thrill of having one of my songs go through the process of a professional recording session and to have so many people give their all on its behalf. Simply to listen to it sitting proudly alongside all the other album tracks was all I ever wanted. I've proved I'm good enough.

We agreed on the album title *Flock*. Yes, as in Indian restaurant wallpaper, but also a razor-sharp indictment on the notion of rock fans as blind followers. Or something. Looking back now, I don't like the record as much as *Shirkers*. It is overproduced and even more inconsistent

So many other songs, some of which I really liked, drifted away from the energy and the power of the live versions, drowned under an over-lush blanket of strings, endless guitar overdubs, backing vocals and swilling reverb. 'Ship of Fools', however, was a merciful exception, kept simple and sounding fresher for it.

Maybe the problem is that I still can't divorce the actual music from the experience of having been there creating it. I remember coming away from Loco utterly drained. Whatever our relative merits as mature and dignified human beings, it is undeniable that *Flock* was recorded against a backdrop of quite unbelievable tension. Chinese whispers, elation, despair, and rows between Confused and Artistic, Artistic and Knobs, and almost every other permutation of the above names you can imagine.

It's a wonder a record was even made. But **studios** do that. They are such an isolated, intense and artificial little universe that everything gets blown out of proportion. Our sanity was sorely tested after barely a month. Imagine what happens when bands take FIVE YEARS to record an album.

STUDIOS – It is easy to see how bands get into debt. While Loco was relatively cheap at around £500 a day, the big London studios can charge £2,000 and more. Fiscal expediency made us incredibly quick workers at over a track every two days, but I remember Tennant telling me '80s soul singer Sade once spent FOURTEEN days doing one line. That's a *vocal* line, Johnnie...

TAKING THE PISTE

Having heard the new LP, Crockford and Burnham still showed no signs of weakening. Amazing. We were assured that a concrete offer was imminent. As far as I was concerned, this couldn't come soon enough because after the brief hiatus, in which our negotiations with Musidisc were governed by courtesy and common sense, things had soon fallen back to their farcical normality.

In the brave new world since the departure of Jeremy and Sheila (yes, even Sheila had recently left for a better job), Frank Bigfield now ruled the company with a rod of iron. No decision was delegated and, more frustratingly, no cheque was signed other than by the Bigfield pen, which made things very difficult in that he was only ever in London two days every two weeks. For the rest of the time, messages were left to percolate through the agonisingly slow cross-Channel Musidisc grapevine. In an industry based on instant decisions, this was a recipe for trouble.

'I will make monaay available if appropriate,' Frank had told me at our last meeting in December before recording the album.

'For touring, for promotion, you geev me a budget and I will look at it. We want zis record to be zuccezful.'

Fair enough.

Unfortunately, promoter Simon Moran had not been blind to Musidisc's inconsistent level of support, and with his interest in us slightly on the wane, it had taken Geoff about two months' work to convince him that we were the right band for the forthcoming 13-date Stiff Little Fingers tour, which included two sold-out nights at the Glasgow Barrowland.

What better way or time to release the punkish new single 'Iron Man' than on the back of playing to 25,000 people across the UK?

My job was to cajole Musidisc into accepting and parting with the money for the buy-on, while Geoff's was to keep Moran sweet in the light of fierce opposition for support, notably from some Manc bunch recently signed to Creation called Oasis.

The problem was that SLF were after a buy-on of £3,500. Crucially, it would take us over our 'minimum contracted tour support budget' into the discretionary 'maximum budget'. Time to beg.

The initial signs were promising.

'He wants you to do the tour' was the word from London HQ.

'Have you told him how much?'

'Yes, we've passed the figures on.'

The timing was critical. On the Thursday, Geoff phoned to say Moran had definitely offered us the tour, but confirmation from us was needed the next day to catch the deadline for ads in *Q* and *Select*. I faxed Musidisc immediately.

On Friday morning, still no word. I called.

'We have to get an answer by today, or else we could lose the tour.'

'We will phone him and speak to him. Promise.'

Still nothing by mid-afternoon, when Geoff called me back. I tried once more.

'Oh, hello Ed. François has gone skiing for the weekend and was too rushed to look at the figures. He'll talk to you on Monday. Hope that's not too great an inconvenience.'

L-o-r-d g-i-v-e m-e S-S-T-T-R-R-E-E-N-N-G-G-T-T-H-H-H-H-H-!-!

Battle-weary, but doggedly determined, I called again first thing on Monday.

'Sorry, still no word, I'll try and contact him this morning for you.'

The minutes ticked by. Lunchtime and still no word. So I did what I should have done previously, and dialled Paris directly.

'*Bonjour. François Grandchamp, s'il vous plaît.*'

Wait, wait, wait. At last. . .

'Hello François, it's Ed Jones, from The Tansads.'

By this time, I had a degree in how to be polite under stress – and boy did I need it. We exchanged small talk. He seemed in a good mood. Eventually, we got on to 'le beezness'.

'I need to know about the tour. The promoter is holding on for an answer.'

'What tour is zis?

Aaaaaaaah!

'Have you not received my faxes?'

'Oh, yes, I did see somesing. Wiz Steef Liddel Feengerz?'

'Yes, that's the one. Only the situation is getting critical, we have-'

'But didn't we do zis tour last year?'

'Yes and it was really successful. Our fan base has grown enormously since then. That was five dates, this is almost three times that. We have done brilliantly to get the tour, as there are many other bands up for it. However, the promoter and Stiff Little Fingers themselves have asked for us to do it.'

'I don't know. Perhaps we should try somezing else.'

Oh, for God's sake, man.

'But you realise how difficult it is to get major supports? This is a considerable result. The agent has been trying for others, but for example, The Beautiful South had thirty bands wanting to pay money. This one is ours if we want it. What better way could there be of pushing the single? Besides Simon Moran has shown faith in us. What sort of signal will it send to him if we pull out now?'

'Simon oo?'

Oh, for fuck's sake!

'SJM. The promoter.'

'Oh yes. Hmmmm, let me look at ze figures. . . it is very expensive, hmm?'

'Well, no, not really. Most buy-ons start around £4,000 or £5,000, some go up to £10,000, £15,000, £20,000, even £30,000. '

'Hmmmm.'

'We just need the all-clear from you . . .'

There was a pause. An increasingly pregnant pause.

'No, I don't sink so.'

'But we—'

'You always ask me for monaay. You ask for too much monaay.'

And that, as they say, was that. It all went downhill from there. Several weeks previously, Gillian from Hall or Nothing had agreed in principle that she would take on the press once again. Great.

We discussed in detail our plans for the Fingers tour, how we were going to release 'Iron Man' as the first single, indicative of the need to develop much more of a guitar-driven, aggressive edge and to that end, push Andrew forward as the figurehead rather than Janet.

Excellent.

We agreed that the *NME/Melody Maker* were a lost cause, that it would make more sense for her to concentrate on by-passing them by going for coverage in all the national broadsheets and large regional rock pages. If the 'comics' followed suit, so be it, but why waste all your energy on people who care nothing for you? Fine, it sounded like a really coherent way forward.

All she had to do was to meet Frank to confirm the deal.

Oh dear.

I don't think they even got as far as talking money. Frank was charming, of course. He always was. He had a lovely chat about 'ze Tanzards', told her how much he loved the 'barnd'. He said how it was time for a change of direction, how we should release one of 'ze ballads from ze alburm, wiz Janet zinging', and God only knows what other nonsense.

'Don't listen to him, Gillian,' I implored when we spoke on the phone. 'That was just a personal choice. He's said we can put out what we want. We'll get the confusion sorted out.'

The damage, however, was done.

It had been one of those horrible weeks of waiting. I had left countless messages and the silence was worrying me. And then everything happened in the matter of half an hour.

First, it was Gillian.

'I'm going to level with you here, Ed.'

I wasn't really listening from there on in. She said it had nothing to do with the Frank thing but, having looked at the situation again, she wasn't going to have time to do us justice, blah, blah, blah. Almost as soon as I put the phone down on her, it rang again. It was Crockford and Burnham.

'We've thought long and hard about this, we like the band, we think you've got a real chance. But it's just not going to work out. We're just not going to have the time. I'm sorry if I got your hopes up. Good luck for the future.'

We knew very well that, in both cases, the time excuse was just a smoke screen; they wouldn't have showed so much interest initially if that were the case.

So why the sudden change of heart?

Was it a coincidence both called me on the same morning? Remember that the music industry is a very small world.

I suspect they were too professional to criticise someone directly but I do wonder what finally tipped the scales against us. The SLF tour fiasco? The confusion over the single? Our contract? The general chaotic way Musidisc went about their affairs? Good old Frank himself? Or a combination of all of these?

Ultimately, it was a direct repetition of the Morton scenario, though played out far more honourably (or clinically, depending on the level of your cynicism). Once they scratched below the surface, they found too much to scare them away.

And, let's face it, who can blame them?

TALES OF THE UNEXPECTED

Destiny had clearly decreed that we were to burn in Musidisc hellfire for all eternity. Following the disappointment of losing in such quick succession the SLF tour, Hall or Nothing, and major league management, not to mention the confidence of such a big player as Simon Moran, we understood that now more than ever.

Better just get on with it then, we shrugged.

The prospect of another meeting, therefore, with Frank did not have me jumping around with anticipation.

'He wants to discuss the album and single,' decreed the London office.

We arranged to come down on St Patrick's Day, March 17th. On arrival, John and I were duly ushered up to the sacred inner sanctum, the kitchen in Frank's (very swanky) first floor flat above the office.

By now, we had learned how best to play him. Assertive was fine, aggressive out of bounds (Morton had proved that), and *always, always* be positive. Not easy in light of recent events.

Head down and boogie, then.

'Hello François, nice to see you again.'

'Come in, zit down, would you like zome tea?'

Rhubarb, rhubarb.

We talked about the album, what he made of it, how it compared to the last one, what shape the band was in, and gradually we eased our way to business. John and I had agreed beforehand that we should express our fears about the staff downstairs and ask whether they were really behind us enough to make the album work. It certainly wasn't a stinging attack, but it took him aback. There was an awkward pause.

'If that is ze way you feel, perhaps it is time to change.'

'How do you mean?'

'I don't zee how we can work togezer if you have no confidence in ze company.'

Naturally I carefully omitted to say we had NEVER had any confidence in the company.

'I don't understand what you're saying.'

'If you can find a buyer for ze new alburm, I am happy to release you from your contract. I want £30,000. I will give you sree monzs. After zat we go ahead and release ze record on Musidisc. Whatever happens, we will release ze single. But you must understand zat I will not do any marketing if you are leaving ze label. If nossing has happened after sree monzs, we go ahead as planned.'

Pardon?

PARDON?

PARDON?

To the cheers of 80,000 delirious fans, I had just scored a last minute goal for Wigan in the Cup Final at Wembley, ripped all my clothes off, and run the full length of the pitch swinging my underpants above my head singing 'You Are My Sunshine' at the top of my voice.

Talk about the unexpected.

Was it really as simple as questioning the ability of his staff? Surely not.

Whatever, this was no time to sit idle. The clock was ticking, and we had three short months to engineer our escape from Colditz.

The way ahead was straightforward enough:

1: Find manager.

2: He or she secures deal.

3: Become pop star.

Easy as ABC.

DISC FIVE

March 1994 – January 1995

THE DYE IS CAST

A crucial period lay ahead. My diary takes up the story. . .

Friday March 18th

Phoned Crockford and Burnham. Surely, everything's changed now. Musidisc are no longer. They say they will call next week. They HAVE to say yes.

Tuesday March 22nd

They've said no. How could they? What better chance do they need to make money? Most of the work has been done. We've already got the fan base, the album, the profile. All we need is a sussed record company. WHY CAN'T THEY SEE THE BLEEDIN' OBVIOUS WHEN IT STARES THEM IN THE FACE? *Shit. We're back in the last-chance saloon. Time to ring Jeremy Thomas, the very same Jeremy Thomas, ex-Musidisc. Two-faced? You bet. There's a fine line between hypocrisy and pragmatism. He is the only person we know who is a) able (maybe) and b) willing (probably) to do the job.*

Thursday March 24th

John spoke to Jezzer this morning. He says he will let us know. Come on Buster, don't you let us down as well. John and I spent all afternoon drawing up 'ideal world' scenarios. Plan A, for a major label, based on 60,000 record sales (don't laugh), was around £100,000, with the band on £100 a week. Plan B (15,000 sales) was £60,000, with us on £50. All very grown-up, though we could just have played a game of Monopoly.

Friday March 25th

Musidisc now want to release BOTH 'Iron Man' and 'Band on the Rainbow' as a double A-side. They really haven't a clue, have they?

Monday March 28th

Cheapo picture session at the Wigan Observer *studio. Brought our own wallpaper for ambiance, I spelled out the word 'Flock' on the sole of my boot with drawing pins and we all wore dressing gowns. And we wonder why aren't successful?*

Tuesday March 29th

Jezzer will do it. Relief rather than elation. On the plus side, he now has an A1 assistant by the name of Danny. On the minus side, Danny told me the cheque for his wages (a pittance by all accounts) has just bounced. Here we go again.

Wednesday March 30th

My 30th birthday. How depressing. Thirty and still on £30 on week. You're meant to have careers, kids, pension-plans by now, aren't you? Or at the very least, have made and lost your first pop-star million. I know I'm not allowed to be miserable at the moment, but this is the end of my youth Please give me a break.

Thursday March 31st

Musidisc have been forced to delay the single for a fortnight. Someone somewhere is having their nails done or something. The single's an irrelevance in the light of us leaving and it's baffling why Frank even wants to go ahead with it.

FRIDAY 8TH APRIL – Following an attempted suicide in Rome, the previous month, Kurt Cobain, the reluctant icon of a generation, was found dead in his Seattle home.

Friday April 8th

Frank has given us a confirmed deadline of June 27th for the album release, that's about 11 weeks for us to get a deal. Gulp. Jezzer wants 20 packs containing copy of LP, biog, and new picture.

Monday April 11th

Twenty beautiful packs (flock wallpaper-lined, for the corporate image, see) have been despatched to J.T. I kissed them all good luck individually.

Tuesday April 12th

Amp-vandalising day. I painted nonsenses all over my bass gear in indelible, fluorescent paint. John lined his Marshall stack with (removable) flock wallpaper. What does that tell you?

Wednesday April 20th

Castle Communications have shown an initial interest. Who?

Friday April 22th

We have no money for wages. We need this deal. BADLY.

Monday April 25th

Frank is taking out adverts in NME *and* Melody Maker *for the single. Why?*

Wednesday April 27th

Jezzer has sent the packages off. The lucky recipients are (in no particu-

lar order): Warner's, Beggar's Banquet, China, EMI, Virgin, Castle Communications, Chrysalis, Island, Go Discs, Echo, A&M, Arista, London, Australian label Mushroom and Pony Canyon, a Japanese indie. Big in Japan. Sounds great. We have to organise a showcase in London.

Tuesday May 10th

Geoff has booked 24 dates for our summer tour, starting next Tuesday.

Tuesday May 17th

DERBY WHEREHOUSE *(£150 fee), the tour begins. Numbers were down from last time to about 80 paying punters. Today Jezzer spoke to Richard Swerrett from Arista, who told him that he would sign us tomorrow if he were head of A&R UK. He's not.*

Thursday May 19th

LEICESTER PRINCESS CHARLOTTE *(£200). Only around 80 again. Stopover at Leicester Travelodge.*

Friday May 20th

RUGELEY RED ROSE *(£150). Around 150 in. I'm feeling tired.*

Sunday May 22th

MORDEN TRAVELODGE, SOUTH LONDON. *No comment. Tomorrow is* VERY IMPORTANT.

Monday May 23th

Showcase at The Ritz Rehearsal Room in Putney. Was this the most crucial day (again) in the history of The Tansads? What a totally surreal experience. Everything was set up exactly for a gig, with a PA, monitor speakers, engineer, lights, soundcheck. The 'set' comprised of six songs ('Ship of Fools' obviously not good enough to be in there). We had an audience of 15 spread over both shows. When they came in, nobody said a word, we weren't introduced, it was kept formal. We gave the full performance monty, nobody clapped, then all filed out again. Jezzer was totally in his element, shmoozing with all the oily rags, you could practically see the slime oozing under the door. Chris Briggs, head of Chrysalis A&R and two others from his office was the scoop. We also had Castle, BMG, Pony Canyon, and a host of others. It was all so artificial. The performing monkeys played the game.

Friday May 27th

Castle have registered a definite interest. Jezzer now wants next week's show in London to be a live showcase. We're going to have to fund a coach down for our supporters, which is costing us £450 and which we naturally can't afford.

Tuesday May 31th

LEEDS DUCHESS OF YORK (£150), supposed release of the single, with 'I Don't Know' as extra track. I can therefore, as from today join the very noble and exclusive Performers' Rights Society. Not that I will get paid any royalties on our sales, BUT THAT'S NOT THE POINT. Back to the gig, and there seems to be a definite pattern to the tour: numbers are static, around the 80 to 100 mark. Shirkers *was out almost 18 months ago now, so it's not altogether surprising. That's not to say the atmosphere at the gigs has been anything but excellent, it just proves how desperately we need to move up a level. Travelodge in Barnsley.*

Wednesday June 1st

HULL ADELPHI (£125) Around 100 in, and another great show.

Thursday June 2nd

LOUGHBOROUGH UNIVERSITY (£100). The best student gig ever? 1,200 people, and most of them listening. Leicester Travelodge, getting ready for the big one.

Friday June 3rd

LONDON KING'S CROSS WATER RATS (Door take, £250) An absolutely incredible night. What an atmosphere, full of supporters. It was unbelievably sweaty, my hands were so wet I couldn't get my fingers to the notes in time, and I felt faint at one point. The crowd were stage-diving, crowd-surfing, dancing on each other's shoulders. Castle and China turned up to witness it, but Arista didn't, unfortunately. Tonight we looked like a band that mattered. The support was great too. They also had A&R watching. They were called **Cast**, *with the bassist from The Las singing. I'm predicting a big future here and now. Janet had her purse stolen from the shared dressing room, then made a massive song and dance about how the band should give her the money again. That's so crap. I mean, a shared dressing room. Why didn't she give it to someone like Simon to look after, for God's sake, and why should the band have to pay for her irresponsibility? We had a vote on it and everybody agreed to give it to her, of course. Cowards.*

CAST – In terms of the bands who supported The Tansads, Cast were the first to attain Top 20 single and Top 10 album status: 'Finetime' reached number 17 in July 1995 and LP *All Change* (the best-ever selling debut album on Polydor) clocked in at number 7. Still, I wonder who did nick Janet's purse…

Saturday June 4th

LIVERPOOL LOMAX (£125) A somewhat jaded performance after last night, but 150 people in and still a great atmosphere. Encouragingly, there were only a few people in from home, the majority having been culled from elsewhere. Everybody was relaxed on the journey up because John and Janet didn't travel with us, having gone straight back home after London. Funny that.

Monday June 6th

Chrysalis have pulled out. The writing was on the wall when they didn't come on Friday. Better news about Arista, who genuinely couldn't make it, and still want to see us live. Jezzer hasn't managed to contact China, but Castle are definitely keen – it's down to those three now. Frank has agreed to postpone the LP until the end of July. Eases the pressure a little.

Monday June 13th

Our single is at 151 in the Charts. Not bad as it has received no airplay and isn't in the shops.

Wednesday June 15th

Castle want to license Flock *for six months before offering us a permanent deal. Read my lips: b-o-g o-f-f.*

Thursday June 16th

No sooner had Jezzer refused their initial salvo than Castle came back with a concrete offer of money, £6,000 in advances, £4,000 in tour support, and the rest in six months. It may be all we get. Jezzer still can't contact China. He's not given up hope, but it seems pretty plain to me they're not interested.

Friday 17th & Saturday 18th June

ST HELENS CITADEL (£800 for both nights. Aahh, wages, bills, food.) Two great sold out shows. What every gig should be like.

Monday June 20th

Arista have pulled out. Shit. Barring an unlikely sudden surge of interest from China, we are now left with only Castle. I was over at John's house when Jezzer rang with the news. I expressed disappointment that our last stab at a major had gone, and he went ballistic. 'Do you realise how hard Jeremy has worked to get this etc?' Yes, of course he has, hats off to the guy, but I still can't help thinking if he'd pushed Arista quite as hard as Castle, we may have had a choice. But Jezzer and Castle top cat Dougie Dudgeon go back a long way, and it's no coincidence. John didn't like that sort of talk. OK, it's a deal, it's secured the life of the band for a time, but who the hell are Castle Communications when they're at home? I'm sorry but it feels like an anticlimax to me.

LEARNING THE LARD WAY

If ever we needed a reminder of why we *had* to escape. . .

Musidisc's supercharged promotional campaign for the single was carried out *without* any knowledge of our impending departure. Frank thought it would be better that way. In other words, they were trying.

Frightening.

Common or garden incompetence is one thing, so too laziness. These are good old-fashioned human frailties. But we were about to receive proof that something far more premeditated was going on.

Russell Fraser had already given us more than enough indication as to his credentials.

As well as the plugging side, Russell had been brought in for his (clear my throat) expertise in helping Frank launch a new dance label. Jezzer told us Frank didn't particularly like dance music, but bands always asking for money gave him headaches, so the one-man-and-his-studio thing appealed.

One of Russell's first 'coups' had been to tempt 80s pop diva Hazel Dean out of retirement. Having pressed thousands of copies, the first single performed the standard Musidisc belly flop. Russell was left with expensive egg on his face, and Frank still didn't like dance music.

I never trusted Russell from the first meeting. He was shifty, and too polite by half, but my suspicions were truly aroused when he asked us if we had any ideas for getting the single aired.

'Hang on, shouldn't we be asking you that?'

I gave him the benefit of the doubt (for now) and reeled off our list of past successes.

'Oh, and there's **Mark Radcliffe.** We were interviewed twice, had a session on *Hit the North* and I know he said for us to keep in touch. You should definitely try him.'

'Right.'

Pause.

MARK RADCLIFFE – Like me, Radcliffe is a failed pop star. The County Fathers, for whom he was the drummer, released an EP *Lightheaded* in the '80s on Mancunian indie label Ugly Man Records – incidentally, I still have the rejection letter they sent me after receiving the Those Famous Red Shirts demo.

'Hmm. Mark, uh Radcliffe, did you say?'

'Yes.'

' Perhaps you could tell me a bit about him.'

Bite your lip. Nice, slow, deeeeeep breath.

'You've not heard of Mark Radcliffe?

'Sorry.'

'He's on Radio 1. Have you heard of *them*?'

Granted he hadn't yet graduated to daytime domesticity with his cuddly and charmingly named sidekick Lard, but Radcliffe had long since left his berth at Radio 5, and his seminal alternative show every weekday evening was prime fodder for all new bands.

The alarm bells were ringing.

'Well, perhaps, you could see if he'll play the single, and give us a session? The show is broadcast from Manchester, so it would be no trouble for us to pop down.'

'I'll get on to it at once.'

So we waited. A week. Two weeks. Three weeks. Finally, I called.

'Russell, any joy with the Radcliffe session?'

'Oh – uh, no. I've tried him, but he says he'll get back to me.'

Another week.

'Russell, have you got an answer on the Radcliffe thing?'

'Yes, he's given me a few dates.'

'Great, why didn't you tell us?'

'Well, I, uh, I didn't want to get your hopes up, you know.'

Another week. We were in June by now and the single was out.

'Russell, any news?'

'He's given me the first week of July, probably the Tuesday.'

'Right, but you will let me know for sure as soon as you can.'

'Absolutely.'

By the middle of June, there was still no confirmation.

'Russell, I'm really going to have to push you for a definite date.'

'Yes, yes, of course.'

The last week of June and still no word. This was getting silly.

'Hi, it's Ed, is Russell there?'

'He's out of the office.'

That was on Monday. On Tuesday and on Wednesday morning the same scenario. So I did what I had to do.

'Hello, BBC Manchester.'

'Oh, hello, can I speak to somebody at the Mark Radcliffe show?'

The interminable hold. Eventually. . .

'Hello, Radio 1.'

'Oh, uh, hello, can I speak to Mark Radcliffe please?'

'Sorry, he's not in yet. Can I help at all, it's **Mark Riley**, I produce the show?'

MARC RILEY – Riley is yet another failed pop star, although his CV reads better than most. After four years as bassist then guitarist with The Fall, Riley branched out on his own as Marc Riley and The Creepers, a gig of whose I actually attended at Shades Nitespot in Lancaster in 1985 (the same place I first laid eyes on my wife-to-be, incidentally, though that was during Claire Spafford's birthday party a few weeks later).

Ahh, the infamous Lardy-boy himself.

'Oh, hi, Mark, it's Ed Jones here, from The Tansads. We met a while back when we did the session on *Hit the North*?'

'Yeah, I remember. Wigan's finest. How are you?'

'Not bad, not bad. Listen I'm sorry to bother you, but I'm having a little trouble pinning our plugger down on this session. I know it's a bit unprofessional to call you direct—'

'What session is that?'

'The session he's arranged for us on the show.'

'I'm sorry but nobody's been in touch about The Tansads for ages. What's his name?'

'Russell Fraser, from our label, Musidisc.'

'No, never heard of him.'

'And he can't have spoken to anybody else?'

'No, all the sessions are arranged through me.'

'But he gave us a date, for next week.'

'No, I'm sorry. We received a copy of the single but, to be honest we didn't like it all that much, so we haven't played it. But please keep sending us stuff. We'll always listen to it.'

Why bother? That's what I never understood. Why bother lying to us for so long about a session which had never existed? Why didn't he just say Radcliffe wasn't interested? How *do* these people get jobs?

Suddenly, in the midst of yet another Musidisc storm, the warm shelter of Castle Communications harbour appeared ever more welcoming.

THE LABEL WHO LOVED ME

It was a straight steal from one of those old spy movies; the nocturnal political prisoner hand-over at some obscure Iron Curtain border crossing, glaring limousine headlights reducing everybody to silhouettes.

A shady-looking character with thick black-rimmed specs and knee-length mac greets another shady-looking character with thick black-rimmed specs and knee-length leather coat halfway across no man's land.

A briefcase full of money is handed over.

Leather Coat gives the sign, the barrier is raised, and tracked by a dozen twitchy machine-guns, the prisoners shuffle tentatively through. When they reach Mac, he turns and escorts them back to the other side, through the second barrier, into a magical land of opportunity . . . where they are immediately rehoused on the 20th floor of a damp Tower Hamlets tenement along with a friendly colony of cockroaches.

Our release took place on July 21st, at the highly salubrious Oxford Jericho Tavern, an appropriately filthy and decrepit hole, but the legendary spawning ground for locals such as Radiohead, Supergrass, and Ride.

I called Jezzer when we got to the venue and received the news we all wanted to hear:

'He's signed it.'

He, of course, was Frankie Bigfield. The deal with Castle had been signed. I leapt into our dressing room like a Greek messenger.

'People, I bring word from Athens! From this day forth, WE ARE OFFICIALLY AN EX-MUSIDISC ACT!!!!!'

That was the good, correction, the *great* news. No more sycophantic phone calls to Paris. No more Holland Park kitchen diplomacy. No more begging for what we were owed. Hmmmmm, what was that sweet perfume? Freedom, by Estée Lauder.

Not for long.

I had been handed the task of chief negotiator. For most of the next ten days, I exchanged endless telephone calls and faxes to Jezzer and to our solicitor Helen Searle from various Toilets across the country. Like playing with a wooden Russian doll set, this involved drawing up ever-decreasing survival budgets, until eventually, on the first day of the eight month of the one thousand, nine hundred and ninety-fourth year of our Lord, we had a contract to sign.

The total amount Castle were guaranteeing to spend on us in three and a half years was £161,500, which included Frank's payoff (£32,500, the bugger pushed for more money at the eleventh hour) and £25,000 for recording the next LP. In all, it was worth over twice as much as Musidisc's contract, and also included a video budget of £7,500. A potential maximum of £96,500 would be paid into our bank account.

My projected figure of £50 each in wages looked realistic-ish, coming in at £63,700 for the full three and a half year period, especially as – let me blow my own trumpet – I had managed to pull off a bit of a coup.

On top of the basic advances (£7,500 for the first six months, £16,000 for year one, £25,000 for year two, and £30,000 for year three), I managed to make them agree to a clause whereby our tour support was advanced to us in monthly instalments, *without* the need to justify every demand, Musidisc-style. In other words, we would actually get paid what was on the contract, i.e. £750 a month.

Castle insisted on a six-month probationary period, with the option to dump us come January. After that, it was the standard one-year option periods. They may not have been the leap to a major we had hoped for, but they were certainly a big step up from Musidisc.

And on the plus side, they were not interested in the publishing, beyond buying out the current deal with Musidisc for *Flock*. Thereafter, we would be able to strike up an independent deal somewhere else: ergo, more money. At worst, then, we knew we had a six-month stay of execution but, in truth, it was highly likely Castle would wait at least one more year to see a return on their investment.

And anyway, we knew full well that as they were (incredible, I know) *really* excited about signing us, they would spend a good deal more than these contracted minimums when it came to advertising and promotion. They had just purchased famous 60s and 70s American folk label Transatlantic (no, I'd never heard of it either) and we were to be the flagship new signing for their planned autumn relaunch.

The bottom line was that they had a serious vested interest in making us happen.

There was a downside, however. Of course. In terms of profile, Castle were probably equally as irrelevant as Musidisc in the eyes of the fashionable press, having made their name reissuing old albums by the likes – ironically – of Stiff Little Fingers, along with a host of other punk legends.

Never mind that, though, they were chucking money about like nobody's business and we were happily in the line of fire. Having been round the block once or twice by now, we knew this could not last unless we had major, and I mean *major*, record-selling success.

But that was all in the future.

For the time being, we took the roof down, put the shades on and cruised along Honeymoon Boulevard.

Sort of.

ME AND UNCLE JONES

However hard I tried to reconcile myself to the fact that Castle had the serious hots for us, that I had been a major player in securing the most money anybody had ever spent on us, that I had a song on the new album, that I had reached an unprecedented level of professionalism as a performer and that the band had never sounded so good on stage, something still didn't feel right.

Castle was probably the beginning of the end for me. Only I didn't know it. Yet.

I suppose it had started with the 'Ship of Fools' fiasco at Loco, and with John planting the seed in my head that I needed to arise from my posterior and start a band of my own. It continued with all the fuss over Frank, my reservations about Jezzer, the Arista disappointment, and my initial reluctance over the deal with Castle.

However, towards the end of April, something completely separate had knocked me out of my stride.

'Mr Edmund Jones?'

You're never at ease when a policeman stands on your doorstep.

'Yes.'

'Are you related to Mr Bruce Jones, of Austin Waye, Uxbridge, Middlesex?'

'Oh, uh, yes, he's my uncle.'

'I'm sorry, sir, but I've got some bad news. He was found dead in his flat this morning.'

Poor Bruce.

The coroner recorded that he had lain for two or three days before a neighbour became worried she hadn't seen him and called the police. Heart failure induced by high blood pressure was the verdict.

Since my Aunt Grace had died in 1983, nobody was really left to look after Bruce. If he had been born 50 years later, he may have been diagnosed as being autistic, or as suffering from obsessive compulsive disorder. There would have been care available, anyway.

But, growing up in the '20s, Bruce was shunned by society and ended up living life as a recluse, cleaning paint pots out for a living. He rented grotty council flats, he had no friends to speak of and his life was a jumble of contradictions.

He was meticulously clean, yet too miserly to use hot water. The flat was filthy, but he always ensured his shoes were polished. He never went out without wearing a tie, but his shirts were threadbare and unironed. He insisted on sprinkling bran all over his food on the advice of his doctor, but survived on leftover chips from the local Wimpy Bar.

The point though, was that he survived. I tried to help, but, speak the truth shame the devil, as the stubborn old mule always said, I didn't do a very good job.

He had visited us in Wigan several times, for which he was always grateful. Two years previously, I had gone with him to buy carpets, spent a weekend cleaning up, and would go down every few months to keep the dust at bay. Lord knows I'd tried to get him some support. But he refused point blank to pay for a cleaner, and the last social worker who had been round had apparently vowed never to return on fear of his life. Incredibly, the police found a loaded gun in the flat. I dread to think why he had that.

The only person he listened to was his doctor, but patient confidentiality prevented him from divulging anything to me. Bruce had lived this way too long, and it was plainly too late to change.

He was an incredibly difficult person to be with; eccentric, bigoted, vitriolic, but at the same time fiercely loyal and in his own way, he cared. In the final analysis, he was still Dad's brother and, to my eternal shame, like a disinterested line of Joneses stretching back to my grandad, I did only the bare minimum.

And now he was gone, alone and unloved.

It was guilt and remorse, rather than grieving which overtook me now. My sister Lucy was five months pregnant and the unfortunate task of dealing with everything fell upon my shoulders. Amazingly for such a busy year for the band, it was a free week. Bruce was considerate to the last.

But that was not all.

The stupid idiot lived like a pauper but had just left Lucy and me over £40,000 each. The inheritance took about two months to come through probate; he died intestate, but there was nobody to contest, so it was quick. Having so much money all of a sudden was a shock to the system.

'You're not giving it to the band,' my dearest wife said to me as she fastened my ankles together and nailed my feet to the floor, 'and anyway, it's only the equivalent of what you've not earned since giving up work.'

Women, don't you just love them?

She had a point, though.

'Don't worry darling, I'm daft, but, contrary to popular opinion in this house, I'm not *completely* stupid.'

Had I been able to guarantee a life of successful rock stardom by spending it all, then I may have done so. But I couldn't. Instead I did the sensible thing and invested it.

Well, most of it.

'I always said I'd take you to Geneva. I've booked the ferry. We're going in August, after the tour is finished.'

I'd not been back since 1982. Unfortunately, the friends I was hoping would put us up were on holiday, so we camped alongside Lake Geneva.

'You pu ze tent eer, it is fessin' zis waay, you do not park ze car, you give me passport, you give me 100 francs or no camping.'

The welcoming Swiss.

We arrived on the day a five-week heatwave broke. While the locals danced in the streets to praise the rain gods, I dragged a long-faced sun-seeking wife kicking and screaming round the (damp) local landmarks.

'See that building? That's where the dentist was. I played on that football pitch, scored a goal. See that road sign for Veyriers? My friend Neil lived there. He was a Man United supporter. That's the supermarket where Mum did the weekly shop. And there's the bus stop she picked me up from after school.'

We went back to the old house, but my rural little childhood memory of fields and freedom had been invaded by a motorway, an industrial estate, and blocks of flats.

'It's horrible,' she said.

And she was right.

So we left after two days and had a proper holiday in the South of France instead. We were away for just over three weeks, but something in me had definitely changed when I got back. Perhaps I had just lost my momentum, or perhaps it was simply having the time to distance myself from it all, and put things in perspective. Maybe sorting out Bruce's affairs had aged me in a funny kind of way, or maybe it was the money blunting my desperation to succeed and giving me a new sense of autonomy over the rest of the band. Probably all of these.

Whatever, my appetite for the band seemed to have diminished at precisely the time when, with the Castle honeymoon barely having begun, I should have been at my most hungry. It might have only been a temporary lull in motivation, but it felt like I was going back to work.

What worse indictment could there be?

MAD ABOUT THE BOY

'JUST FUCKING GET OFF HIS BACK. IF IT WASN'T FOR HIM, YOU WOULDN'T EVEN BE HERE, YOU UNGRATEFUL BITCH!'

I'd never shouted at anybody so loudly.

Andrew had let it slip that Simon, who was on the door at our recent show in Wigan, had allowed six well-known blaggers in without paying, halfway through the gig. If there was one thing guaranteed to inflame Janet, it was the sniff of perceived injustice and, boy, was that nose now working overtime. She was on the prowl for a scapegoat, gnawing, scratching for information.

Suddenly aware of having let a particularly hissing, flea-infested cat out of the bag, Andrew tried to bundle the beast from whence it came.

'I don't know, maybe, uhh, maybe I got it wrong. I thought, I, uh, heard him talking about something, but, uh, you know, I—'

Too late. Hiroshima had just entered *Enola Gay*'s viewfinder.

'He had no right to let people in like that! Who the hell does he think he is? There's a lot of my friends who had to pay. And now he lets those bastards in for nothing. I'll bloody 'ave 'im.'

In his absence, my buddy, my trusted, loyal, friend, was being mercilessly crucified. Simon worked tirelessly with little financial reward. He was one of the rocks on which the band had been built. Yet here he was being castigated.

'It makes me sick. He knows how broke we are. How could he do it? And them. Of all people.'

I tried to ignore her at first, but the inexorable tide of her accusations built up momentum. The more she said, the more I bit my lip. Then it was one insult too far.

'YOU MAKE ME FUCKING SICK! DO YOU KNOW HOW MUCH MONEY THAT FUCKING BLOKE HAS PUT INTO THIS FUCKING BAND, DO YOU KNOW HOW MUCH EFFORT HE'S PUT IN?!'

Deep, straight, powerful first service.

'YOU'RE JUST SAYING THAT BECAUSE HE'S YOUR MATE! YOU'RE ALWAYS STANDING UP FOR HIM!'

Janet's surprise at having the bass player hijack her inquisition was quickly replaced by a desire to get even. The return was solid.

'NOBODY ELSE FUCKING DOES, WHY SHOULDN'T I? THAT'S WHAT FUCKING FRIENDS ARE FOR, ISN'T IT? YOU SHOULD HAVE THOUGHT ABOUT THAT BEFORE FUCKING SLAGGING HIM OFF IN FRONT OF ME!'

Top-spin backhand down the line.

'WHAT ABOUT ME? WHAT ABOUT FUCKING JOHN AND ME? WHERE D'YOU THINK ALL OUR PUBLISHING MONEY'S GONE?'

Janet got a racket to the ball, but only managed to push it tamely back over the net. An empty court beckoned.

'YOU'VE NOT PUT FUCKING NINE THOUSAND QUID IN, HAVE YOU, YOU SOFT COW?'

Unreturnable smash.

'YOU'VE NOT PUT NINE FUCKING THOUSAND QUID YOU'RE NEVER LIKELY TO SEE AGAIN INTO A BAND YOU'RE NOT EVEN FUCKING IN!'

I had no idea where all this anger was coming from.

'THAT'S NOT THE POINT, THAT'S NOT WHAT THIS IS ABOUT!'

In a last ditch effort, she scrambled in vain to reach the ball. But it was all over.

'WHAT DO YOU MEAN IT'S NOT THE FUCKING POINT? IT'S EXACTLY THE FUCKING POINT! YOU DON'T EVEN TRUST SOMEBODY WHO HAS PUT NINE FUCKING THOUSAND QUID INTO THE BAND!'

If you can get louder than the top of your voice, I was heading to that place, and fast.

'SIMON WAS ON THE DOOR, HE CHOSE TO LET SOME PEOPLE IN. WHAT'S THE FUCKING PROBLEM, THAT'S WHAT HE WAS THERE FOR, WASN'T IT?

Allegro.

'YOU'RE FUSSING ABOUT A FEW LOUSY QUID, WE'RE NOT THAT FUCKING HARD UP!'

Fortissimo.

'JUST GIVE THE GUY A BREAK! IF HE CHOSE TO LET THOSE PEOPLE IN, HE MUST HAVE HAD A GOOD REASON, AND YOU'VE GOT NO FUCKING BUSINESS QUESTIONING HIS DECISION OVER A FEW LOUSY FUCKING QUID!'

And the final crescendo . . .

'WHAT DOES IT FUCKING MATTER IF WE'VE LOST TEN, TWENTY, THIRTY QUID, FOR FUCK'S SAKE? WHAT DOES IT FUCKING MATTER, WHAT DOES IT FUCKING, FUCKING, FUCKING, FUCKING MATTER!!?'

An eerie calm descended upon our big blue van. The rest of the band had just sat open-mouthed, the fear in their eyes being less to do with my wrath than about basic self-preservation.

We were riding at sixty-five miles per hour in the middle lane on a busy stretch of the M6 motorway and I was at the wheel. Throughout the tirade, my increasingly reddening features had been turned 180 degrees to face Janet, who sat directly behind me

They thought they were all going to die.

Nobody spoke for the rest of the journey. We were on our way to record our first single after signing the new record deal. The survival of the band, after a long, hard struggle, had just been secured. Optimism was at its highest for years.

DODGING THE ISSUE

Castle insisted on recording 'Band on the Rainbow' again as the first single. We were whisked in at short notice to (very pleasant) Lindford Manor Studio in Milton Keynes, and a (very pleasant) producer by the name of Spong and a (very unpleasant) episode ensued.

The vehicular contretemps with Janet on the way down soured things for starters. Obviously. I apologised to her later that day, not that I felt I had done wrong, but I thought it might help smooth things over. No chance.

The next morning was no different, as Janet still walked out of rooms I entered and refused point blank to acknowledge my existence. Real school playground stuff.

'How long do you reckon it can go on?' I asked Guy.

'Well, you know Janet. . .'

It would take a whole 22 days.

Janet, though, wasn't my main gripe. That accolade belonged to her other half. John's reaction to the Castle contract had been the antithesis of mine from day one. Where I was lukewarm and battle-weary, he was the hyperactive psycho-child who had just guzzled four Big Macs and a gallon of Extra-Caffeine Super Saccharine Cola. Intensity was an integral part of his make-up, but this was enthusiasm overload.

When we got to Lindford Manor, he was demented from the word go. I tried to ignore the excitement and tension that fizzed out of his body. But it's hard when somebody tells you exactly what your part is, hovers like a wasp in your face, and all but plays your damn instrument for you. I had been through all this before, of course, and it used to faze me. These days I was more confident. It just annoyed me.

'John, please leave me alone.'

'I'm only trying to help.'

'Well, you're not. Come back in half an hour.'

Whether or not he was truly happy with the bass line I never bothered to ask, but it survived onto the final mix, so I presume it must have met with satisfaction. Or maybe they just ran out of time in which to redo it.

A video-recording session was booked to aid the single's release. The script (written I think by John and Robert, of course) had us cavorting through a forest, standing halfway up a slagheap, before looking moody in a disused hangar.

Hmm.

John was, again, unbelievably pumped up for the filming, which took place for some reason in and around Slough. John Betjeman was right about that place. It poured down all day, the van was broken into, and everybody's clothes were stolen. Swarms of flying ants also attacked us, the shoot was hours behind schedule, and we ran out of food. A planned 10.00 p.m. finish ended up with us finally placing ear to pillow at 6.00 a.m. after a twenty-two-hour day.

The words 'aaaaannnnnd playback' rang in my brain for the next week and I still can't listen to the track without feeling spasms in my right arm and my left knee caving in.

John was unbelievable.

Even at 5.00 a.m., after we had listened and mimed the song (with feeling) approximately 678 times, he was *still* shouting at us to concentrate and stop mucking about. That boy was in a Porsche 911 on the fast lane to Nervous Breakdown City.

Worse was to come when the issue of the *Flock* album cover came onto the agenda. We gave Simon the brief of a sheep (sheep, flock? Oh yes), but his ovine pictorial was deemed too 'indie' by Dougie Dudgeon at Castle, who subsequently commissioned his own designers to provide alternatives.

They came up with two ideas. One featured – surprise, surprise – a sheep, while the other was a close up of the Chinese Terracotta Army. How these were any less 'indie' I don't know. For that matter, I don't know what precisely constituted an 'indie' cover anyway.

The truth, of course, was that all this had nothing to do with album designs, it was good old-fashioned ego. They wanted theirs, we wanted ours. Simple. Something had to give and what followed upset me then, and upsets me now when I think about it.

Castle having no loyalty to Simon I can fully understand. The fact Jezzer was being oily for the sake of diplomacy annoyed me because he was meant to be on our side, although given the nature of the beast I suppose it was to be expected.

However, what I cannot forgive is the way John and Janet turned against their most hard-working foot soldier, without whom, let us not forget, they wouldn't even have been in this position to make the choice in the first place. Remember, not only had Simon injected £9,000 into the band, spent an inordinate amount of time designing everything from demo covers to album covers via T-shirts and newsletters. He had also travelled round the country's lesser venues and enjoyed many a lonely hour standing around draughty corridors behind his merchandising stall at no financial gain to himself. And, for his sins, he had also moved in with them.

John's not a nasty bloke at heart, far from it. He's just driven. In an ideal world, I'm sure he would have loved to give Simon time to redesign the sleeve and fight the battle. But expediency was the crucial factor now. Dougie was pushing Jezzer for a quick answer because the album was due out the following month, and we were in danger of missing printing deadlines.

Solution?

Easy, wheel in your old friend democracy, let the band vote on it and ease your conscience into the bargain (ring any bells?). I don't remember for certain if people were fully aware of the facts when they arrived at the house on September 14th, and were shown the three images. I seem to remember the whole idea was to make them choose a cover without knowing who had designed which, in order that an 'objective' opinion could be formed. Delbert confirmed this was the case, but Guy tells me he knew which was which. Whatever, I was the only one to vote for Simon.

Oh dear.

'If we don't think Simon's cover is as good, we owe it to him morally to give him another chance,' I suggested.

Familiarity must have been breeding contempt as far as my defending Simon went, however, because the protest didn't make much of an impact. Outvoted six to one.

Whether the majority genuinely believed the Terracotta Army to be the better cover is not really that important. I still maintain that we should have fought for Simon on principle. Besides, everybody liked his cover at first, before the politics intervened.

And that was the problem.

Tansads diplomacy decreed that, had John wanted Simon's design, there would not even have been a vote. Castle had more to lose by delaying the LP than we had, and they would surely have buckled if we, and Jezzer for that matter, had held firm on the issue. The bottom line, however, was that John did not think album design an important enough issue to risk sullying our still pristine relationship with Castle, and by extension of course, his or the band's career.

Whatever the level of everybody's knowledge, Simon was ultimately let down by people he had done so much to help. When it came down to it, it was simply a case of *him or us*.

Loyalty becomes inconvenient eventually.

'We all have to take rejection,' John said to him afterwards.

'Simon has to learn to fight his own battles. He cannot just rely on the band all the time,' John said to me.

What a cunt.

The not-so-secret ballot had taken place on the Wednesday. 'Band On The Rainbow' was released the following Monday, the tour started a fortnight later, we needed to rehearse a new set, I had to book all the accommodation, there was a newsletter to write, the accounts to do and a thousand other pressing jobs. At the same time, Jezzer was pushing us to sign his management contract, one of the stipulations of his getting us a deal.

The fact that the Simon issue was quickly brushed aside because there was so much else going on, left a very ugly taste in my mouth. Did I really want to be associated with people who could be so cruel to their friends?

Hmmm.

The early signs for 'Band on The Rainbow' (Spong version) were good when it was named Alternative Record Of The Week in the industry circular the *Tip Sheet*, ahead of tracks by established indie names such as Gene and Portishead. This was a major achievement.

Our experience with Musidisc was such that we were amazed when it

TIP SHEET – Started by former Radio 1 DJ and industry shaker Jonathan King, the *Tip Sheet* is circulated weekly to record companies, shops, agencies, promoters and the like to give advance notice of what's hot and what's not.

actually made it into shops, with the CD priced at just £1.99 as arranged. Suddenly we had a real record company.

But not for long.

For all the big push, it reached number 101 in the Gallup chart. OK, it was our highest-ever position, but new press pluggers Partridge and Storey failed to achieve any significant reviews. You may have changed companies, snarled the *NME*, but we still know it's you. Partridge and Storey eventually changed their name to Coalition and became The Verve's PR agents, a company nobody now says no to. But by then we had long gone.

On the radio side, meanwhile, Castle's plugger Steve Payne – surprise, surprise – failed to get it played anywhere, never mind a sniff of a playlist. Even our self-help plan backfired, when following a piece in our newsletter urging everyone to lobby Radio 1 to play the single, Mark Radcliffe refused to comply on principle because he had received, quote, 'too many requests'. Honestly, you just can't win sometimes.

Geoff booked a 25-date tour, starting in mid-October. It was by far our most compact to date. And, true to rock-'n'-roll form, he also arranged a low-key, unadvertised warm-up gig a couple of weeks beforehand, at Sunderland Poly.

I agreed to do it because we were headlining, the money was good at £350, and we needed the practice after two months without playing live. When we got there, however, we discovered we were not in fact headlining. That treat belonged to a band called **Dodgy**, and our fee was only £300 (I should have heeded Morton's advice and sacked Geoff months before, as the boy was clearly out of his depth).

DODGY – Signed to A&M, their single 'Staying Out for the Summer' had already crept into the Top 40, and it would not be long before bigger hits followed from their debut LP *Homegrown*. A second successful album, *Free Peace Suite*, appeared in 1996 and the band has recently decided to carry on despite the departure of singer Nigel Clark.

But I didn't mind. Not really. There wouldn't have been a lot we could do about it had we kicked up a fuss and, to be fair, we had suffered far worse 'gig trauma' anyway. Yes, pride was dented slightly, but we were still well treated, it was still a profitable show, and the headliners actually turned out to be really pleasant compared to other future pop stars we had come across.

Besides, by recent standards, this Dodgy business hadn't even measured on the Richter Scale. I was becoming too tired to care.

FACT OR FACTION

When 11 of you are wedged in the back of a van, albeit a very nice one, for weeks and thousands of miles on end, it is only natural that factions develop. There were five main sociological groupings:

1.Mummy and Daddy, also known as ***The Sensibles:*** John and Janet.

- Habits: Always seen together, tending not to venture far from the van during day times, or the dressing room during the evening, always first to bed. Conversation usually restricted to matters musical or culinary.

-Might be heard saying: 'What's for tea, Queen?' 'Have we got a rider tonight, Ed?'

2. ***Countryfile***, otherwise known as ***The Van-dwellers***: Andrew, Andy and Terry.

-Habits: Would always peel their eyes at the countryside speeding past outside, occasionally pointing to the sky and nudging each other. Treated the van as home, with some justification, as it was. The rest of us were temporary intruders into their universe, tolerated during the day, but in the evening, in that tedious lull between soundcheck and gig, the van was strictly out of bounds. They may or may not have consumed copious quantities of a substance, derivatives of which can be used in the production of rope.

-Might be heard saying: 'Wood-pigeon!' 'Jackdaw!' 'Has anyone got a surface?'

3. ***The Pub Club***: Guy, Simon, and sound engineer Big Dave (to whom you have not been introduced yet). Honorary low-alcohol intake member: me.

-Habits: Very quiet until the van dropped anchor. Then, automatic pilot would guide them to the nearest hostelry, before liquid injection of life. I tagged along most of the time, letting the side down by going off for walks and showing interest in the world around me. PC members would spend as little time as possible in and around the venue, always preferring the shelter of a good pint. Then, they would stay up half the night in the Travelodge bedroom performing one or more of the following routines.

a) Being locked in the bathroom by Big Dave with the light turned off.

b)'Piley-on', whereby a chosen victim, usually Delbert, would be instantly submerged by everybody else. With Big Dave measuring in at 6 foot 7 inches and weighing 18 stone, this was potentially life threatening.

c) Laughing at Delbert attempting to punch Big Dave.

d) 'Raps', featuring a deck of cards and bleeding knuckles, the perfect pastime for musicians.

e). In the morning, after Big Dave had emptied the rubbish bin onto the floor and stuck cold tea bags to the ceiling, boring old me would attempt to undo the damage. The rooms were booked in my name.

-Might be heard saying: 'Your round, Simon.' 'Very funny, Dave.' 'Piley ooooooooon.'

4. ***Earth Calling Planet Bob***: Robert was a *van-dweller* without being a member of *Countryfile*.

-Habits: Usually involved a packet of Rizlas.

-Might be heard quoting Blake, or singing Dylan.

5. ***Delbert***: Occasional member of *The Pub Club*, but basically on his own (or 'with your mates again are ya Del?' as Big Dave would say).

-Habits: Had the dubious honour of sharing a double bed with Dave, and every night therefore had to endure the Chicken Tikka Masala Pasty Methane Endurance Test, involving his head being forced under the sheets and being made to imbibe Dave's awesomely fierce posterior gases. Long-term, this obviously had a detrimental effect on his brain because he spent most of his days reading Barry Manilow's autobiography.

-Might be heard saying: 'Daaave, nooooo.' 'Yeah, but he's a brilliant songwraaaater, tho'.'

Keeping out of each other's way on the road was a safety valve against friction, a sign that far from building a solid foundation for the future, we were finding ways of tolerating the present. That was worrying. Touring had always been the last remaining genuinely exciting vestige of band life. If even that spark was being eroded away, what long-term hope remained?

None, in a word.

And it had all started so well for the Jones boy. John decided to fix a set for the whole tour, and included 'Ship of Fools' as the first encore track. That was where the good news ended.

I woke on the morning of October 10th, three dates into the tour and the day *Flock* was released (an omen?), to find a kamikaze milk float had destroyed both itself and the back of our van in an orgy of twisted metal and broken bottles.

Great.

Have you ever tried explaining to somebody else's insurance assessor, whose knowledge of the music industry extends as far as the last Celine Dion CD his wife bought him that, as well as spending thousands of pounds on repairing our splitter van ('Does it break off into two pieces, then?'), he also has to fork out for a replacement vehicle and a motel room on 20 separate occasions because the gigs are contracted and the floor space in the hire van only fits two sleeping bags instead of the usual four?

I knew that if we didn't honour our dates, we would lose not only long-term, career-threatening credibility, but also short-term tour support from Castle. Having made the commitment to go ahead, which ran into thousands, I also knew if the insurance company didn't cough up, we would be bankrupt. In other words, the future of the band could depend upon the outcome of the claim, responsibility for which fell upon my shoulders. Fortunately, though, the matter did resolve itself and we got our money.

Despite much greater backing than *Up the Shirkers*, *Flock*'s release proved one thing to me: the band was going nowhere. Eventually, it sold around the same number of copies, a pathetic 5,000 or thereabouts (though I can't prove that figure). Aside from the obligatory gushing support from *Folk Roots (*'The Tansads' splendour is undiminished. Yet more praise, oh dear'), generally, the profile was down. The video was a white elephant, having achieved no exposure whatsoever, while plugger Steve Payne was promising a session on Radio 1 and GLR with our 'old friend' Johnnie Walker, but precious little else.

Partridge and Storey achieved just one significant review, from John Crosby in *Q* magazine:

'The energy of their live work translates well to the new album. . . a gutsy performance which confirms that if John Kettle is the group's creator and prime-mover, singers Andrew Kettle and Janet Anderton are the focus for individual performances. . .'

Q – Madonna's *Bedtime Stories*, Gloria Estefan and ex-Eastenders' Michelle Gayle's eponymous debut score a mere two stars. Three stars puts The 'Sads on a par with Dodgy's *Homegrown* and *The Return of the Space Cowboy* by Jamiroquai, while four stars are bestowed upon Nirvana's *Unplugged in New York* and The Black Crowes' *Amorica.*

Incredibly for us, it was a review devoid of all sarcasm. But, however welcome 120 friendly words were in 'the UK's best-selling rock mag', it hardly constituted much of a media hype. Of the other monthlies, only *Select* carried a review, though they took it upon themselves to call the album *Fleck*, list it as a Cooking Vinyl release (Lord have mercy on us if music journalists ever take over the planet) before soundly slagging it off as 'pseudo-Celtic jiggery-pokery from – smirk – Wigan' (they wouldn't get away with the last bit today, would they, pop-pickers?).

There was nothing, not even a slating, in the *NME* or *Melody Maker* (though the former did condescend to carry our tour dates) and no coverage in the broadsheets, or the big regional papers.

What little presence we did muster hardly advanced the cause. *Making Music* surmised: 'Sixth-form poetry rears its crusty head, everyone plays too much all at once and the M11 still gets built'; Bournemouth University mag

The Nerve didn't mince their words either: 'Amateurish production, woeful lyrics and outdated arrangements, I could make some joke involving the punchline 'Flock Off'. Or mention that the group's name is nearly an anagram of 'Sad Nads'. But I really can't be bothered.'

My skin had grown thick enough to appreciate witty jibes, and the worrying point was that I agreed with most of them.

No matter how much we had tried to shake off the Levellers-clones/crusty tag, half the songs on the album perpetuated the myth, and there was still no sign of the heavyweight media ally who would lift us to a higher plane and make such quibbles insignificant.

A happy exception to prove the rule came in the *Exeter Express and Echo*, where a man with obvious good taste and fine judgement by the name of Rob Baker went overboard in his 'Wavelength' column:

'The highlight for me is 'Ship of Fools', nothing whatsoever to do with Erasure or World Party but perhaps one of the liveliest, most, catchy pop songs you're likely to hear all year.'

Thank you, Rob, though, unfortunately, you didn't work for the *NME*.

The sad truth was that, in the main, we had become an irrelevance to the music industry.

Castle would catch on sooner or later and drop us and, when they did, it would be only a matter of time before the band started going downhill, because we would struggle to get another deal as lucrative. This might be two months down the line (though highly unlikely) or (probably) twelve months later.

But I knew there was only one way the band were going.

THE HEATER AFFAIR

My Kettle-toleration threshold was plummeting faster than holiday bookings in Yugoslavia. In retrospect, I can see our deteriorating relationship had as much to do with my negative state of mind as with John actually being a twat. At the time, though, the latter was very much the focus of my disenchantment; and in that I was not alone.

John had always possessed the ability to be an obnoxious control freak at gigs, but it had become an alarming and regular habit lately.

'That mix is all wrong in your monitor, Guy, the treble's a mess, you need more five K.'

'But that's how I like it.'

'Sorry, there's not enough five K. You can't possibly play with that.'

'Look, you can't put your amp there, Ed, Del won't have enough room.'

'But he chose that spot.'

And so on.

Organising everything on stage was only a minor irritant, as was his increasingly humourless demeanour. The major source of embarrassment was the arrogance he had started to display in dealing with PA companies at venues, precisely the sort of attitude we had always actively decried. Everybody (except *Earth Calling Planet Bob*, oblivious to anything within ten thousand light years of his body) began uniting against *Mummy and Daddy*.

Not that anybody ever said anything to their faces, of course.

The first time John really lost the plot was in the van as we travelled along the M4 one afternoon. In a (successful) attempt to while away motorway boredom, Big Dave was tormenting Janet; ruffling her hair, poking her in the ribs, flicking her ear, and so on.

'Stop it, Dave.'

She, admittedly, saw the funny side, but in doing so made the fatal mistake of reacting.

'Dave, stop it!'

This carried on for five minutes, then ten minutes, and then fifteen minutes.

'Daaaaave!!'

Janet giggled as the overgrown child pulled at her shirt.

Then came the thunderbolt.

'DAVE, JUST PACK IT IN!! HOW WOULD YOU LIKE IT IF SOMEBODY DID THAT TO YOUR GIRLFRIEND??!!'

Talk about missing the point.

Another source of irritation to John were the games Delbert and I played on stage. It had all started during an absolutely awful gig in the (unlit, stageless, audience-free) back room of a pub in (happening) Leighton Buzzard. I had switched off the keyboard in the middle of a song. Del retaliated by pulling the lead out of my amp, and so another silly on-the-road tradition was born.

Being the consummate professional, I would always make my move during the gaps where he wasn't playing, knowing full well that there was time for him to switch his gear back on.

Alas, Delbert, the great keyboard-playing lummox, was not so considerate, and disconnected my bass in the blackout at the start of our Liverpool Lomax set. John kicked in as normal, which cued Terry to throw on the lights, revealing a bass player on all fours scrambling to plug his lead in, and a keyboard player in stitches.

The guilt of schoolboys discovered making faces behind the teacher's back prevented us from playing up the next night, at Bedford Esquires but, during the soundcheck at the Leicester Charlotte the night after, I was happy to discover my power supply had been sabotaged.

In the dressing room afterwards, however, we duly stood charged with behaviour not in keeping with members of The Tansads.

'I've had enough of this messing about. I want it to stop.'

It was the style rather than the content of the reprimand that instantly pissed me off. Had John said, 'Look lads, your pranks are getting a bit out of hand, can you just make sure it doesn't affect the show,' I would probably have just apologised. But his avuncular tone was offensive.

'I beg your pardon?' I replied.

'All this pulling leads out and switching amps off. I'm not happy about it.'

'What the hell business is it of yours? I will behave exactly as I wish on stage, you overblown arse.'

That's what I should have said.

'It's just a bit of fun,' was my actual, rather tepid, reply.

'A bit of fun? It looks crap. And I want it to stop.'

'Come off it, people get off on seeing bands enjoy themselves, what's the big deal, that's what we're supposed to be about, isn't it, entertainment?'

Well, that was it. To use another Big-Dave-ism, he just went pop.

'IT'S UNPROFESSIONAL AND I AM TELLING YOU TO STOP IT!!'

'YES SIIIIIR,' I shouted, rather childishly giving a military salute, before heroically stomping off to the pub with the boys (Big Dave actually bought me a pint by way of congratulations, a first, I do believe).

Relations were strained.

It was quickly overtaken, however, by more pressing matters, namely our next gig, a headline at The London Forum on October 18th. Castle had insisted on booking the best venue in town as a showcase for all the Transatlantic bands.

I wonder if it cost as much as Frank Bigfield taking over the Hotel Martinez in Cannes? It did about as much good.

Anyway, miraculously, 600 people turned up from nowhere to create something approaching an atmosphere and none other than Johnnie Walker compered the evening.

'Great', I said to Steve Payne, 'I take it you've sorted out a session date with him, then.'

'Aah, there's been a snag in that direction.'

This is the same Johnnie Walker, remember, who had played 'Up The Revolution' twice in one show because he liked it so much, whom we had just met again backstage and been told that he was a big fan, and who then introduced us as one of the greatest live bands in Britain.

Steve Payne would now have us believe that Walker had initially agreed for us to do the sessions on Radio 1 and GLR, but had now changed his mind at the last minute because he had 'lost interest'.

Can there possibly be a lower life form on the planet than radio pluggers?

I'm not saying that those two sessions would have been the making of us. Probably not. But they symbolised something crucial, the fact we still mattered. Their sudden disappearance was definitely another turning point.

Our next gig, at Portsmouth Wedgwood Rooms, was not until the following night, so, after the Forum show, we were now detained at the pleasure of the M4 Heston Travelodge for a full day.

And this is where the real trouble started.

When we checked in on the way down, Andrew had sneaked into *Mummy and Daddy*'s room, closed the windows and turned the wall-heater on full. On returning from The Forum, eight hours or so later (by which time we'd forgotten all about it, of course), the Pub Club contingent settled down to its usual post-gig diet of Big-Dave- inspired hotel room diatribe.

'Dave, stop flicking the TV over, will you?'

'Seen yer arse have ya, Jonesey?'

'Fuck off Dave, I'm not in the mood.'

'Aaah! Seen it.'

A loud knocking rudely interrupted the intellectual discourse.

'WHO HAS TURNED OUR ROOM INTO A FUCKING SAUNA?'

'Oh, hello Janet, nice to see you.'

'SOMEBODY LEFT OUR HEATER ON FULL BEFORE THE GIG, AND NOW IT'S UNBEARABLE. WE WILL NEVER SLEEP IN THAT TEMPERATURE. COME ON, WHO DID IT?'

How much more innocent could five innocent boys look?

'I'm sorry but we don't know anything about it. Are you sure it wasn't on when you arrived this afternoon?'

An absolutely majestic use of the straight face.

'OK, PLAY IT THAT WAY IF YOU LIKE, BUT I'LL FIND OUT.'

Exit stage left, with the door slammed for extra emphasis. A severe case of sense of humour failure.

I don't think I've mentioned before the fact that Simon shared a Travelodge bedroom with *Mummy and Daddy*. The berk had (voluntarily) drawn the short straw the first time we had stayed out as a band, and the arrangement simply stuck. As you can imagine, he now endured a grilling of Russell Hobbs proportions over The Heater Affair. He swore to me he held firm, and I believe him.

Andrew, however, more pertinently, towards whom the finger of suspicion inevitably came to point, didn't, and things almost came to blows. Over a fucking wall heater.

The near-assault took place the following night. In the interim, thanks to our Steve Payne-engineered limbo, the band spent approximately 24 hours drinking solidly.

Ah.

The night began innocently enough watching football on TV and with a pillow fight between Guy and Simon. But then Big Dave got involved and the mattress was thrown across the room, and the bed ended up turned upside down, breaking one of its legs and the wall lamp in the process. The contents of our bags were sprinkled over the carpet, the bins were emptied, and the hotel literature started flying through the window. Mercifully, they were not followed by the symbolic TV set.

'Pack it in, lads, it's booked in my name, remember,' I said, scrambling to repair some of the damage.

'FUCK OFF, JONESEY,' came the collective reply, accompanied by a volley of pillows and obligatory mass piley-on.

I give up.

Luckily for me, the boys eventually got bored destroying our room, and gravitated next door.

Peace.

Knock, knock.

What NOW?

'Mr Jones, we are going to have to ask you to keep the noise down, there have been complaints from the other guests.'

'Uhh, look, uuh, yes, I'm ever so sorry, I'll go and have a word with them.'

Thankfully the hotel manager didn't ask to come into the room; otherwise we would have been kicked out on the spot. By the time I arrived next door, noise-abatement was the last thing on my mind, as Simon and Andrew were at each other's throats.

'Look, mate, I didn't say anything to her.'

'Get away from me, or I'll hit you.'

'Andrew what's the matter, mate?'

Andrew stormed out of the room, quickly followed by Simon, who just wasn't getting the message. I went after them, realising he was drunk and stupid enough to get himself into trouble. I caught up with them up on the grass outside.

Simon just seemed determined to have his head smashed into smithereens.

'Look, I don't understand what I've done, mate.'

'Just fuck off, or I swear I'll fucking hit you.'

'Andrew, mate?'

'I'M WARNING YOU!'

'But—'

Thankfully, fate intervened.

Simon's glasses, superglued together after a cricketing accident at silly point, fell off, with a lens coming away from the frame as they landed. He immediately started scrambling around in the dark looking for it.

Time to jump in.

'Andrew, I'll look after him. Look, he's just pissed.'

We escaped to the motorway diner for a sobering cup of coffee.

'Simon, what the hell is going on?'

'I think I've had enough of all this, buddy.'

Of course it was the ale talking, but I had never seen him so low. He spent half an hour tearfully pouring his heart out to me about how he was at the end of his tether with the way people took him for granted, how betrayed he felt over the album cover, how I was the only one whom he trusted, how he was wasting his life, etc, etc.

Bass player, accountant, psychiatrist . . .

'As for Andrew,' he continued, 'he just went for me. All I said was that I didn't tell Janet about the heater.'

That girl was driving a wedge through the band.

'Look, let's go and find him, and thrash this stupid nonsense out.'

I can't remember the exact sequence of events that followed, but I know

I talked to Andrew, he apologised to Simon, we all became friends again, and found ourselves in one of those drunken honesty sessions, analysing the way the band was falling to pieces. We all agreed John was a twat, but that the real focus of our grief was Janet, whose attitude just seemed to be at a complete tangent to everyone else's.

'Sack her and we'll be great' was the conclusion. Yeah, right. Up the revolution.

Eventually, in the early hours, after solving all our ills, we retreated to our various resting-places, ready for some welcome shuteye.

Ah-ha, not so fast. Guy stood up.

'Look, lads, I've got something to say to you all. There's no easy way to put this, but I can't carry on in the band any longer.'

'WHAT?'

Oh God, here we go . . .

'It hasn't got anything to do with you. It's me. I just can't afford it any more.'

As he broke down in a haze of alcoholic tears, we heard about a £2,000 Visa debt, about Angela, his seven-months-pregnant wife, running out of patience with his lifestyle, of an immediate need for income, and of his humiliation in having to let everybody down.

'I'm sorry, I'm really sorry' was all he could say in the end.

Much, much later, I asked him whether he wanted me to tell the rest of the band in the morning.

'Would you mind?'

What a day it had been. Beer and boredom. Truly a lethal combination.

THE SOUND OF SILENCE

The morning after the night before.

When we were all assembled in the van ready to set off, I stood up and told everybody about Guy. Once I was finished, John rose to his feet.

'I want to say something as well,' he began. 'I think it's time we sat down and chatted as a band. I'm very worried about people's motivation generally. Let's get to Portsmouth first and do it after the soundcheck.'

The unhappy cocktail of impending summit meeting, heady words of the previous evening, Guy's announcement, not to mention a collective hangover, created an unbearable sense of foreboding as we travelled down the A3. October 20th was definitely not going to be just another ordinary Tansads gig.

After the soundcheck, as threatened, John rounded up the troops and we headed towards the dressing room.

Deep breath.

John called for honesty, but I knew that, if everybody was as forthcoming as they had been the night before, anything could happen. It might clear the air and we could all start afresh, on the other hand the band might collapse there and then.

I knew for a fact that a majority of the seven people in that room – Guy, Del, Andrew and me – wanted Janet sacked. I also knew categorically that the four of us thought John needed to be brought down a peg or two. *Earth Calling Planet Bob* was (no doubt literally after what he had consumed that day) a floating voter, which left only *Mummy and Daddy* in the other corner.

What I had unfortunately overlooked was that I had been relatively sober the night before. In my case, it hadn't been the ale talking.

'You asked for honesty, John, so here it is. I, like everybody else, including you, am worried about the way the band seems divided. But what I find particularly worrying is the way you seem to have become so arrogant of late. There's an attitude there which grates on all of us, and I believe that's creating a lot of the tension.'

'What do you mean?' said *Daddy*, accompanied by a very, very stern look.

Absolute silence. And inevitably, I just dug myself deeper into trouble.

'Look, it's not personal. No, that's a daft thing to say. It is personal, obviously, but I just feel it's important we are honest with each other, like you said. And there is a lot of tension within the band, much of it directed at you.'

'Nobody's said anything to me about it.'

'Well, I am doing now.'

I told him how the band were fed up with his ego, with the way decisions were made, and I listed other ills, from the way he tried to organise everybody to the patronising way he dealt with people in and out of the band.

John was deeply hurt, unsurprisingly. Tact has never been a particular virtue of mine.

'Is this the way everybody feels?' he asked, looking at the others.

Not a word.

Come on, I've laid the foundations. Tell the man what you think. Nothing. Not a word. Eventually, Del did muster something.

'Yeah, I'm not happy about you keep ordering me where to put me' amp, laak.'

Is that it, boys? Is that all the support I get?

An intense, squirming, embarrassed, silence followed, in which not another single word was spoken.

Thanks, lads.

What to do next? Retreat, or play the Janet card? If I told John over half the band wanted to sack not only one of its singers but also his paramour, one of two things would happen. We would either split acrimoniously on the spot, or, bearing in mind the immediate precedent, nobody would admit to anything, and I would look like the Machiavellian schemer in all of this.

It was too late. As nobody had followed me onto the battlefield, what should have been a unified front degenerated into a straight fight between John and me, precisely what I had been trying to avoid. Maybe.

'Nobody's backing you up. I don't see any evidence of what you claim. It must be all in your mind. The power's gone to your head,' said John.

'No, no, you've got the wrong end of the stick.'

'I don't think I have. You talk about my ego, What about yours? I mean, I've been keeping the band afloat.'

'I'm sorry?'

'You piss people off too, you know.'

'What?'

'I've seen the way you talk to people. It's you that's arrogant. You're not as indispensable as you think you are.'

'What are you talking about?'

The meeting achieved nothing except to aggravate an already hypertense situation. Diplomatic relations weren't just strained any more. It was time to evacuate the embassy.

LUCY IN THE SKY'S A DIAMOND

The last place John and I wanted to be right now was stuck in a van with each other. So what was next on the agenda? Yup, you've guessed it, six overnight stays on the trot.

*Fan*tastic.

John's tactic was clear from the outset. When we arrived at Thames

Valley University in Ealing for the first show, he set his amp on the stage, left straight away again without uttering a syllable to anybody else, and neither he nor Janet communicated with me all day or all evening.

Pure Spinal Tap.

The gig was awful, exceptional only for the support act and their incredibly sexy girlfriends. The music didn't really do that much for me, but the band was so tight and confident, the musical translation of flares with 70s rock chicks thrown in.

I phoned up Geoff to tell him the next morning.

'They were called The Kays. Try and get hold of a tape. They are going to be massive, honestly.'

They changed their name to **Kula Shaker**.

KULA SHAKER – Crispian Mills, son of famous English actress Hayley Mills (daughter of Sir John Mills) hadn't discovered Indian mysticism when The Kays supported us, but the Eastern influences are very much apparent in their 1996, number one debut album, *K*. They reached number 2 on the singles chart in February 1997 with 'Hush', a release that is best described as workman-like in its similarity to the Deep Purple version of the Joe South original.

Things hardly improved over the course of the six days, the factions cutting deeper than ever. John and I didn't speak in Exeter, nor in Gloucester, Tunbridge Wells, or Coventry. We didn't speak for a week at home when I wasn't invited up to record demos and the following weekend we didn't speak before, during, or after a gig in Leeds. Then we didn't speak when we got home again.

I was in a rut and in desperate need of a catalyst to shake me up and say, 'Sort out your life, soft lad, and do SOMETHING!'

For my sins, as Martin Sheen said in *Apocalypse Now*, I got one.

'Hi bro, how you doing?'

'Oh, hi sis. Not bad, you know. Well, things are a bit crap in the band to tell you the truth. I'll explain some time. How's the baby?'

'She's lovely.'

'And you? How are you doing?'

'Well actually, that's what I have to talk to you about. They've found a lump on my breast.'

The tumour was quickly diagnosed as cancer. It had seemingly flourished during the later stages of pregnancy, and now, a mother of barely three months, Lucy was rushed into hospital for surgery followed by chemotherapy, radiography and all their hideous associations.

An unerring familiarity came over me, an uncomfortable reminder of something I hadn't felt for a very long time.

Absolute blind panic.

I dropped everything and went to be near her in Brighton, the petty disputes at home suddenly thrown into sharp perspective. The early signs were good, the operation looked to have been successful. There was to be a six month initial danger zone, then regular check-ups. The odds for total recovery were excellent, notwithstanding the physical and emotional stress involved not only in the operation itself, but in Lucy not being able to care for baby Emma as she would have wished. Basically, though, she got the medical thumbs up.

Phew. Don't *do* that again, will you?

But she did. Just three short years after first contracting cancer, Lucy lost her battle at 6.00 a.m. on the morning of her 35th birthday, September 9th. Her timing was atrocious. She died three days after the funeral of Diana Princess of Wales, and the whole country had just gone mad.

I was so fucking angry.

My grief was usurped as Britain wallowed in a nauseous, institutionalised sorrow. Everybody, but just *everybody*, understood what I was going through.

'Oh yes, We've *all* felt it this week.'

FUCK OFF!

I tried to stay calm throughout the whole Diana episode. I was determined to maintain my dignity, but when I finally saw Lucy's gently smiling body at the hospice, all the bottled up angst exploded into an uncontrollable tide of tears. I had bought a card for her birthday, embossed with a sunflower, her favourite. It seems so futile looking back, but I handed it to her husband Ray. The inscription read: 'May the sunflowers grow big and tall and forever wherever you are. Say hello to Dad for me, Baby Bro xxx.'

What hurt me most was that Lucy hadn't wanted, and then wasn't able, to speak to me in the final few weeks. I was forced to feel her gently extinguishing light down a telephone line, groping for information from nurses who didn't know anything about me, or about her. A couple of days after she died, I called Ray to see how he was. He didn't reply, but the answerphone message clicked in.

'Leave a message for Lucy, Ray, or Emma after the beep. Please talk slowly as the machine is a little hard of hearing.'

It was the last time I ever heard her voice.

The service was held a week later. I knew I wouldn't have the courage to speak, but maybe I would manage a song. What a terrible idea. The cliché only hit me when I was actually there before the mourners, standing in my wedding suit, acoustic guitar clumsily hanging from my neck. Elton John had beaten me to it.

I've been dreaming of summer,
By staring at the snow,
I can see the sun, everywhere I go,
Despite the icy wind that blows.
Hope will spring where there's no hope,
Just make yourself believe,
You can see a light when all around is dark,
Or your regrets will never leave.

'What a beautiful tune, the words were perfect.'
'I loved that song.'
'What CD is it on?'
'Is the band still going?'
'How come you're not playing any more?'
'God, you performed that so well.'
'Who are you signed to?'
'Have you still got a deal, then?'
Go awaaaaaay.
Of course, by this time I had left the band.

TAXI FOR JONES

'If you're unhappy, baby brother, do something about it', Lucy had told me one day at the hospital, when she was first diagnosed with the cancer.

'Work out if you want to stay or go, talk about it with Alison and make a decision. By the way, I love your song on the album.'

Unlike Mum, Lucy had always been supportive of the band. It helped that she understood rock-'n'-roll of course. She faithfully bought the CDs and it upset me that – through no fault of her own – the only gigs she had managed to see were really crap ones.

Dad's death had created a special bond between us as children, especially as we had been so far from home together at boarding school. For many years we were very close but, now that I lived so far away, sometimes we would go months without talking, and I felt slightly ashamed it had taken Emma's birth and now this initial crisis to bring us back together.

If anybody was going to knock some sense into me, I suppose it had to be big sis. I got a blank sheet of paper, picked up a pen, and drew up a list of pros and cons about leaving the band. It more or less boiled down to this. On the plus side, I would instantly shed all the unwanted baggage of Tansad-dom, namely tension and that infernal folky tag.

I would be in total control of my destiny, and I could use the knowledge, ability, and contacts gained over the previous five years to start my own band, write and play the songs I wanted in the style I wanted with the people I wanted. Realistically, given my age, I had only one more shot, so I had to get things right.

On the minus side, I would lose some security, starting from scratch, no publishing deal, no management, no rehearsal facilities, and no van.

But crucially, no ties.

Put that way, it seemed a pretty straightforward choice. Who wants security when you can have freedom? There was one other thing, though. The Pete Best syndrome. What if I was being premature in dismissing our chances? After all, the gigs were going well, the band had never sounded as professional, and Castle were still really keen. What if I left and The Tansads made it big time?

Whether it was the two weeks apart or the news about Lucy, when I got home, inter-band relations had improved marginally. At least John and I were sort of talking again. My mind was not made up to leave by any means, although I was much closer to a decision. However, just to confuse matters further, we enjoyed another string of great gigs.

One of these was at Oxford Jericho Tavern to a packed, sweaty full house. We went off to soaring applause and, for the first time in ages, I received a flattering bit of extracurricular attention.

I was the first to emerge from the dressing room after the show, to be greeted by four nubile, fresh-faced, belly-button flashing girlies.

'There he is!'

I'm bound to have turned the colour of an overripe tomato.

'Can you sign this for us, please?' one of them asked, handing me a copy of *Flock*.

'Yeah, me too.'

'Of course, I'll just nip backstage and get the others to do it as well.'

'Don't bother, it's only you we're bothered about.'

Whey-hey-hey, I may have turned 30, but I could still pull those teenage babes. I was too faithful to do anything about it, naturally, besides, *four* at once? Even in my prime I used to struggle with just the one.

Our gig the following night was at The Mean Fiddler in London, and a truly farcical evening edged me ever nearer the decision-making precipice. Castle brought a contingent from France to see us, with a view to giving us a big push over there. Jezzer introduced me to a rotund, dishevelled-looking bloke in a suit called Jean Marc something, while whispering in my ear:

'Give it your best blarney old boy, this chap's the *grand fromage*.'

'Yes we lurve ze barnd,' said Monsieur Cheese.

Now where had I heard *that* before?

'Great, you think it would work in France?'

'Yes, yes, off curs. Ze market is hot for ze Celtic musik, ze folk-rock, yes?'

Lord preserve us.

After the gig, Castle laid on a get-to-know-you-better soirée at a restaurant in Queensway.

'They're really up for it,' Jezzer said, 'I want you to sit with them and turn on the old ambassadorial French charm, this could be crucial.'

Brilliant.

I reluctantly parked myself between two of the French knobs, opposite Jezzer, who introduced us.

'Ed is the band's resident Francophone.'

'*Aaah, vous parlez français?*'

'*Ouais, je suis né en Suisse.*'

Blah, blah, blah.

This is a nightmare, I thought. I was still sweating from the gig, and I had nothing to say to these people, except, 'John and I have fallen out, nobody can stand the sight of Janet but haven't got the bottle to do anything about it, the drummer's jacking it in because he's broke, and I want to leave and start a three-piece grunge band because I'm fed up playing second fiddle to a bloke who's liable to regrow his moustache at any time. And I hate FOLK-FUCKING ROCK!'

'Excuse me, I just need to go to the toilet before we order.'

When I returned, I found my seat occupied by Jean-Marc Big Cheese. Jezzer made a gesture as if to say 'Sorry, old boy, what could I do?'

I tried to look disappointed, undoubtedly failed, and, grinning like a Cheshire Cat, spent the rest of the meal telling dirty jokes and having food fights with Big Dave at the other end of the table.

French folk-rock?

Come on, even Pete Best would have run away from that one faster than you could say *le finger dans le ear*.

EXIT MUSIC (FOR A BOOK)

Although it had been building for months, I finally made my mind up in a instant. The evidence had been staring me in the face all along, of course, but then, that's the thing about big decisions, the fundamental issue is often so obscured by bullshit you get thrown off the scent.

Ultimately, it wasn't Castle, folk-effing-rock or anarcho-Celtic urban warriordom. It wasn't *flock*, Jezzer, radio sessions, press officers, money, freedom or wondering whether I had enough contacts to make it alone. It wasn't really about falling out with John either, or about Janet, nor the fact that nobody was prepared to speak their mind in the band. It wasn't Pete Best Syndrome, or songwriting politics, or deranged kamikaze milk-floats. And it wasn't even about not enjoying it any more either.

The penny just dropped one day.

Our minuscule amount of success had generated all this grief, imagine what the situation would be like if we made some real headway. I realised that even if we sold fifty million albums I would still resent being in The Tansads.

ALISON says, *'I suppose I just felt relief when it was all over, that maybe we could just get on with the rest of our lives again. I didn't make him leave, but I did feel a bit guilty in case he thought I did. It was his decision in the end, but I'm sure the rest of the band thought it was my fault. You didn't leave because of me, did you?'*

I finally decided to quit the night we supported The Oyster Band at Cambridge Junction. After the gig, everybody (except *Mummy, Daddy,* and *Earth Calling Planet Bob*, naturally) trooped off to the pub in a rare bit of social solidarity, and I broke the news.

'Please don't tell *Mummy and Daddy* just yet, I'd rather go and see them myself.'

I used the band kitty to buy a couple of rounds.

'I can't see this happening again once Janet gets her hands on the purse strings,' I said.

The tragic thing was that, whenever those two weren't around, we always got on so well.

My farewell was two sold-out shows at the Citadel on December 16th and 17th. I don't remember John's reasoning for not wanting Andrew to announce from the stage I was leaving but I made sure to spread it round one or two people before we played the second night, if only to alert some of the regulars.

John did pay me the courtesy of picking 'Gelignite' as the final encore on the Saturday night. It had been a great gig, but as we waited backstage to come back on one last time, something was missing. I suppose my pride felt a little dented that the occasion hadn't been officially marked as my Tansads swan song.

Never mind. Just 'Gelignite' to go and you're a free man.

I emerged from backstage first, as always at the Citadel, because my perch was furthest from the door. As I made my way across the stage, Terry upped the lights and a great roar erupted from the floor.

The crowd started singing: 'Eddie Jones, Eddie Jones, Eddie Jones. . .'

For ages.

What do you do when that happens? Blush? Wave? I can't recall, but it was a really touching moment, and one that has stayed with me.

'You escaped lightly, mate, I wanted to rip all your clothes off and chain you to the crush barriers,' Big Dave told me afterwards, 'but John wouldn't let me because he said it would spoil the gig, the boring bastard.'

At least we could still agree upon something then.

REGRETS, I'VE HAD A FEW

When I started writing this book, a parallel universe began to develop, whereby the same things were happening as had done to the band, except a demo in the publishing world is called a synopsis. I got loads of rejections, became incredibly despondent, carried on blindly, and eventually, there was a breakthrough. Within days of sending off my manuscript to Canongate, I got a positive reply: remember, when it happens, it happens. A contract with loads of *heretos* and *hereunders* followed, along with advances, royalty rates, and all the rest of it.

ALISON says, *'And now we have this. Just when I thought it was over, he writes a stupid book about it all and wants to know what it was like for me. Listen, I didn't find any of it funny when I had to live through it the first time round, I'm hardly going to enjoy reading about it, am I? I wonder if he'll ever grow up...'*

And, of course, it was another excuse to put the real world in the pending tray.

As the terminal pessimist, however, I fully expect the book to do as well as a Tansads comeback single on Musidisc. But it would tickle me if it sold more copies than the band sold albums (somewhere around the 12,000 mark would be the magical figure I guess), and therefore, more people ended up knowing The Tansads because of the book than the records.

Would that make me a successful failure or a failed success?

Actually, I may have been a little premature in assuming The 'Sads never make it. You wouldn't recognise them (only *Mummy and Daddy* remain) but at the time of writing, the band is still going and, as you read this, John may finally catch up with that rainbow he's been chasing all these years. The last I heard, he had hooked up with a management company in the US and was in Nashville, Tennesseeeee, laying down some hot new licks.

Would it bother me if he made it?

Well, I'd be gutted. That's what you want to hear, isn't it? I'd be lying if I said anything else. Jealousy is part and parcel of being in bands, it's far more important than playing your instrument in some cases; a manifestation of the massive insecurity which affects all musicians.

That's why I could never love The Verve, or whatever solo projects emerge from them in the future, because however great it is, I have an excuse, petty, convoluted, and distant though it may be, to be envious.

And envy may arise its head again concerning a band called Witness, the latest starlets-in-making off the Wigan production line. The singer and main man Gerard Starkey was in a band called More Perfect Watchers, who supported us at the first-ever Mill at the Pier gig. The band changed their name to Embryonic (whose demo I reviewed in the column shortly before leaving the paper), before appearing as Witness, signing to Island, being managed by Verve press officer Tim Vigon and handled by agent Geoff Meall. The world goes on merrily spinning round.

My departure from The Tansads signalled the end of an era. Simon, Guy, Terry, Andy and Big Dave all followed suit, with animosity levels ranging from medium to extremely high in Simon's case, after he asked for some of his money back. He didn't need it, but felt the principle at stake outweighed his loyalty to John and Janet.

'I would advise you never to come back to Wigan again. I'm warning you, I may not be held responsible for my actions if I ever see you again,' said John to Simon.

After we all left, replacements were sought and, as predicted, following another year of Toilets-trading, during which time Castle funded the release of a live LP (embarrassingly called *Drag Down the Moon*), the band were dropped. The funny thing is that at the fourth or fifth time of trying, The Tansads started selling out The UK Toilets circuit, the momentum of three solid years' touring finally taking positive effect. But, by then, the press had disappeared, the interest from London was non-existent, and – of course – the money had run out.

A further exodus took place when Castle moved off the scene, leaving just *Mummy and Daddy* to slug it out alone, under a new monicker, Jane Doe (incredible, John actually managed to come up with something worse than The Tansads). When no promoter was interested, he reverted to the old crap name, and started from scratch with the new recruits.

The Tansads do make it into a couple of rock music anthologies. I can't really say anything about *The Virgin Encyclopoedia of Popular Music* because I helped to compile the entry, but a very nice man by the name of Phil Udell writes an informed and sympathetic piece for *The Rough Guide to Rock*, neatly nestled between Tangerine Dream and The Teardrop Explodes.

He correctly notes that 'The British music business has always had at least two parallel scenes. On the one hand, there's the media-driven, London-centric whirl of the music press, radio stations, and gossip columns. On the other, the distinctly regional world of small labels, transit vans and incessant gigging. The Tansads are a band straight out of the latter environment . . .' A pretty accurate history follows, whereupon he concludes, 'Don't expect this situation to change much, and don't expect The Tansads to give a damn.'

That's where you're sadly mistaken, Mr Udell. We cared so much it virtually destroyed us.

I started my three-piece grunge band as promised, became axe-monster and chief warbler, roped Guy into joining, found a bass player called Chris Cookson, and called ourselves Frame 313 (that's when the bullet enters the head in the Kennedy assassination footage).

Just as we were beginning to show signs of focusing, Chris lost interest and, after a year's hard work and one gig (at The Citadel, of course), the twat walked out, and everything collapsed. Another musical bud perished in the spring frost of apathy.

So at 9.00 am on Monday January 16th 1995, Dad's anniversary and one thousand and four days after leaving the *Wigan Reporter*, I walked back into the office and settled down at an empty desk.

'Welcome back to the real world, Jonesey,' said a voice behind me.

WHERE ARE THEY NOW?

In order of departure...

SHRUB – Lives and (used to) work in Chester. After a succession of short-term jobs, including a spell at a video production company and Next menswear department, is, at the time of writing, unemployed but currently recording an album of material entitled *My Little Ice Age*.

DOM – Last heard of having passed his HGV driving license and working for a laboratory supplies company. Nothing unusual about that until I tell you he was a militant vegan with more than a passing interest in animal rights...

CHRIS aka BUG – Earned a First Class degree in applied physics and applied mathematics from Manchester University. Currently completing a doctorate. Told you all drummers were thick.

CUDO – Moved into his dad's caravan after amassing so much recording equipment that the bed had to be sacrificed. The digital audio gadgets habit continues to be funded by drumming covers at his local working man's club. Recently wrote and recorded his own album on CD, called *Is It Safe?* Distribution: one caravan, and that's the way he wants to keep it.

GUY – After three years selling Nissans, he recently switched to Hyundais; with every car sold, Kegsy chucks in six months free road tax and a Tansads or Railway Children compilation tape for the stereo. Recently joined a band by the name of Murf (I kid you not), whose members have a combined age less than his.

DELBERT – Formed his own group called Elusive, who went on to sign a record deal worth no money and are so far more than living up to their name. Hence he helps out his dad in the kitchen game, laaak.

ANDREW – Has thought up 57 reasons why he hates his job at the Heinz factory but keeps up the woodpigeon-spotting programme with voluntary ranger work for Wigan Parks Department. Writes his own songs these days.

ROBERT – After completing a course in English literature at Manchester University, is currently making plans to open up 'Blake-Away', the World's first metaphysical song-lyric drive-in, on wasteland off Montrose Avenue.

And the significant others...

SIMON – The only one of us still actively involved in showbiz. He designs the glossy programmes for major festivals, big rock tours and major comedians. He is also a design consultant for Radio 1's promotions department, works with the Prince's Trust and is a partner in promotion company Foundation, who handle Belle and Sebastian among others. Here is a sample of people he has recently met and worked with: Paul Merton, Eddie Izzard, Jack Dee, Lee Evans, Paul Heaton...and Chaz Smash of Madness. Recently decided to write off the Tansads' debt to posterity.

DAMIAN – Still a frustrated psychology lecturer at Wigan and Leigh College, or Wigan University as it shall probably soon be known. He has published four textbooks, and hopes to bring out a fifth himself in the New Year. Ever the diplomat, he also manages to be friends with both John and me.

JEREMY THOMAS – Jezzer was last heard of living in Greece and writing a play. Naturally.

GEOFF MEALL – Now a director at The Agency. His roster includes Space, Super Furry Animals, The Barenaked Ladies, Cornershop, Bis, Gene, Hurricane No.1, Idlewild and Witness.

NIGEL MORTON – Somehow survived his Sad Tans ordeal with an unblemished reputation. Ahem. Now a booking agent for the F.A.B. world-music agency, and also manages Eliza Carthy. May God watch over her...

PHIL TENNANT – Founded a label called Big Star with Musidisc President François – Frank Bigfield – Grandchamp, which was subsequently sold to bigwigs Universal. Now manages Mike Scott of The Waterboys among others but keeps his hand in behind the desk producing new bands.

MUSIDISC – The sale of Musidisc UK formed part of the above Big Star deal with Universal. The London office is still just about open, but doesn't operate as a label anymore. Or rather, *still* doesn't operate as a label.

CASTLE COMMUNICATIONS – Following its sale to UK banking company Rutland Trust, Castle continue to ply their trade on the cutting edge of the reissue market. You can buy the entire Tansads back catalogue through them if you wish. Please, they need the cupboard space.

And as for little ol' me? Well, at the time of typing this out, I haven't written a song for over two years. Says it all.